I0793002

IMAGES
of America

ITALIANS IN WEST VIRGINIA

On the Cover: This is the Order of Sons of Italy in America (OSIA) William Marconi Lodge No. 1140 in Clarksburg, West Virginia, in the 1920s. (Courtesy of John B. and Mary Ann Angotti.)

IMAGES
of America

ITALIANS IN WEST VIRGINIA

Victor A. Basile and
Judy Prozzillo Byers

ARCADIA
PUBLISHING

ISBN 978-0-7385-8750-9

Published by Arcadia Publishing
Charleston, South Carolina

Printed in the United States of America

Library of Congress Control Number: 2010942068

For all general information, please contact Arcadia Publishing:
Telephone 843-853-2070
Fax 843-853-0044
E-mail sales@arcadiapublishing.com
For customer service and orders:
Toll-Free 1-888-313-2665

Visit us on the Internet at www.arcadiapublishing.com

In memory of the Italian immigrants who settled in West Virginia and all American Italians whose impassioned love of history, heritage, and ancestry are keeping the Italian spirit alive

Contents

ACKNOWLEDGMENTS

This book would not have been possible without the impassioned love of history and heritage of my late brother-in-law John B. Angotti Sr., who collected archival photographs while working at the La Rosa Coal Company, and of his wife, Mary Ann Basile-Angotti, who conserved and organized the collection in their home library. I would also like to thank the executive committee of the West Virginia Italian Heritage Festival (WVIHF) for selecting me as the 2001 Italian American Man of the Year and connecting me with my coauthor, Dr. Judy Prozzillo Byers, a former Italian American Woman of the WVIHF. Both Dr. Byers and her husband, Dr. George Byers, have made significant contributions and editorial revisions to the book. We want to thank the following scholars, archivists, collectors, photographers, religious interviewees, computer specialists, graphic designers, and members and friends of the West Virginia Italian American community who played an invaluable role in authenticating the text and assisting us in meeting the expectations of the book:

Scholars and Archivists: Nicholas P. Ciotola, Jack C. Goushian, Esq., David Hourhin, Barbara Irwin, Jim and Phyllis Wilson Moore, Ryan Rutkowski, Mary Palmer, CSJ

Collectors and Photographers: Thomas C. Martin, Rocco Muriale, Sal Olivito, Ron Rittenhouse

Religious Interviewees: Rev. Colombo Bandiera, Rev. Hilarion Cann, Angelina Cavallaro, CSJ, Rev. John V. DiBacco

Computer Specialists, Technologists, and Graphic Designers: Cathy Calkins, Greg Krinsky, Tammy Holden, Tim McMurtay, Mary Rogers, Maurice Scaglione

Members and Friends of the West Virginia Italian American Community: Nick Ameli, Robert A. and Mary Beth Angotti, Rosa Mazza, Frances Oliverio Phares, Kim Smith.

INTRODUCTION

ITALIANS IN WEST VIRGINIA: FROM ITALIAN EMIGRANTS TO AMERICAN ETHNICS

Both of the authors, Victor A. Basile and Judy Prozzillo Byers, have been an Italian American Man or Woman of the Year of the West Virginia Italian Heritage Festival (WVIHF). This Images of America book celebrates the rich regional history of West Virginia's Italian neighborhoods, scattered coal towns, and cities. It offers a new understanding of how Italian laborers, merchants, and families were assimilated into West Virginia's regional landscape. The transmigration from Italian emigrant to American ethnic is a long and intense journey. This process not only effects one generation, it transcends several generations. The impact of Italian traditions and customs, originating in small villages of southern Italy, being relocated and readjusted to life in the coal towns and cities of West Virginia is the thematic focus of this book.

Two transatlantic events were occurring in the 1860s. In 1861, Italy became a unified nation; in the United States, the Civil War was occurring. In 1863, West Virginia seceded from Virginia, became a separate state, and joined the northern union of states. Italian officials were establishing a variety of programs to make Italy a global country. For example, they were allowing their citizens to travel to Africa and North and South America with limited documentation. At the same time, West Virginia legislators were formulating policies to exploit the state's abundant resources of timber, coal, natural gas, and oil. In 1864, they authorized the appointment of an immigration commissioner. The first immigration commissioner encouraged farmers to immigrate to West Virginia from Switzerland and other northern European countries.

Early efforts to stimulate immigration met only minor success due to lack of adequate roads and rail transportation. West Virginia's abundant resources could not be exploited until transportation improved. The Civil War delayed efforts to develop railroads through central and southern West Virginia. Soon after the war, the Chesapeake & Ohio Railroad opened up the coalfields and forests along the New and Kanawha Rivers.

Coal and lumber companies used the available West Virginia native labor. To expand, they turned to recruiting black workers from the South and emigrants from Europe. Recruiting efforts took several forms. Some companies stationed independent labor agents in port cities such as New York, Philadelphia, and Baltimore and paid the agents a fee for each worker who arrived in West Virginia. Other techniques included sending recruitment brochures to European countries describing the advantages and opportunities of work in West Virginia and promising free transportation to the New World. Sometimes, an advance on wages was offered as an added inducement. Finally, early, contented immigrants encouraged family members to immigrate by telling them of the high wages being paid. Recruiters found a fertile field among those who sought to escape the Jim Crow conditions of the American South and southern and eastern Europeans who were trying to improve themselves economically and socially and saw work in the mines or timber operations as the way to accomplish their goals.

Attracting and using immigrant labor created a conflict between the great need for workmen and existing prejudicial attitudes toward immigrants and blacks. West Virginia's population at the end of the Civil War, with the exception of a small number of blacks, was almost exclusively white, Anglo-Saxon, and Protestant. The power structures, public and private, reflected general negative attitudes toward immigrants, especially those from southern and eastern Europe. Newspaper articles, official documents, and actions by state officials and private companies reflected the dichotomy of a need for and a disdain toward the immigrants. In 1903, the Society for the Protection of Italian Immigrants sent Gino C. Speranza to West Virginia to investigate a number of companies that were holding workers and forcing them to work against their will. Speranza's visit stimulated the investigation of charges of peonage against several West Virginia companies. Peonage is a legal term meaning that a person is being held against his or her will in order to work off a debt. Unlike slavery, which is a permanent condition, the peon would, hopefully, be freed once the debt was paid. Italian immigrants fell prey to the practice of peonage when they accepted free transportation to West Virginia and food and lodging from companies for which they worked. Bringing workers to West Virginia in this manner was called bring them "on transportation," and each was expected to reimburse the company that footed the bill. In 1907, Gov. William Dawson denounced peonage and the conditions of lawlessness in the coalfields.

Between 1880 and 1930, over 13 million Italians left their homeland, launching the largest recorded migration from a country in world history. Fleeing agricultural turmoil, social unrest, and a failing economy, in 1910, there were 17,286 Italians in West Virginia. In 1920, there were 14,147, and in 1930, there were 13,190. The 1910 census disclosed that Italians constituted the largest group of European immigrants in the state.

Based on the 2000 census, the John D. Calandra Italian American Institute at Queens College/City University of New York ranked the number of Italians in the United States by state. West Virginia's ranking was 21st; it was preceded by Louisiana at 19 and California at 20.

The 10 highest-ranking states with the number of Italians were Rhode Island (1); Connecticut (2); New Jersey (3); New York (4); Massachusetts (5); Pennsylvania (6); Delaware (7); New Hampshire (8); Nevada (9); and Vermont (10). West Virginia's ranking is in the median category.

One

Almost Heaven, West Virginia

Most of the 19th-century artists who went to Rome did so in the belief that a painter was a poet, a historian, and a moralist, and that Rome was the inspiration and school for humanistic tradition in art. For over a century, American artists and writers, such as Thomas Cole and Nathaniel Hawthorne, compared the landscape of America's frontier to that of classical Italy. At that time, Europeans were searching for a utopia that would offer economic opportunity and the chance to start over again. In the late years of the 1800s, the West Virginia frontier landscape was one that attracted the transnational immigrant. Don Antonio Arena, an early contented immigrant to West Virginia, described its romantic landscape in a 1920 Italian document. "The West Virginia landscape includes a diverse countryside which is mountainous, and at different points truly picturesque. . . . The hills are covered with luxuriant vegetation reminiscent somewhat of our Calabrian/Lucanian villages. Its terrain is rich and productive. . . . It has healthy air, a temperate climate, and a very charming place for a foreign residency" (Order of Sons of Italy in America Grand Convention, Clarksburg, West Virginia, 1925). Upon receiving these notices, many Italians went to the ports of Naples and Genoa, where they booked passage for the sea journey to "La America." Most emigrants traveled in the least expensive manner possible. Steerage travel consisted of dreary quarters in the lower levels of the ship, where engine noise, heat, lack of adequate facilities, and poor ventilation made the journey unpleasant. After a transoceanic voyage that lasted 10 to 14 days, immigrants arrived in the port cities of New York, Philadelphia, and Baltimore. US immigration officers performed a battery of tests on the immigrants. On leaving the immigration centers, the recent arrivals were approached by labor agents recruiting for the coal mines. For each worker who arrived in West Virginia, the agent would receive a fee. Additionally, family members of recent immigrants were encouraged to immigrate when they heard of the high wages being paid. Southern and eastern Europe was a fertile field in which to recruit those who sought to improve themselves economically and saw work in agriculture, forestry, railway construction, and coal mining as ways to accomplish their goals.

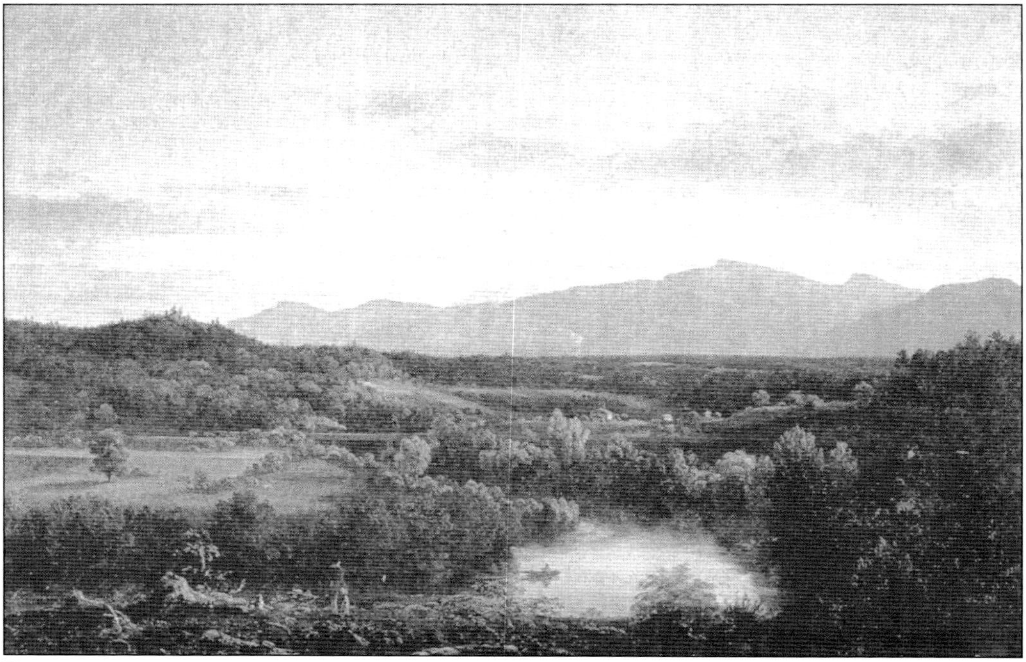

THOMAS COLE LANDSCAPE PAINTING AND HELVETICA, WEST VIRGINIA. Classical Rome and its landscape had a tremendous impact on American artists and writers of the 1800s. American landscape painters, such as Thomas Cole, Washington Allston, and George Innes, painted and traveled in Italy; they often compared the classical Roman landscape to America's romantic mountains, valleys, lakes, and rivers. America's frontier was a popular subject for the New England and Hudson Valley schools of painters. In 1864, just one year after its secession from Virginia, the West Virginia Legislature authorized the appointment of an immigration commissioner. The first immigration commissioner encouraged farmers to immigrate to West Virginia from Switzerland and other northern European countries. In Helvetica, a colony of Swiss immigrants began a farming and dairy settlement. (Above, Authors' collection; below, courtesy of West Virginia and Regional Collections, West Virginia University Libraries.)

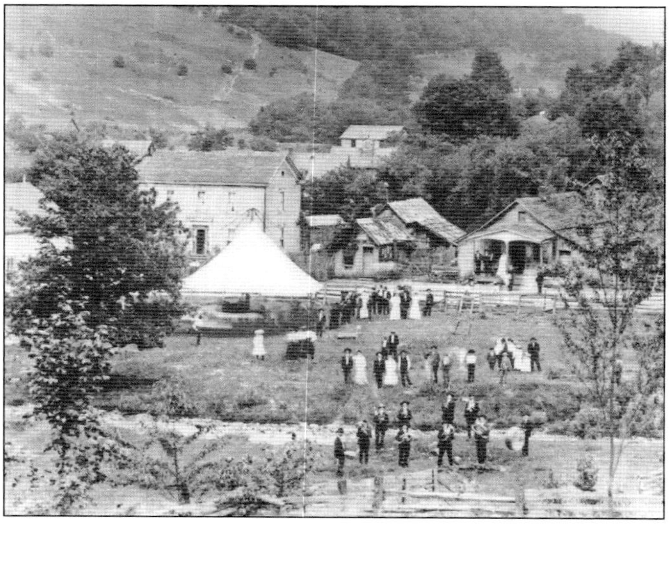

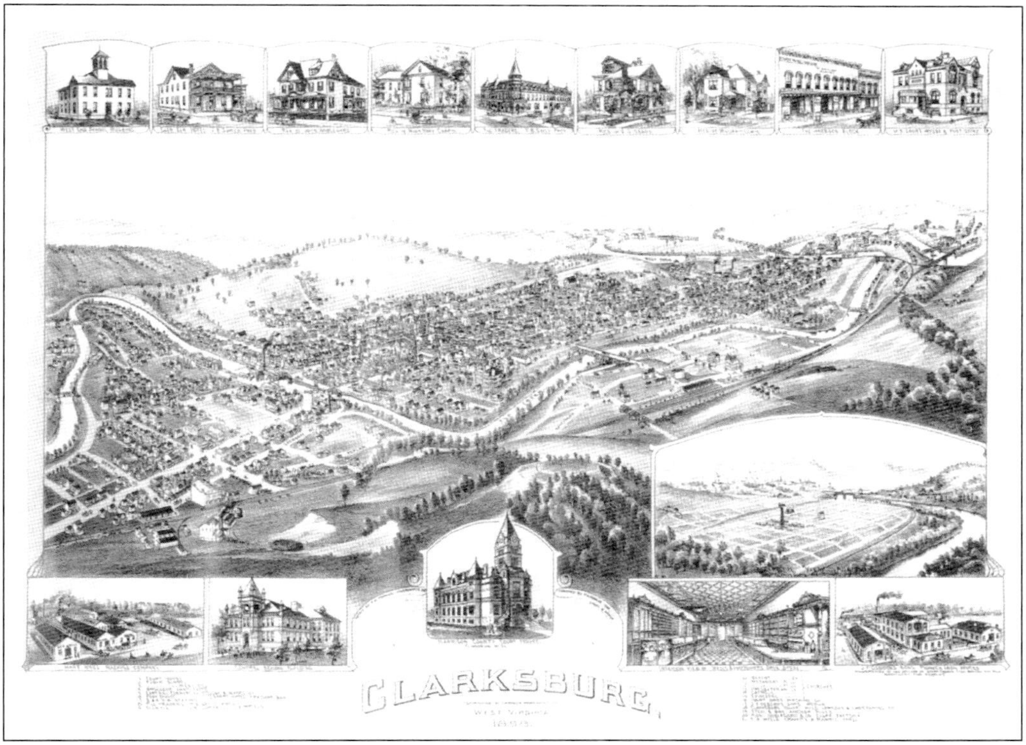

PANORAMIC VIEW OF CLARKSBURG, WEST VIRGINIA, 1898, AND ORDER OF SONS OF ITALY IN AMERICA (OSIA) BROCHURE, WEST VIRGINIA, 1925. American authors Henry James and Nathaniel Hawthorne described classical Italy and its landscape in their writings. In the process, America's social, political, and aesthetic concerns were reflected. These romantic passages lured European travelers to America. Don Antonio Arena, an early Italian immigrant, describes West Virginia's landscape in an OSIA brochure. He writes, "The West Virginia landscape includes a countryside which has numerous mountains . . . large swiping valleys that adjoin the plains and winding creeks and rivers. Little houses are grouped here and there, and are stretched along the railway at the bottom of the valleys. . . . The hills are covered with luxuriant vegetation reminiscent somewhat of our Calabrian-Lucanian villages." (Above, courtesy of T.M. Flower of Morrisville, Pennsylvania; below, Authors' collection.)

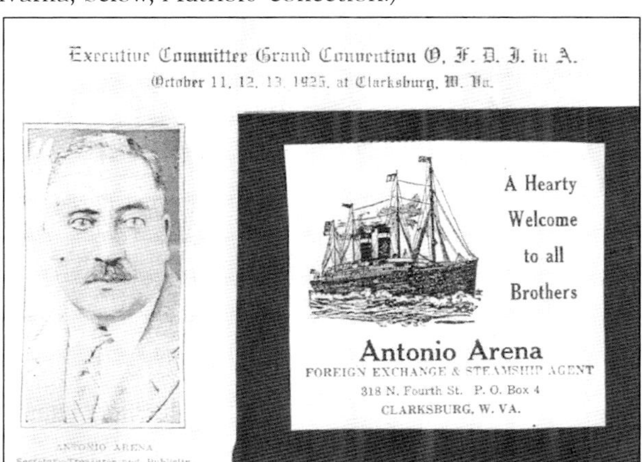

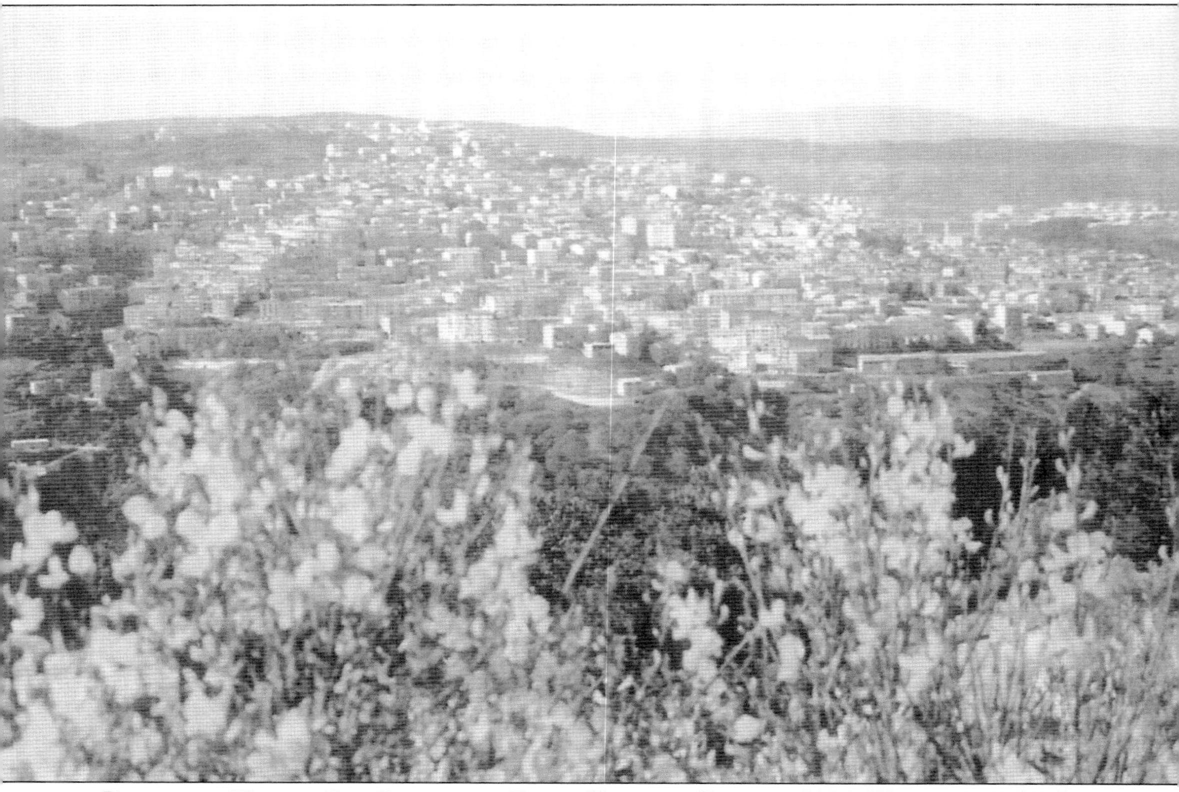

PANORAMIC VIEW OF SAN GIOVANNI IN FIORE, CALABRIA, ITALY, C. 2000. The romantic landscape of the Italian villages and towns of southern Italy are similar in layout to the hill towns and cities of north central West Virginia. San Giovanni in Fiore is a hill town located at the confluence of the Neto and Arvo Rivers. It is one of the major sites to be found in the Sila Grande. Because of its location in a great pine forest of Italy, the natives are noted for their farming, forestry, and animal husbandry. It is the hometown of Joachim of Fiore, the 12th-century monk who founded a religious order of monks and built the Florens Monastery. San Giovanni in Fiore was well known for its handicrafts, such as carpets, colored materials, and gold working. The abbey and the Norman arch are noted landmarks in the town. (Courtesy of Sal Olivito.)

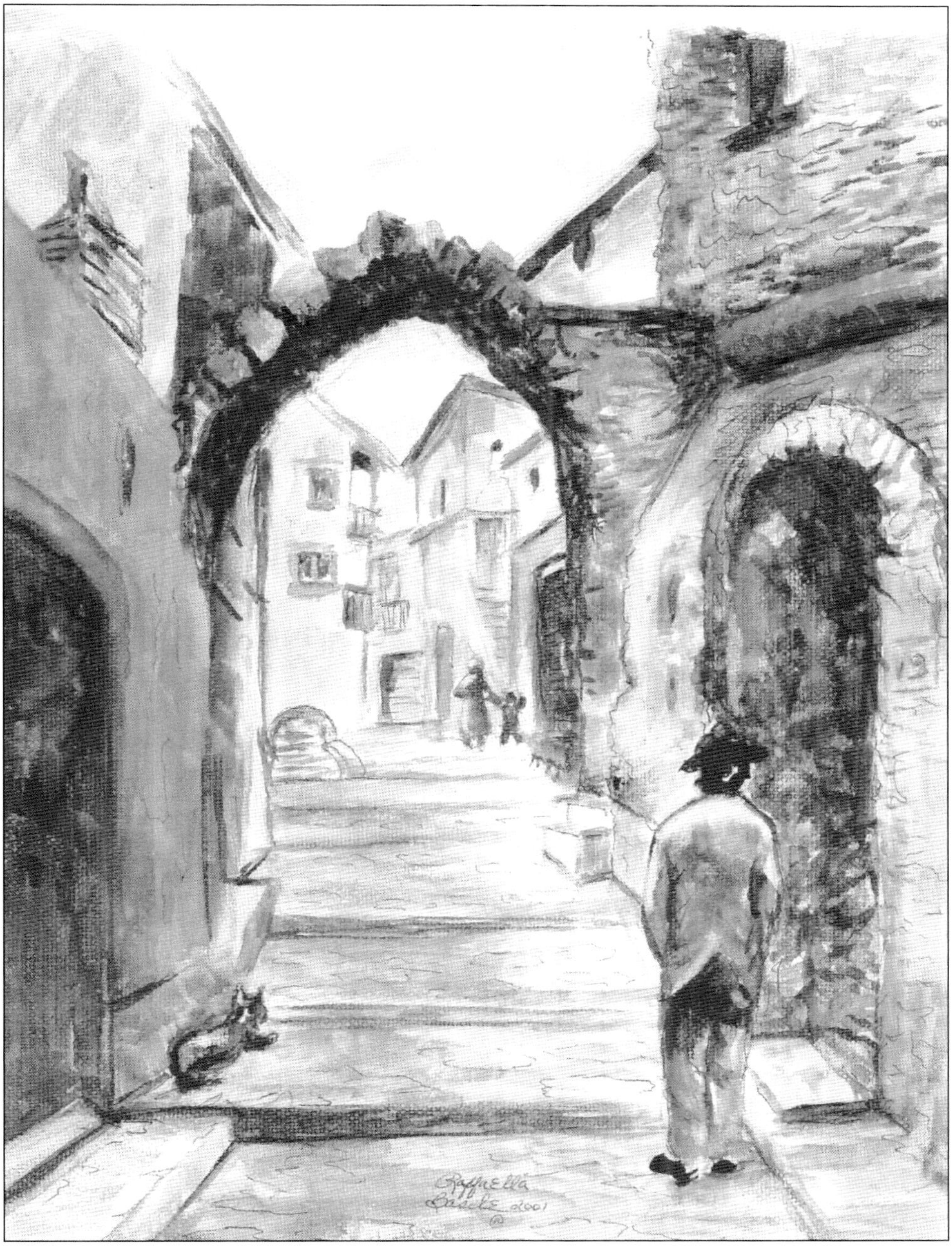

PAINTING OF THE NORMAN ARCH DEDICATED TO JOACHIM OF FIORE, C. 1980. An Italian emigrant is passing through the Norman arch and leaving his historical picturesque town of San Giovanni in Fiore, Calabria, Italy. The arch is a landmark named after Joachim of Fiore. The equilateral arch gives a wide opening of satisfying proportions useful for doorways, decorative arcades, and large windows. The structural beauty of the arch means, however, that no set proportion had to be rigidly maintained. In the architecture of some Italian cities, semicircular arches are interspersed with pointed ones. Raffaella Romano Basile, a West Virginian artist, painted the Norman arch while touring and researching her ancestry in San Giovanni in Fiore. (Authors' collection.)

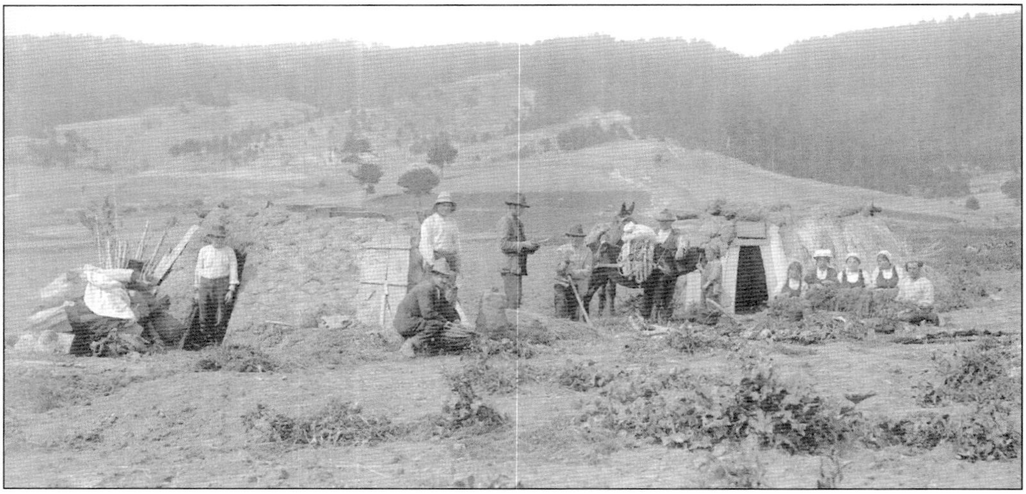

FONDO SAN BERNARDO, 1929. Southern Europe was a fertile region to recruit emigrants who were fleeing agricultural turmoil, social unrest, and a failing economy. The Calabrian peasants were hailing from a landscape that promoted agriculture, forestry, and animal husbandry. At the end of the 19th century, West Virginia officials recruited immigrants who could develop the abundant resources of the state. Early efforts to stimulate immigration met minor success due to lack of adequate roads and rail transportation. West Virginia's abundant resources of timber and coal could not be exploited until transportation improved. Railroad, coal, and lumber recruiters utilized the available native West Virginia labor force. To expand, they turned to recruiting emigrants from southern and eastern Europe. (Both, courtesy of Saverio Marra.)

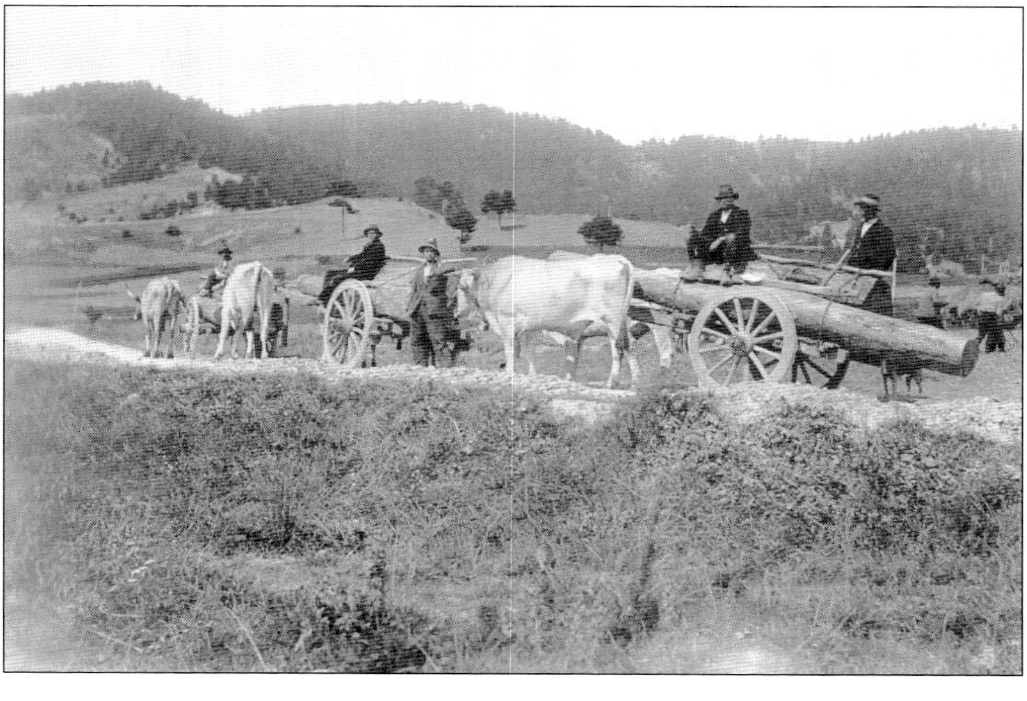

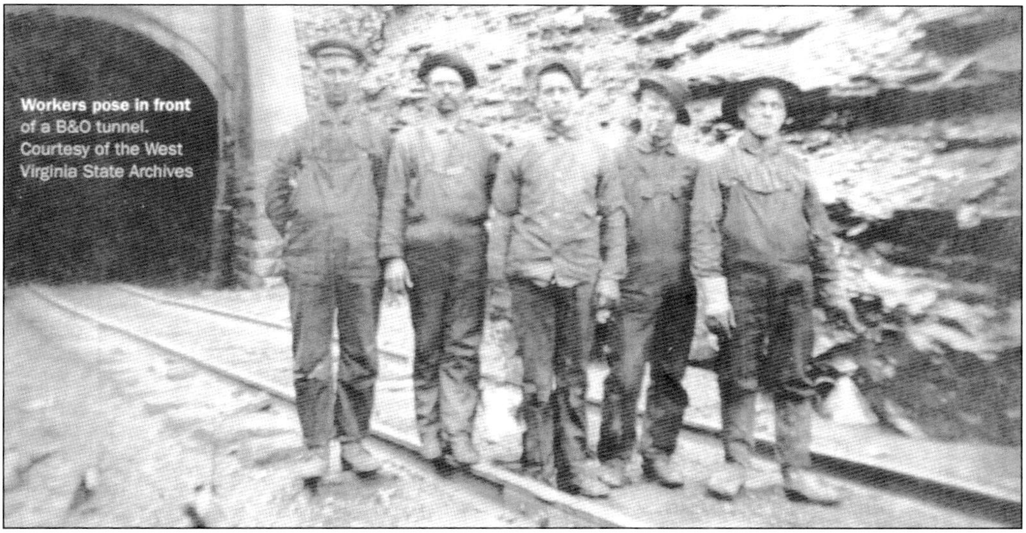

WORKERS ON THE BALTIMORE & OHIO RAILROAD AND WEST VIRGINIA COAL MINERS, C. 1850S. The rapidly expanding nation had a growing need for resources. The rich natural resources found in the central Appalachian Mountains of West Virginia attracted railroads to bring timber and coal commodities to market. In the middle of the 19th century, the Baltimore & Ohio Railroad constructed a major railroad in the state. The north central counties of West Virginia had approximately 115 coal mines in operation in the 1900s. Coal mining was the principal industry of the region, with thousands working in the mines. Approximately 3,000 miners were of Italian origin. They descended daily thousands of feet into the bowels of the earth. (Above, courtesy of West Virginia State Archives; below, courtesy of Russell Marano and Russell Bonasso.)

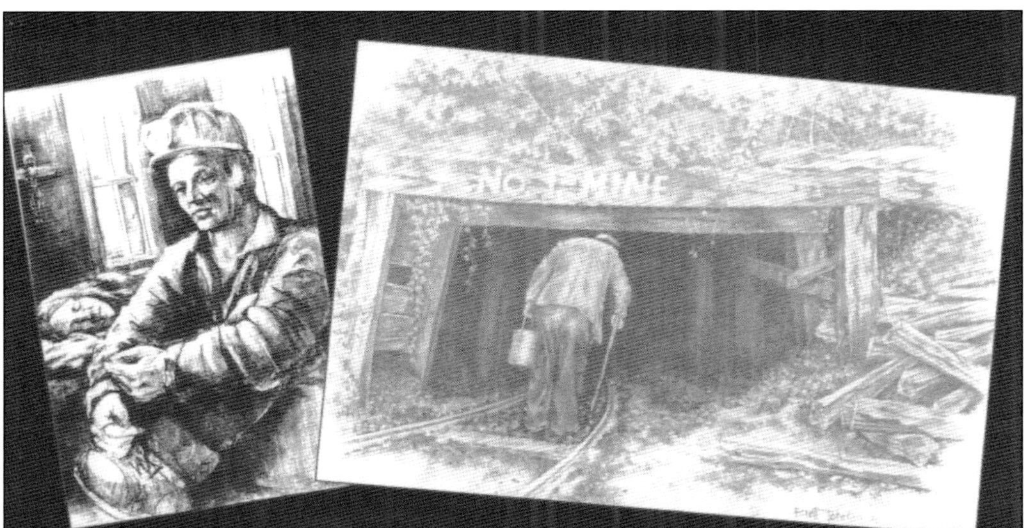

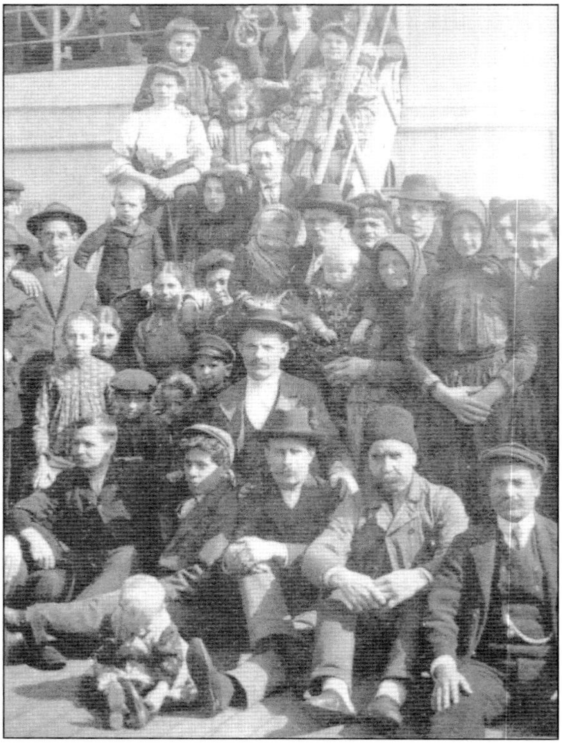

EMIGRANTS LEAVING GENOA AND *LA DOMENICA DEL CORRIERE*, 1906. There were two main embarkation points for emigrants traveling to the United States. Southern Italians left from Naples; northern Italians left from Genoa. Some Italian emigrants traveled overland to Le Havre, France, and boarded ships there in order to avoid the inferior conditions commonplace on Italian ships. Passage to America was rough and dangerous. The White Star Line transported many Italian immigrants on their transoceanic passages. Here, the publication *La Domenica del Corriere* covers the rescue mission of passengers aboard the Italian ship *Sirio* near the coast of Spain. (Both, courtesy of Vincenzo Gentile.)

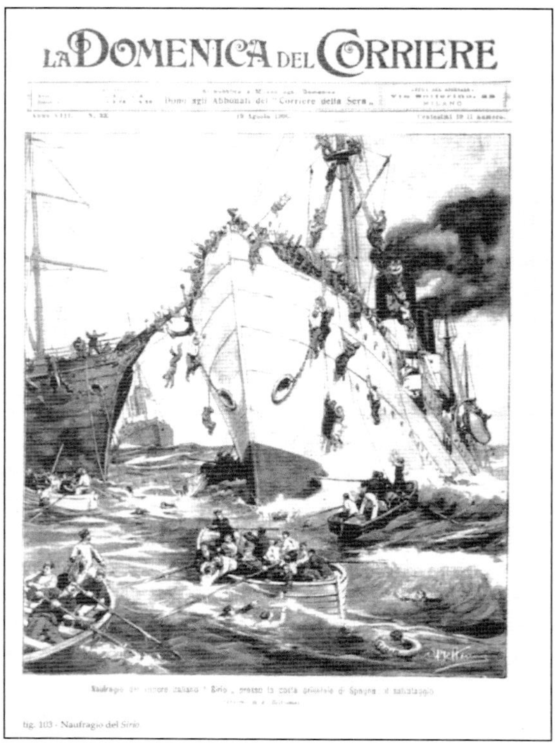
LA DOMENICA DEL CORRIERE

Dono agli Abbonati del "Corriere della Sera"

MILANO

fig. 103 - Naufragio del *Sirio*

STEERAGE PASSENGERS ABOARD THE SHIP, C. 1900. Most emigrants traveled in the least expensive manner possible—steerage. Contrasting sharply with the first-class accommodation on the upper decks, steerage travel consisted of dank, dreary quarters in the lower levels of the ship, where engine noise and heat, lack of adequate comfort facilities, and poor ventilation made the journey one of unpleasantness and difficulty. Emigrants went often to the upper deck of the ship in search of fresh air and relief from the interior conditions of the lower decks. When the sea was rough and passengers were confined to lower decks, motion- and seasickness resulted. (Both, courtesy of Vincenzo Gentile.)

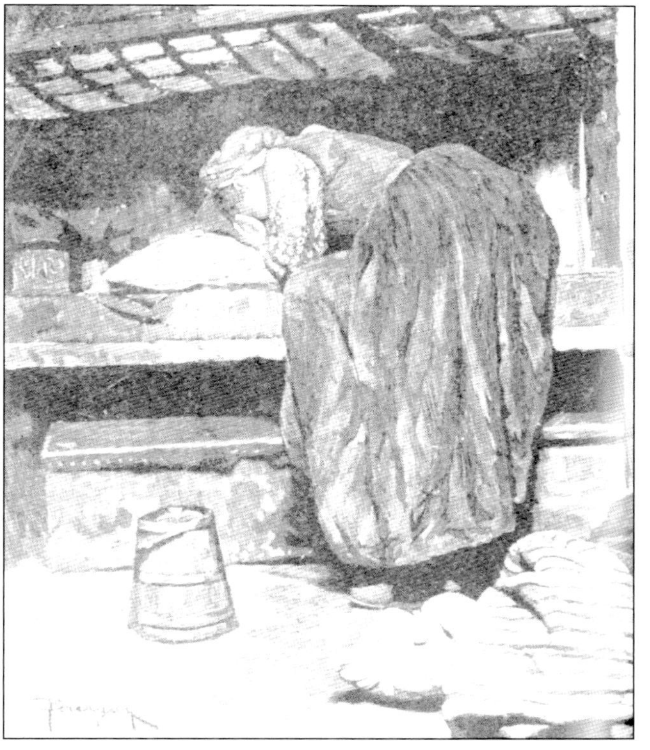

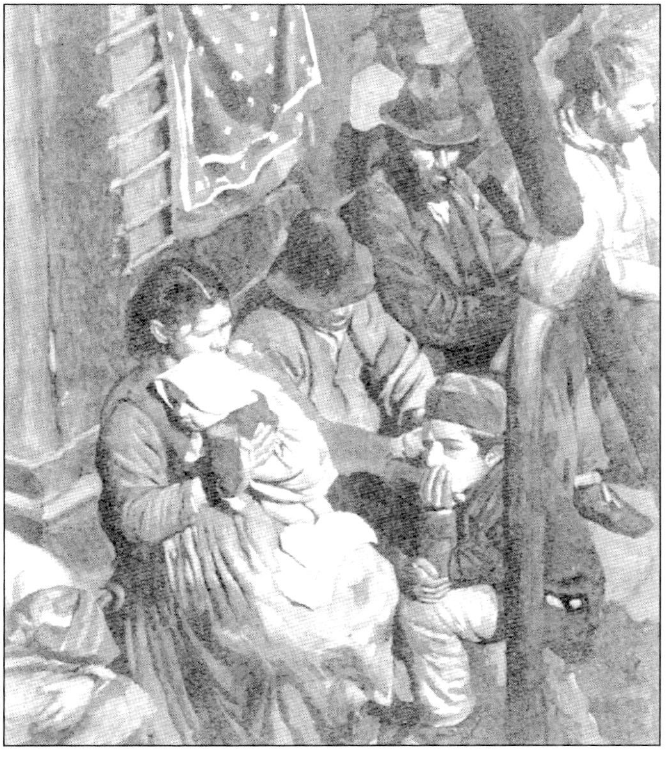

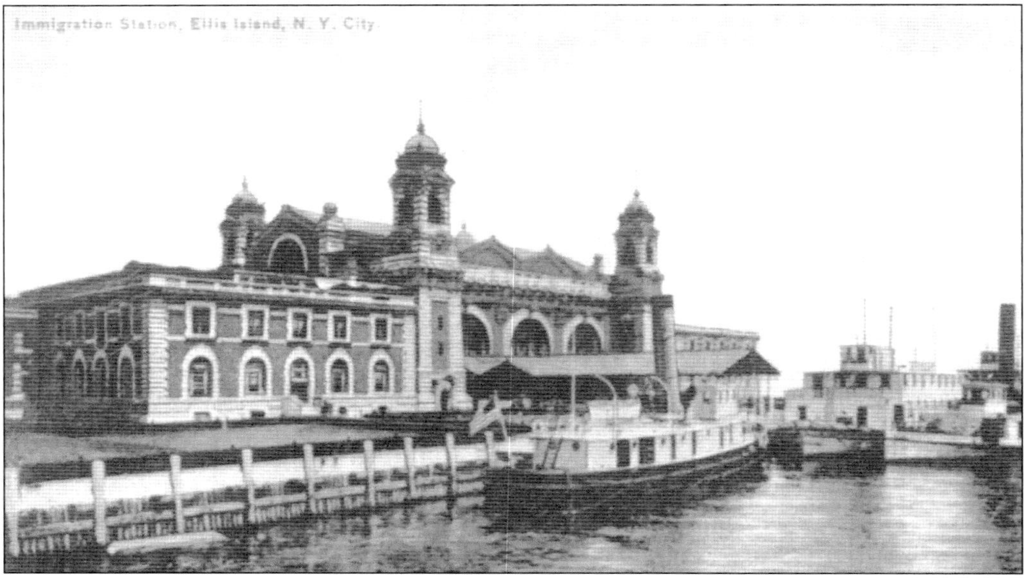

Ellis Island and Interior of Immigration Center, 1915. Upon arrival in New York, immigrants had to pass through customs. First- and second-class passengers were processed aboard the ship and allowed to enter the United States immediately upon arrival. Steerage passengers took ferries to Ellis Island, where they underwent a series of inspections designed to keep out undesirable immigrants. If papers were in order and further examinations deemed unnecessary, immigrants could pass through the stations in Ellis Island in a matter of hours. Others had to remain in the facility for days before finally being granted passage to the American mainland. In a single workday, Ellis Island officials could process more than 5,000 arriving immigrants. (Both, courtesy of the Library of Congress.)

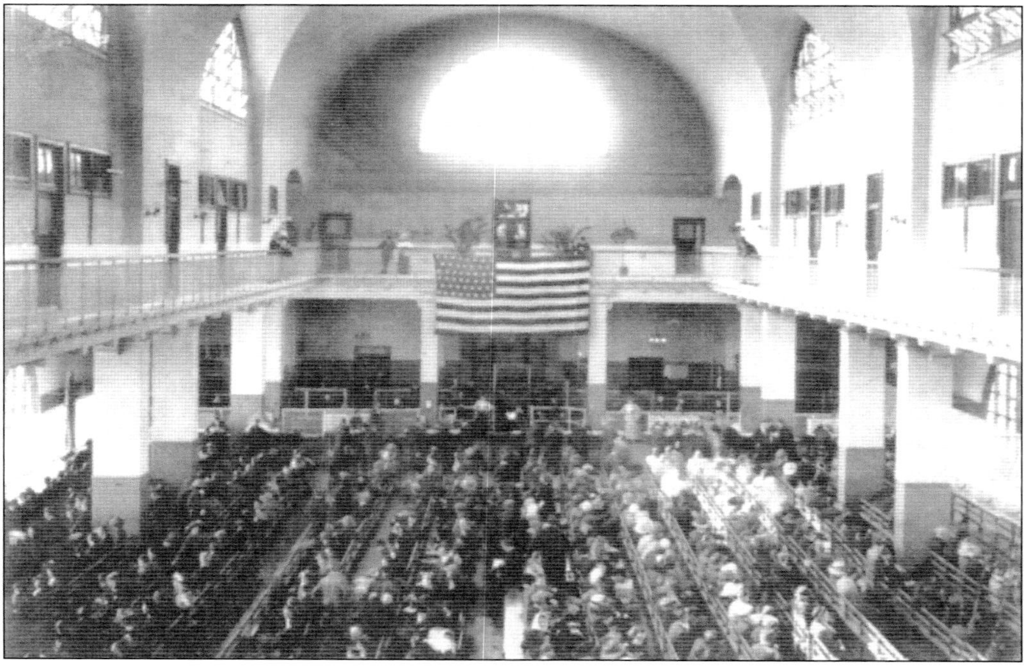

MEDICAL EXAMINATIONS AND IMMIGRANTS LEAVING INSPECTION CENTER, ELLIS ISLAND, C. 1915. One of the major stages in the screening process involved doctors examining immigrants to identify physical handicaps, mental illnesses, or contagious and infectious diseases, such as trachoma, tuberculosis, or leprosy. Immigrants diagnosed with such disorders were quarantined to the Ellis Island Hospital. After leaving the custom inspection center, immigrants would board boats that would transport them to the mainland. On arrival, most would be met by spouses and sponsoring relatives. Others would be greeted by contract laborers. In the 1920s, the federal government passed a series of acts that restricted immigration to the United States and lessened the importance of Ellis Island. By the 1930s, immigration inspectors had begun to inspect and process immigrants on the arriving ships rather than at Ellis Island. (Both, courtesy of Ellis Island Archives.)

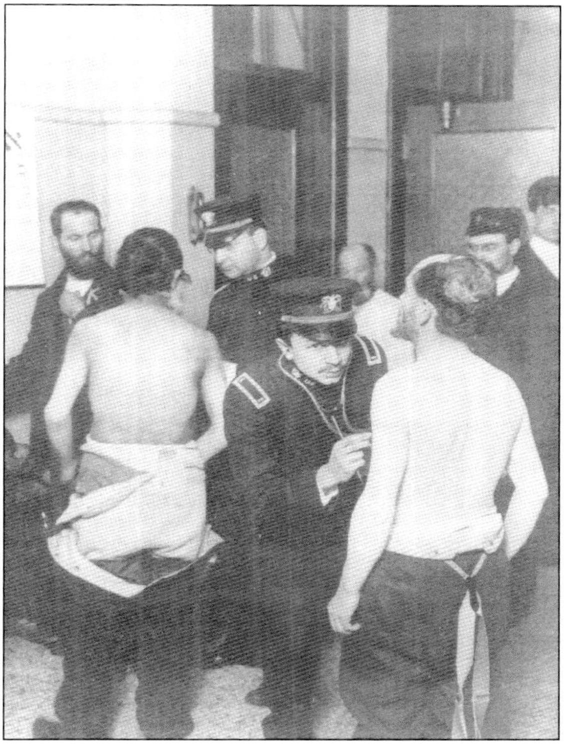

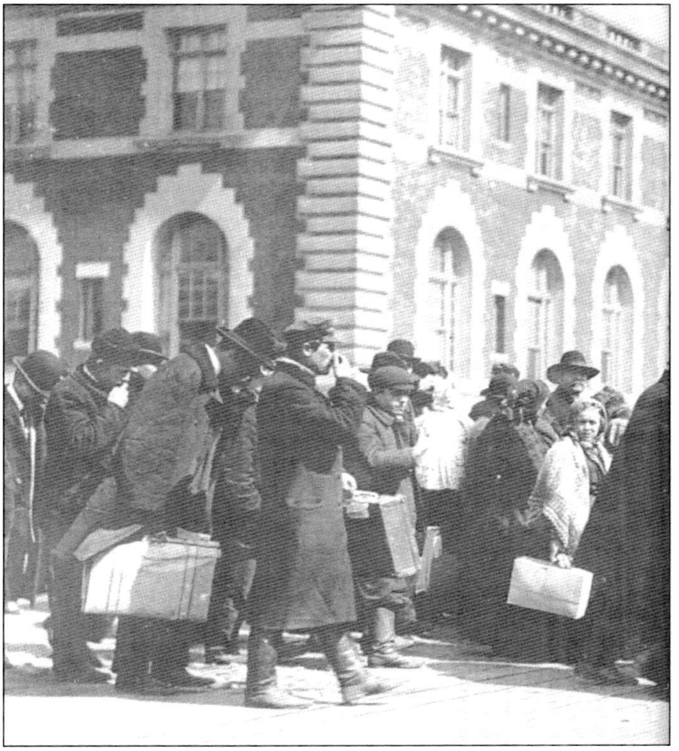

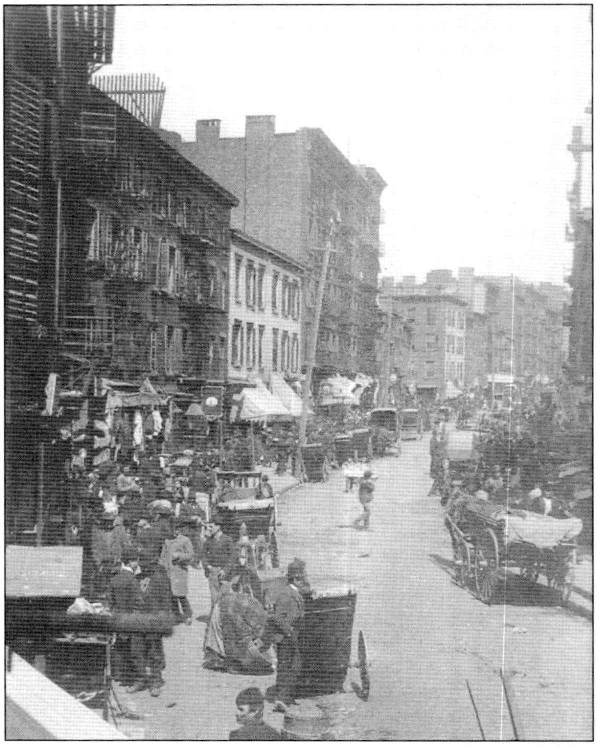

MULBERRY BEND AND COAL LOADERS WITH MULE, WEST VIRGINIA, 1908. Contract agents for coal companies gathered in Mulberry Bend in New York City to review the arriving immigrants. For each worker who arrived in West Virginia, agents would receive a fee. In some cases, free transportation and housing were given to the promising immigrants. Italians who accepted such offers became victims of the practice of peonage. Below, a 1908 photograph shows young boys who are coal loaders with a mule-driven cart. Most Italian immigrants worked as coal loaders. Dirty, backbreaking work, coal loading entailed shoveling coal into mule-driven carts while removing impurities such as shale and clay. The carts were pulled out of the mineshaft in order to be weighed. Miners were paid by the tonnage of coal that they mined in a shift. (Both, courtesy of the Library of Congress.)

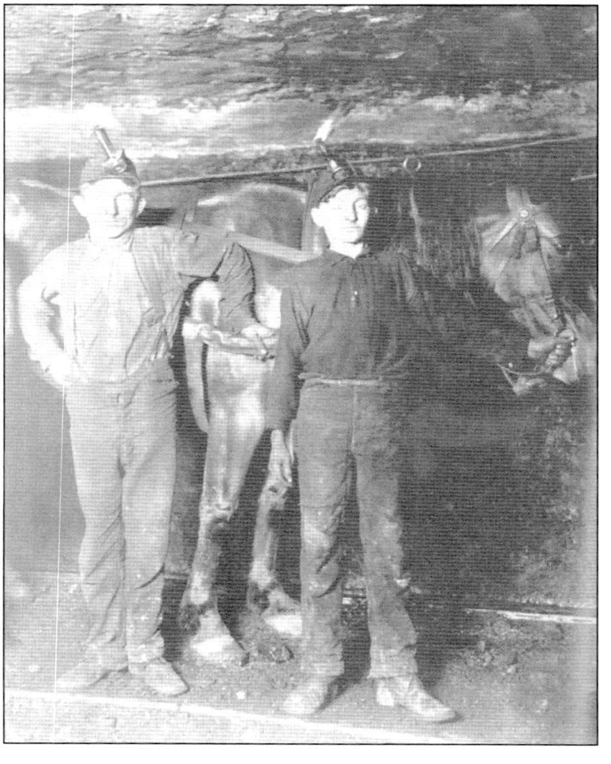

EMOTIONAL PAINS OF IMMIGRATION, 1910. It is easy to minimize the emotional cost of immigration in recounting three generations of success in the Americas. However, the separation of spouses caused by emigration hurt deeply. The graffiti written on the side of this house is particularly applicable to the emigrants who left Italy and went to work in the coal mines. It reads, "A woman is like the sea, all the rivers are estuaries; a man is like carbon, when ignited it burns; when it is extinguished it is still tinged." The empty chair in the lower photograph indicates that the emigrant husband is missed. The hat on the chair signifies that he is still the head of the family. However, his post as head of the family has been temporarily relegated to his oldest son. (Both, courtesy of Vincenzo Gentile.)

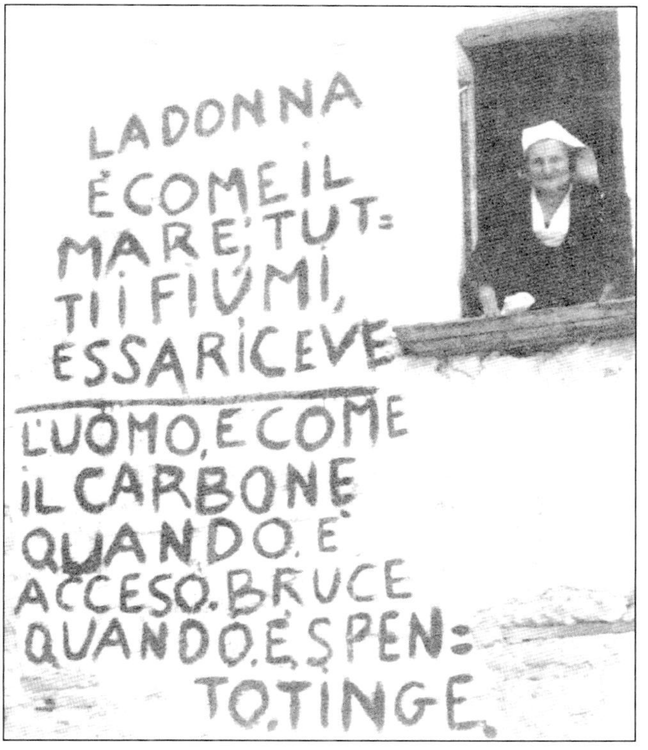

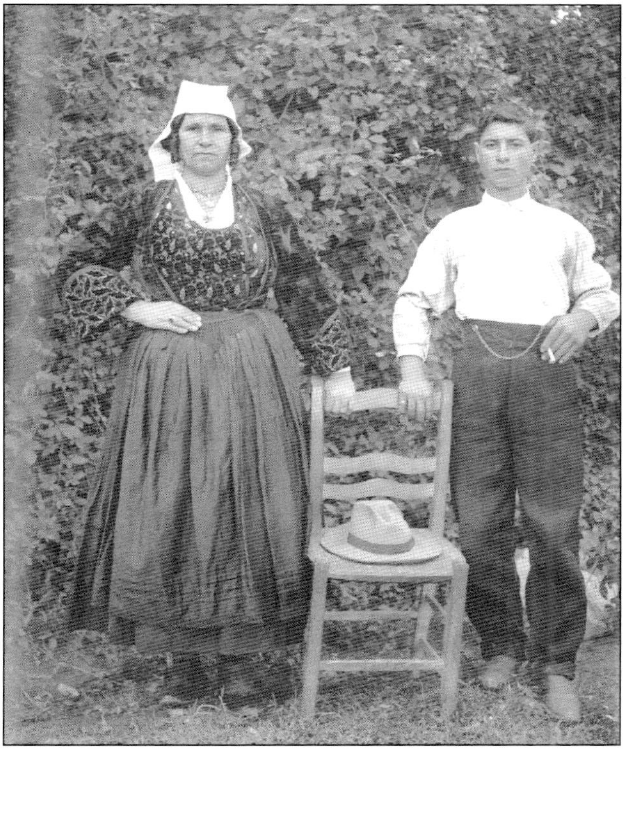

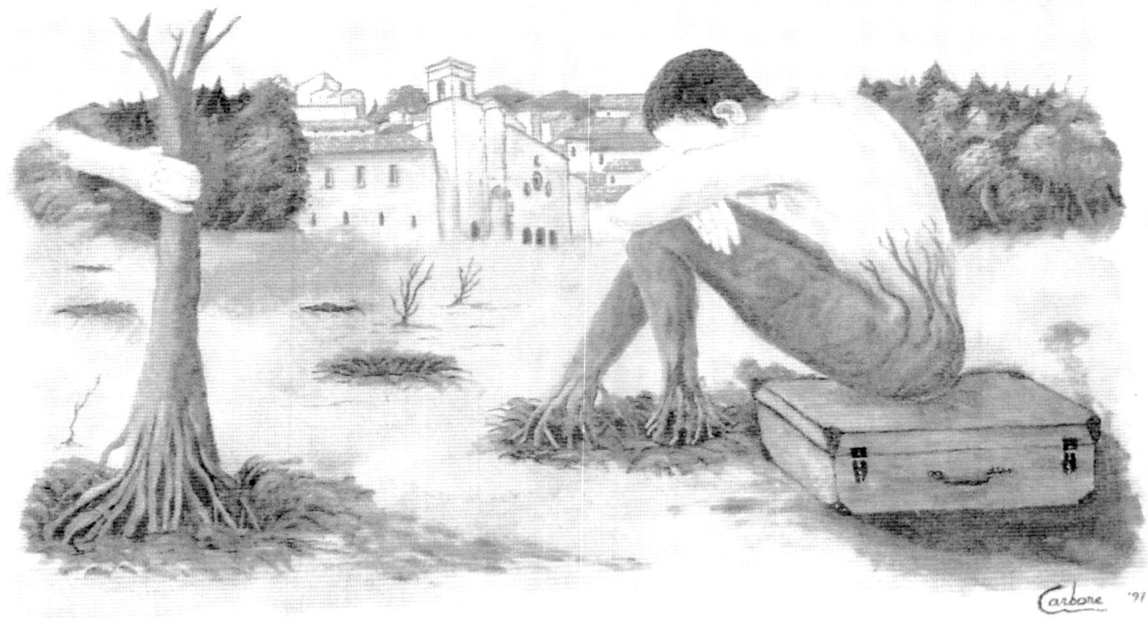

EMOTIONAL PAINS OF EMIGRATION, ITALY, 1910. This etching displays the pains experienced in emigration and the nostalgia for native villages. Anna Paletta Zurzolo expresses this in her book *Bread, Wine and Angels*. She writes, "Just as the roots of a tree are ingrained into the slope, I could have been flexible and elastic. However, having been dragged around the world, my root system has not been broken, but still remains firm and attached to the environment of my native village and the morning dawn in the beautiful hills of San Giovanni in Fiore." (Courtesy of Carbone.)

Two

Work and Disaster

The southern Italian emigrant was a desirable candidate for West Virginia's reconstruction and industrialization. Italians laborers were basically farmers, woodsmen, and stonecutters, and at the beginning of the 20th century, these working skills were in demand for West Virginia's booming initiatives of agriculture, forestry, railway construction, and coal mining. Industrial companies had policies that in some cases were unjust to the immigrant laborers. Promising workers were given free transportation and housing by the coal companies to work in the coal mines of West Virginia. Italians who accepted such offers became victims of the practice of peonage. Unlike slavery, a permanent condition, the peon would, hopefully, be freed once his debt was paid. However, workers who lived in company housing were paid in unofficial currency called "scrip" that was exchangeable only at the company store. In addition to food and clothing, the peon was required to furnish his own tools and blasting powder, which he purchased at the company store. In 1907, a mine disaster in Monongah, West Virginia, temporarily slowed down Italian immigration to the region. On December 6, 1907, the worst coal mine disaster in American history killed a reported total of 425 men and boys, leaving 250 widows and over 1,000 children displaced. Approximately 171 of the victims were Italians who emigrated from the provinces of Calabria, Abruzzo, and Molise. Their heroism and valor were recognized at the 2007 Centennial Observance Ceremony, held in Monongah on December 7. *The Monongah Heroine*, a granite statue, was unveiled in tribute to the dead miners, but especially to their wives and children, who persisted and moved forward after the disaster. Eventually, immigration declined, and the Italians were able to move forward, work in safer coal and coke industries, organize mutual aid societies, and open small businesses.

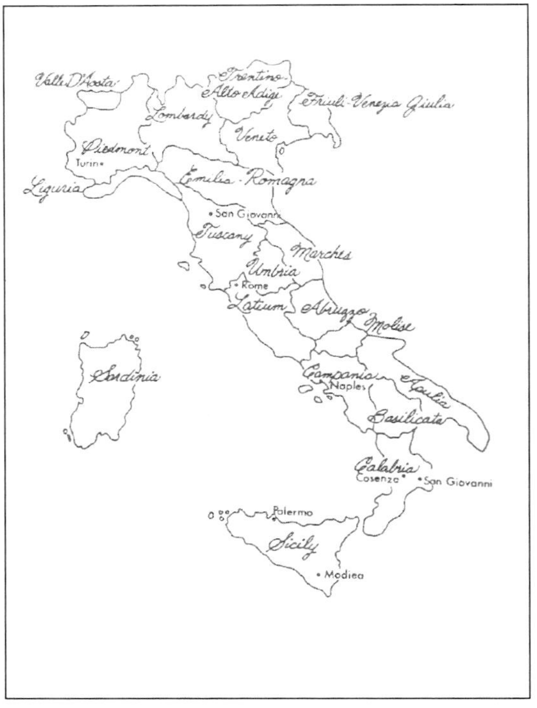

PROVINCES OF ITALY AND FARMING IN WEST VIRGINIA, 1910. Between 1880 and 1930, over 13 million Italians left their homeland, launching the largest recorded migration from any country in world history. In 1910, there were 17,286 Italians in West Virginia; in 1920, there were 14,147; in 1930, there were 13,190. The regions from which Italians emigrated included Calabria (45 percent); Molise/Abruzzi (15 percent); Campania (10 percent); Sicilia, Basilicata, and northern regions (5 percent or less). The US Census of 1910 showed that agriculture, forestry, and animal husbandry accounted for 37.5 percent of the jobs in West Virginia. Since Italians had the additional skill of stonecutting, they went to work in the coal industries. In 1910, 44 percent of West Virginia's Italians worked in the mines; in 1920, 45 percent worked in the mines. (Left, Authors' collection; below, courtesy of West Virginia and Regional Collection, West Virginia University Libraries.)

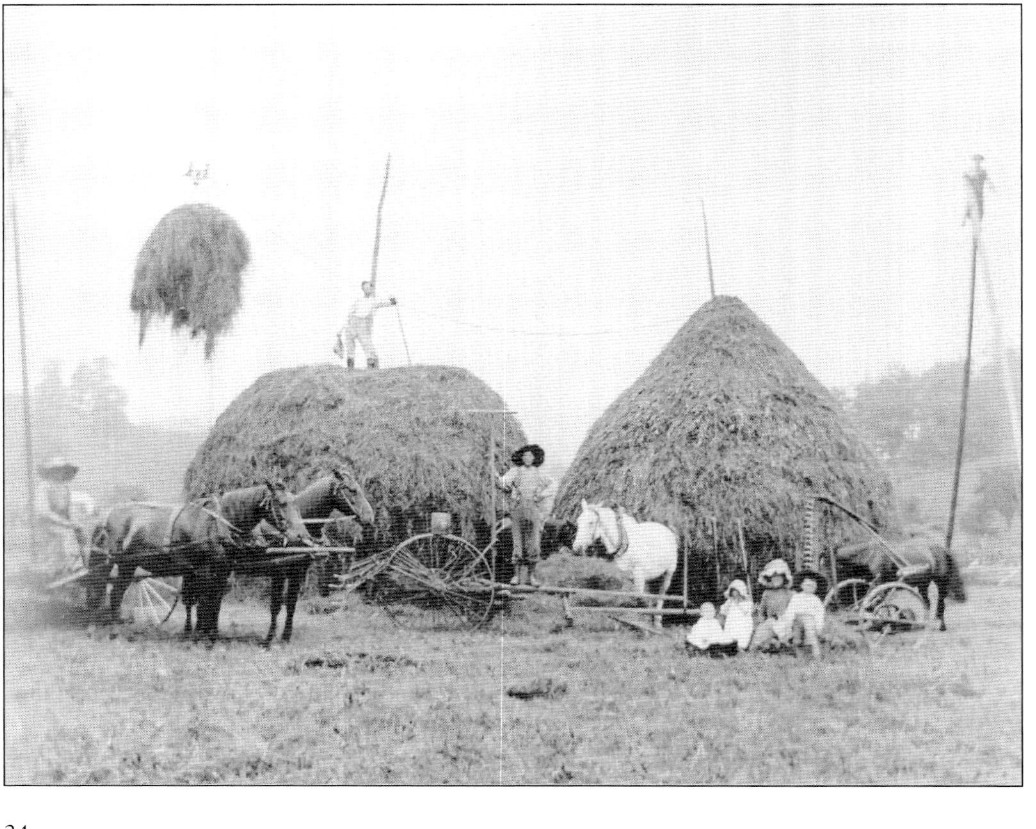

RAIL VIADUCT CONSTRUCTION AND TURKEY KNOB TIPPLE CREW, 1900s. The craft of stonecutting was most applicable to rail and viaduct construction. In order to get the coal out of the mountains, first the timber needed to be removed and railroads had to be built to transport the coal. The Turkey Knob Mine's tipple crew at Macdonald, south of Oak Hill, posed for the photograph below in 1908. The Italian laborer was a promising candidate for West Virginia's reconstruction and industrialization. His skills could be applied to West Virginia's booming initiatives in railway construction and coal mining. (Left, courtesy of West Virginia State Archives; below, courtesy of Library of Congress.)

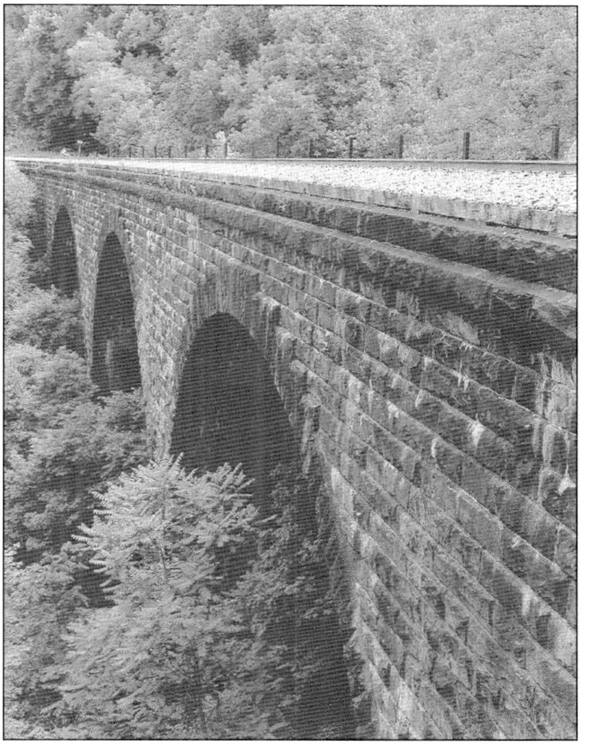

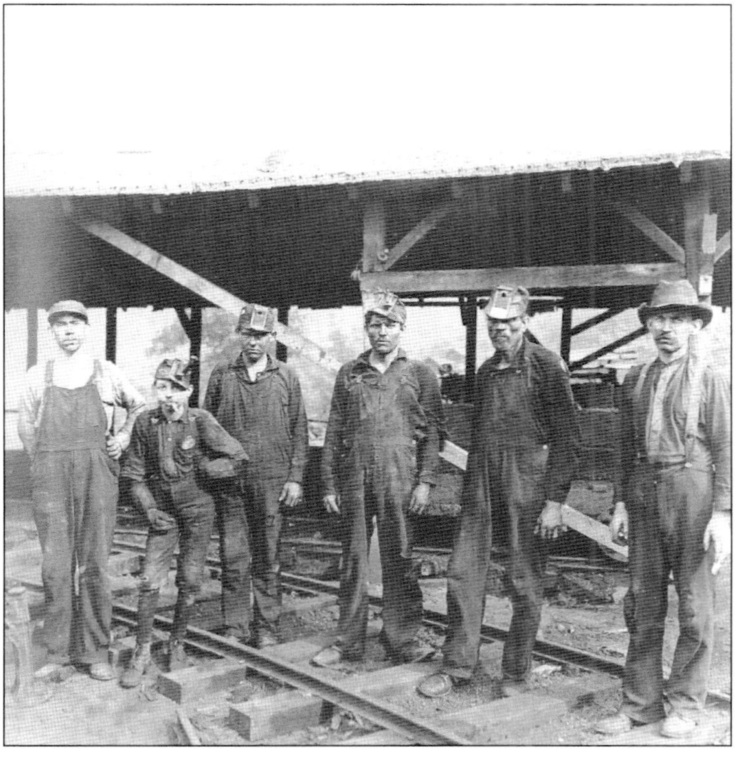

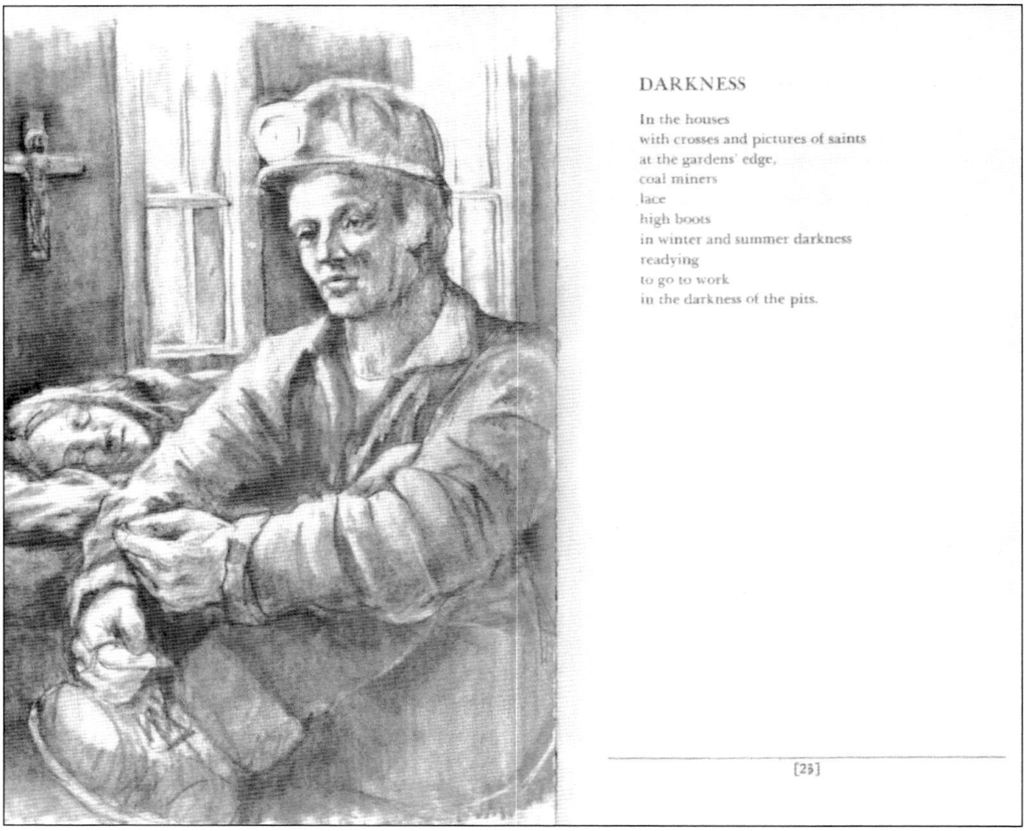

Coal Miner and Mining Town, Monongah, 1900. Historically, coal mining has been a very dangerous, destructive, and dislocating occupation. Russell Marano expressed the perils of the coal miner in his poem "Darkness." Monongah (pictured below) is a mining town in Marion County, West Virginia, along the West Fork River. It was incorporated in 1891. Its name is abbreviated from Monongahela, the river formed by the confluence of the West Fork and Tygart Valley Rivers a few miles north of the town. (Above, courtesy of Russell Marano; below, courtesy of Ron Rittenhouse.)

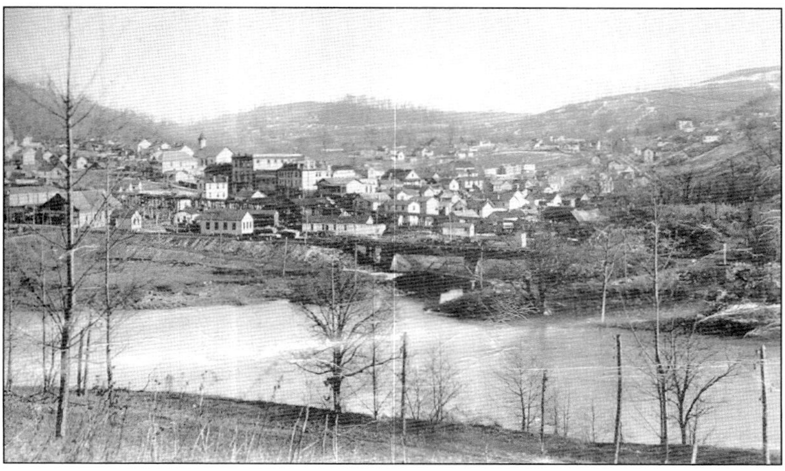

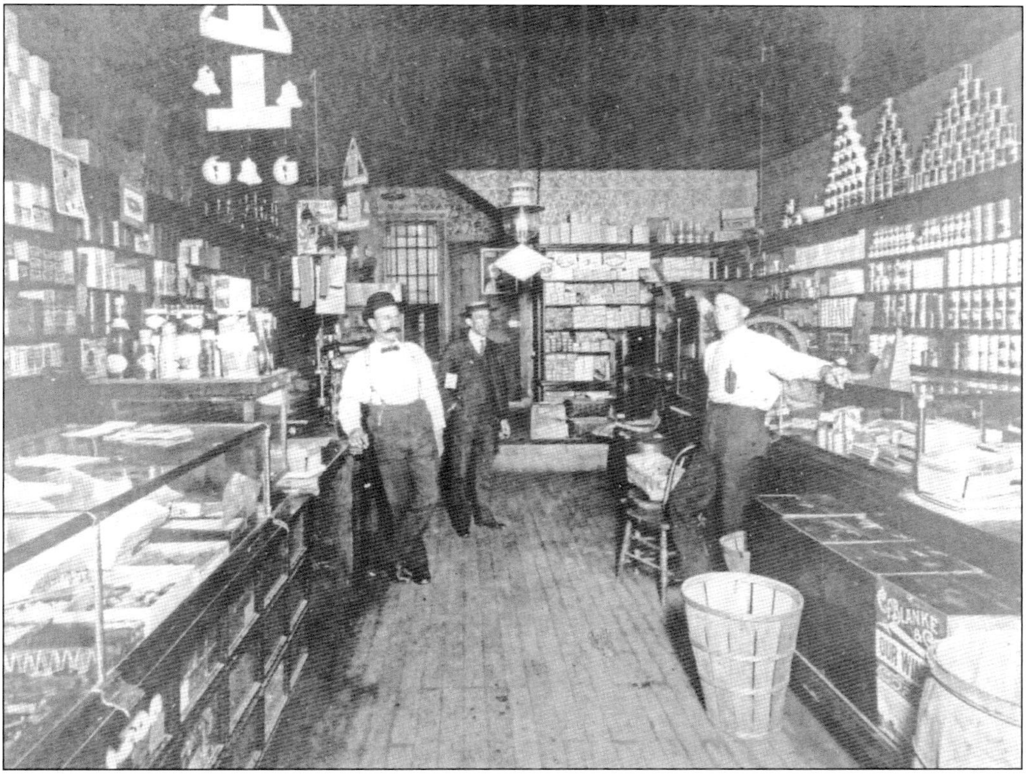

MONTANA MINES COMPANY STORE AND OLD MONONGAH MEAT MARKET, MARION COUNTY, 1900. In the 1880s, coal companies built and owned entire towns, while mine workers were often required to live in company houses and shop at the company store using company scrip in place of cash. These practices added to the company's financial stability and made it more difficult for miners to get out of debt and go on strikes. This system was similar to the feudal system (coal companies being the "barons of the manor" and the coal miners being the serfs). (Above, courtesy of West Virginia and Regional Collection, West Virginia University Library; below, courtesy of Ron Rittenhouse.)

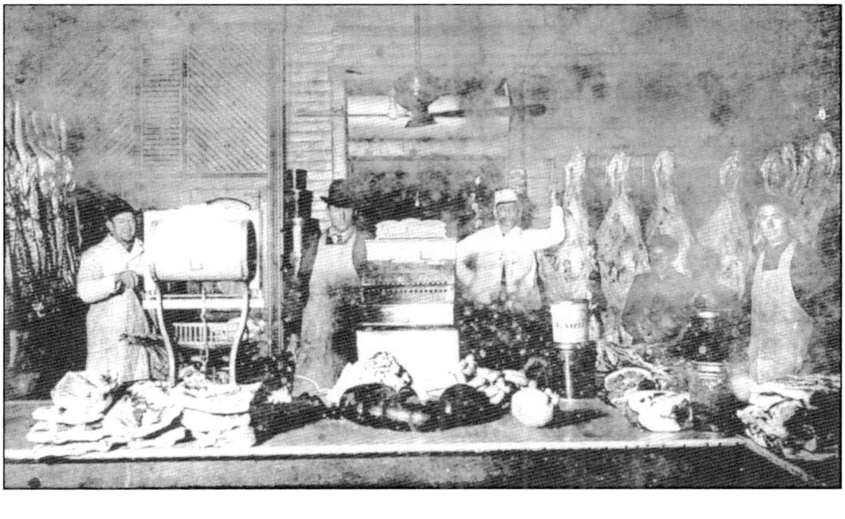

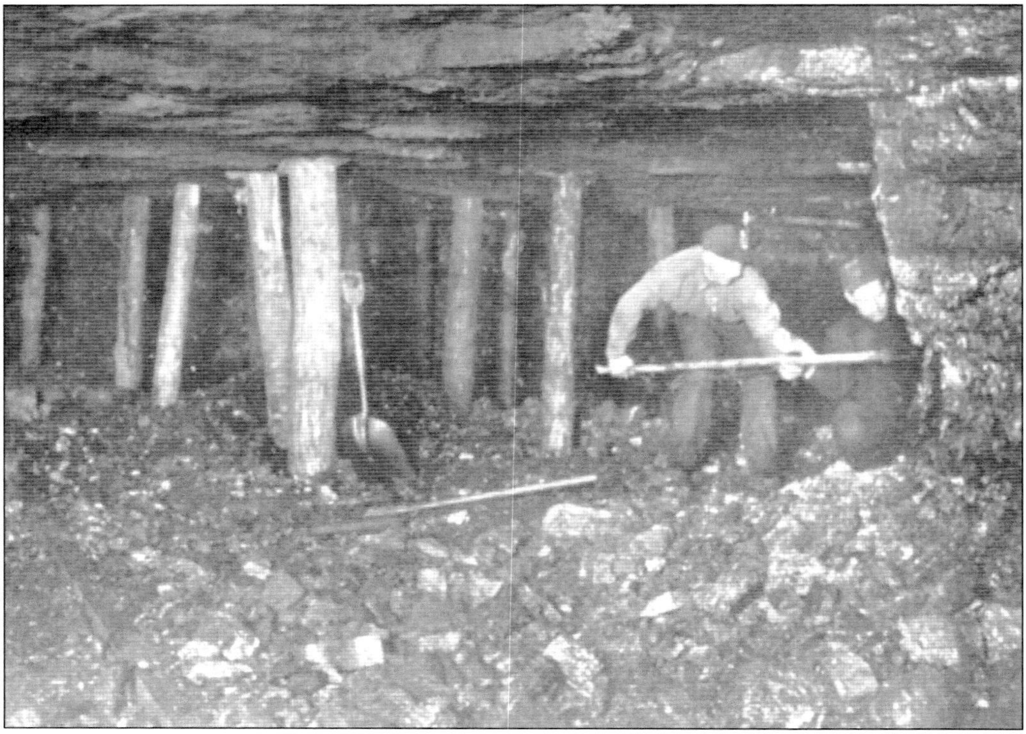

MINING CONDITIONS AND MONONGAH MINE NO. SIX, 1907. Prior to unions, working conditions in the mines were very hazardous for miners. It has been described as being "the meanest life in the world." Miners spoke of bad air, being trapped behind smoke, and being unable to get out. Pins would not hold, which caused the slate to fall. Water seeped into mineshafts and made working conditions damp and cold. Working stooped over in a narrow seam of coal or laboring on their knees in a puddle of water for the entire duration of a shift was sheer physical agony. Below, three miners are pictured standing in the Monongah Mine No. Six pit mouth. This is how it appeared before the explosion of December 6, 1907. (Above, courtesy of the Library of Congress; below, courtesy of Ron Rittenhouse.)

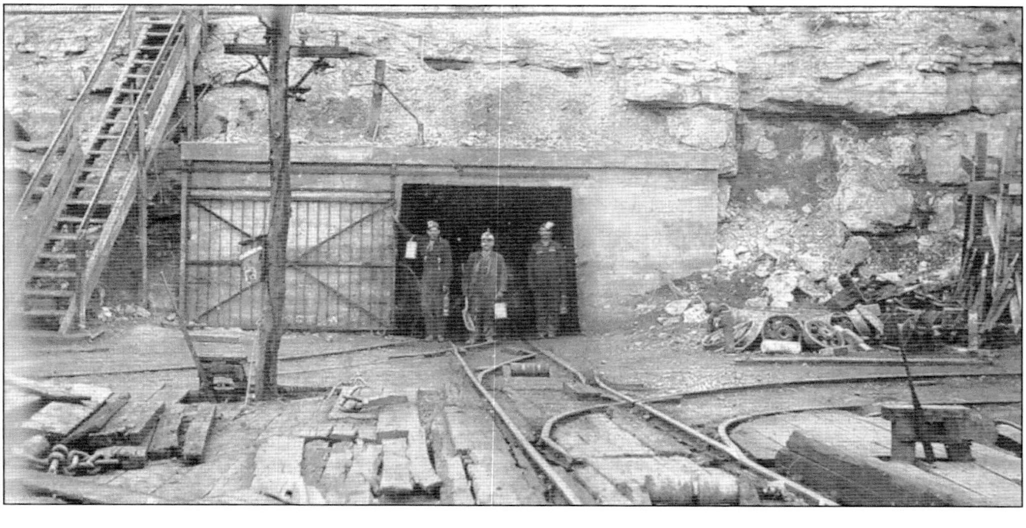

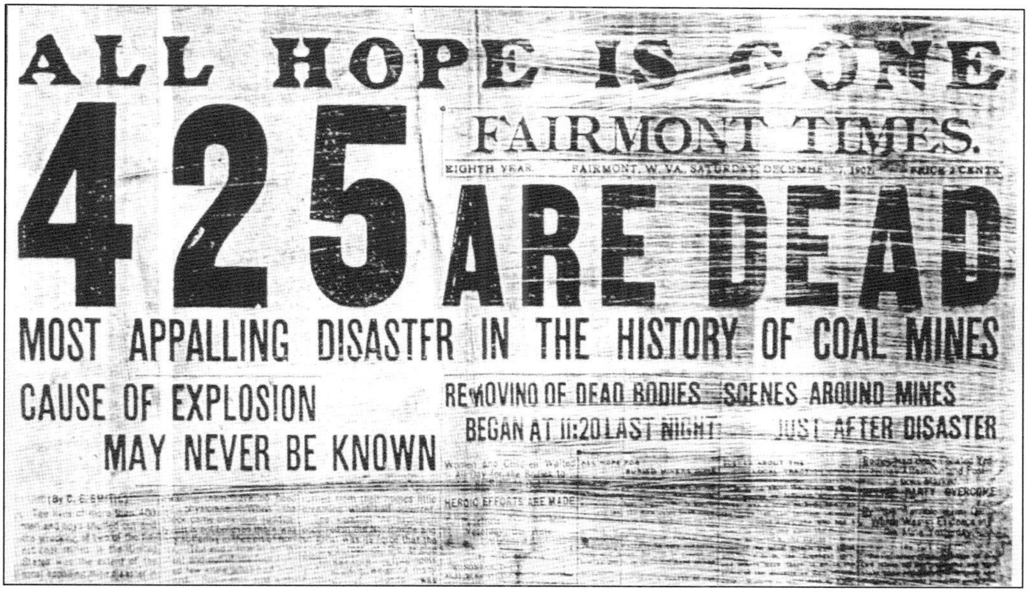

ALL HOPE IS GONE

FAIRMONT TIMES.

EIGHTH YEAR. FAIRMONT, W. VA. SATURDAY, DECEMBER 7, 1907.

425 ARE DEAD

MOST APPALLING DISASTFR IN THE HISTORY OF COAL MINES

CAUSE OF EXPLOSION MAY NEVER BE KNOWN

REMOVINO OF DEAD BODIES BEGAN AT 11:20 LAST NIGHT

SCENES AROUND MINES JUST AFTER DISASTER

HEROIC EFFORTS ARE MADE

***Fairmont Times* Headlines and Men Waiting for News, Monongah, 1907.** The worst mining disaster in American history occurred in the community of Monongah on December 6, 1907. The paper reported a total of 425 deaths of men and boys, leaving 250 widows and over 1,000 children without support. The explosion disrupted the ventilation systems, causing an effluence of deadly gases to be trapped within the mines. Those on the surface concluded that the men and boys who survived the explosion and cave-in succumbed to the gases. The mine officials, as well as the officials of the Baltimore & Ohio Railroad Company, took an active part in the relief, and many acts of bravery were performed by volunteers who entered the mines in search of the victims. (Both, courtesy of Ron Rittenhouse.)

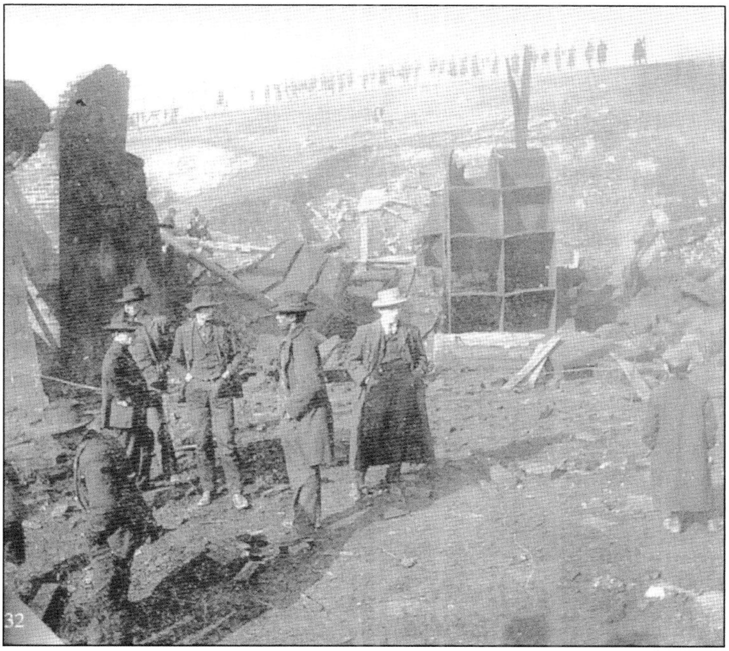

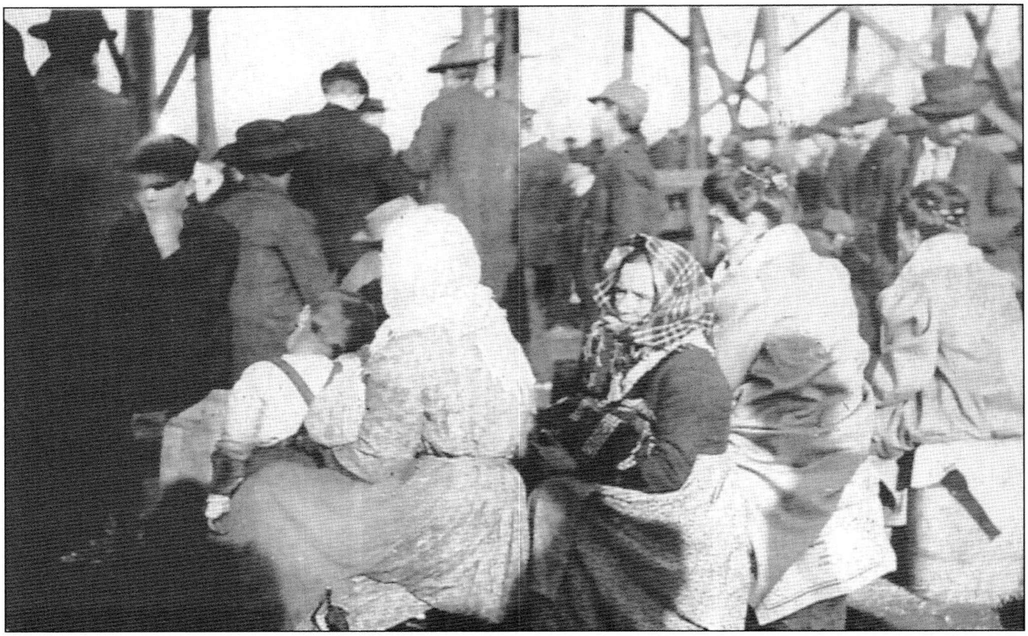

WOMEN AND CHILDREN WAITING FOR NEWS AND VIEWING THE DEAD, MONONGAH, 1907. Crowds gathered at the entrances of the mines and waited for news about their friends and family trapped inside. The scenes at the mines during the rescue efforts were pitiful. For several days, frantic women grouped about the openings of the mines, and there were shrieks of agony. Grief-stricken mothers, wives, sweethearts, and sisters waited, watched, and wept. A temporary morgue was set up in a bank building to accommodate the victims. Bodies were identified by their personal effects. Some were never identified, however, and these victims were placed in wooden caskets that were put out in the street with lids open in the hope that family members could identify the men inside. (Both, courtesy of Ron Rittenhouse.)

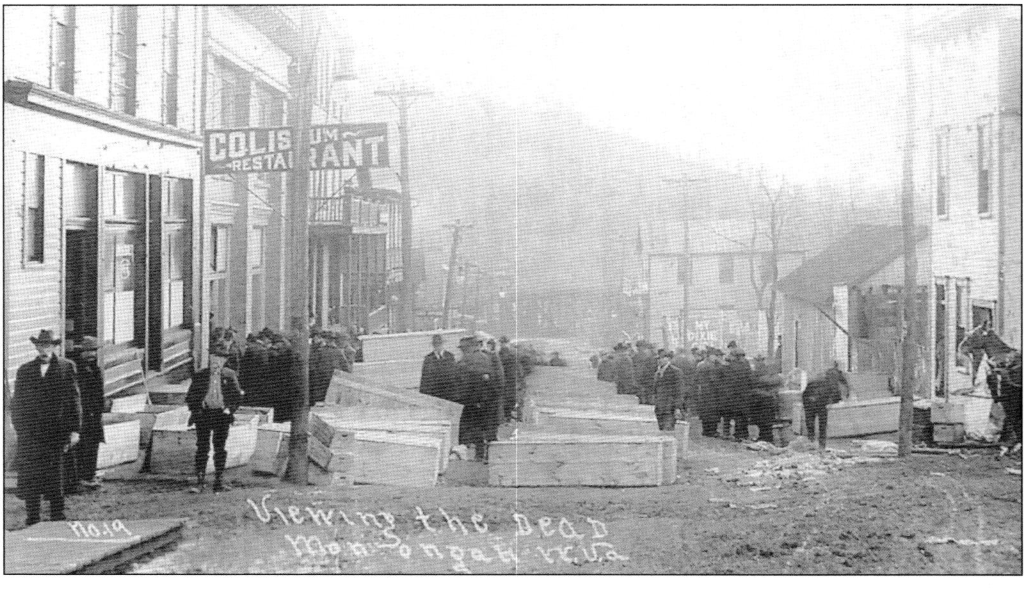

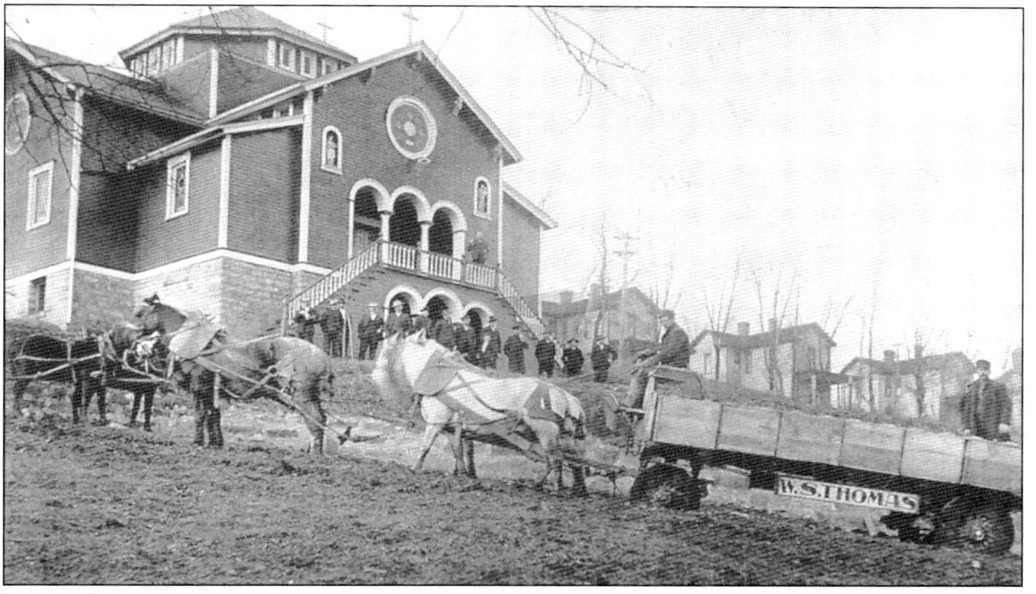

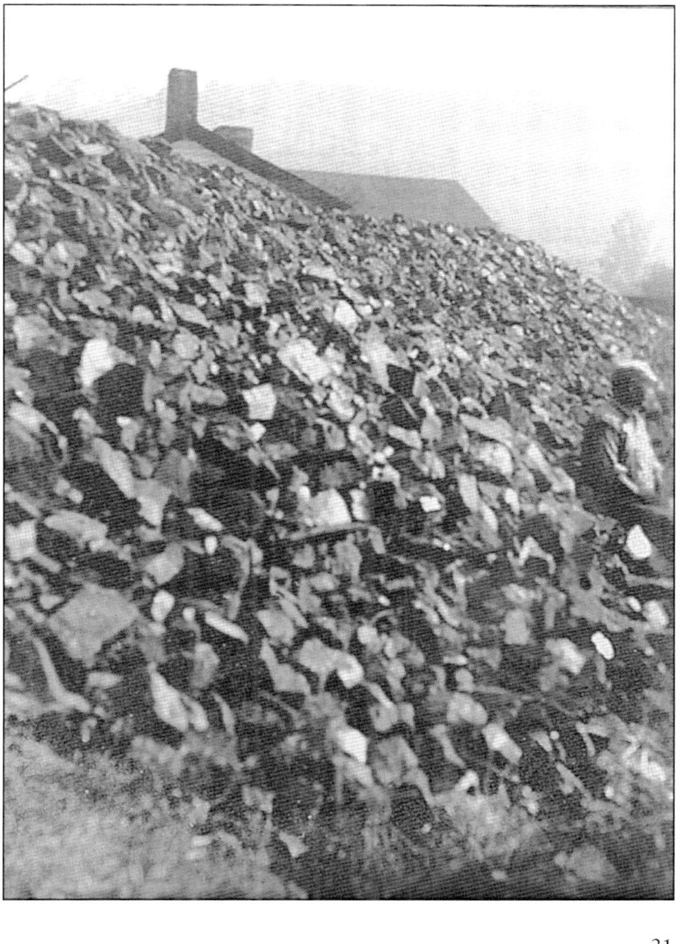

POLISH CATHOLIC CHURCH AND CATHERINE DAVIA'S MEMORIAL MOUND OF COAL, MONONGAH, 1907. W.S. Thomas of Fairmont, a hauling firm, devoted its equipment to transporting caskets from downtown to churches and the cemetery. Many of the victims were Italians who had emigrated from villages in Calabria, Abruzzo, and Molise. Among the hundreds of mineworkers who lost their lives in the explosion was Victor Davia. His wife, Catherine, was so traumatized by his death that she began hauling coal from the mine portal to her house to build a black mountain memorial. Four times a day for 29 years, she walked a mile and a half to the portal, filled her sack with coal, and then trudged back home with the loaded sack. In those 29 years, Catherine walked 125,000 miles carrying her coal. (Both, courtesy of Ron Rittenhouse.)

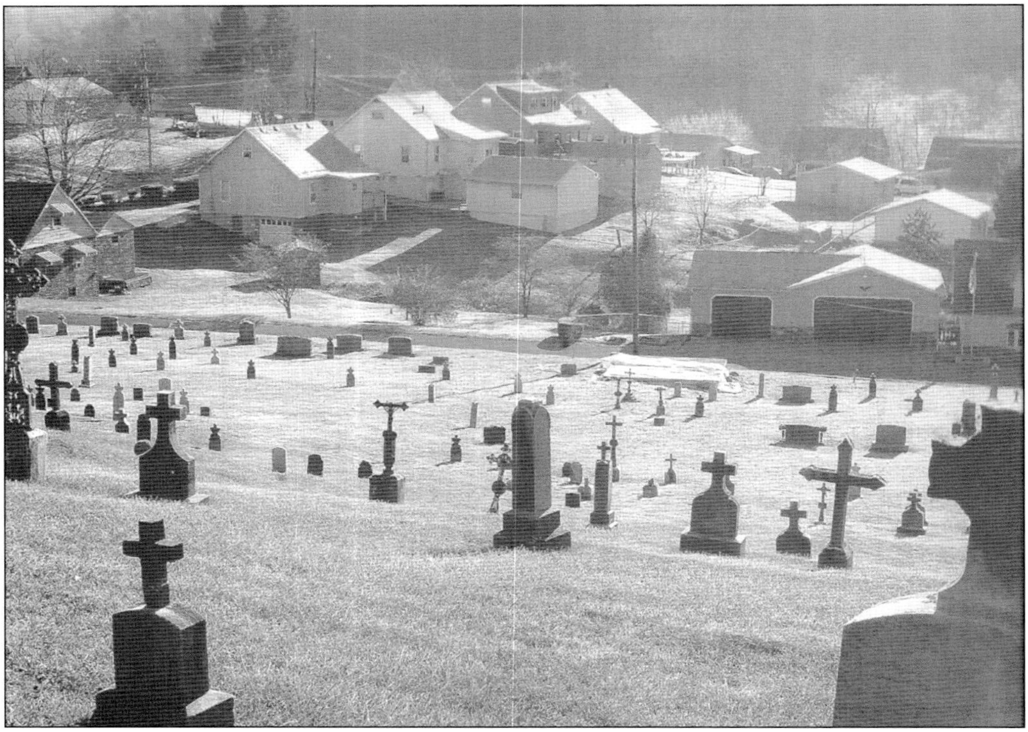

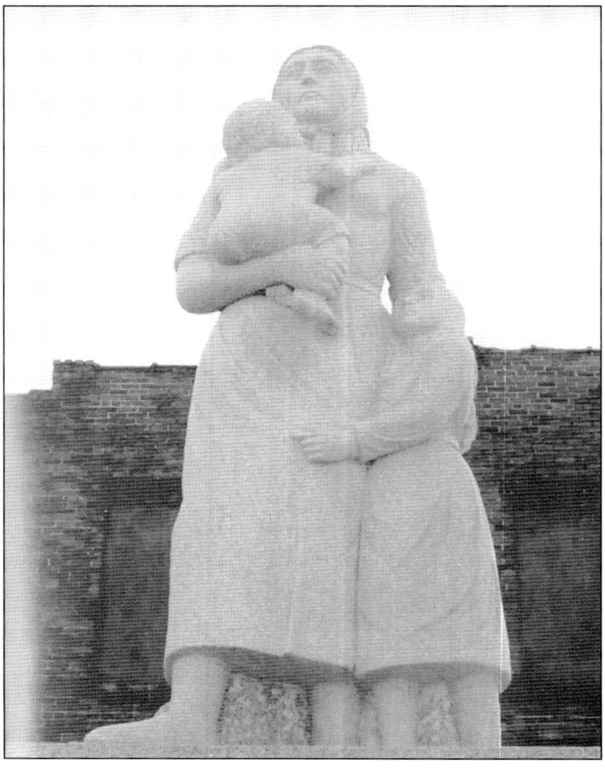

Mount Calvary Cemetery and *Monongah Heroine*, Monongah, 2007. Fairmont Coal Company donated the land for the final resting place of the victim miners. The mining disaster at Monongah increased the awareness of mine owners and the federal government. Inadequate safety conditions and lack of operational knowledge in the mines were addressed; however, the Bureau of Mines had no power to enforce the regulations. The *Monongah Heroine* statue faces towards the hillside and is a tribute to the mothers and wives who had to go on after the disaster. The late Russell Bonasso, a native on Monongah, West Virginia, and a community leader, organized a fundraising campaign to commission the sculpting of the statue and to observe the 2007 centennial memorial service of the Monongah Mine disaster. (Both, courtesy of Ron Rittenhouse.)

Three

Americanization and Political Activism

The assimilation of the Italian community in West Virginia was a "bottom up" process rather than a "top down." Americanization took place within mutual aid societies and through informal community channels of communication and rebellious acts of reform. The OSIA chapter founded in Fairmont, West Virginia, in 1923 encouraged and assisted members in becoming American citizens. In 1925, at the second OSIA state convention, held in Clarksburg, West Virginia, 14 West Virginia lodges participated. An important function of the mutual aid societies was the establishment of life insurance policies for their members. The 1920 census disclosed the occupations of West Virginia Italians. Approximately 70 percent worked in the coal and coke industries, and 30 percent worked as merchants. Mark J. Choate, in his book *Emigrant Nation: the Making of Italy Abroad*, explains that the Italian expatriates who sold goods became the leaders in developing the "Little Italy" communities in the Americas. Promoting an Italian identity was in their economic interest. Growing immigrant communities in West Virginia cities and coal towns demanded new service-related businesses. There was a need for Italian specialty foods, workmen's clothing, and shelter. A number of Italian corner stores and boardinghouses sold and served Italian food. Hotels, saloons, and pool halls catered to the immigrant workers. Eventually, there were a number of Italian barbershops, bakeries, laundries, and clothing and shoe repair shops. The mutual aid societies and the businesses established by Italians were centers in which members discussed their political activism. OSIA members and businessmen actively supported West Virginia's 1924 presidential candidate, John W. Davis. He campaigned on the platform that no individual, regardless of race or color, should be deprived of a civil right to vote. Most of the Italians favored his platform.

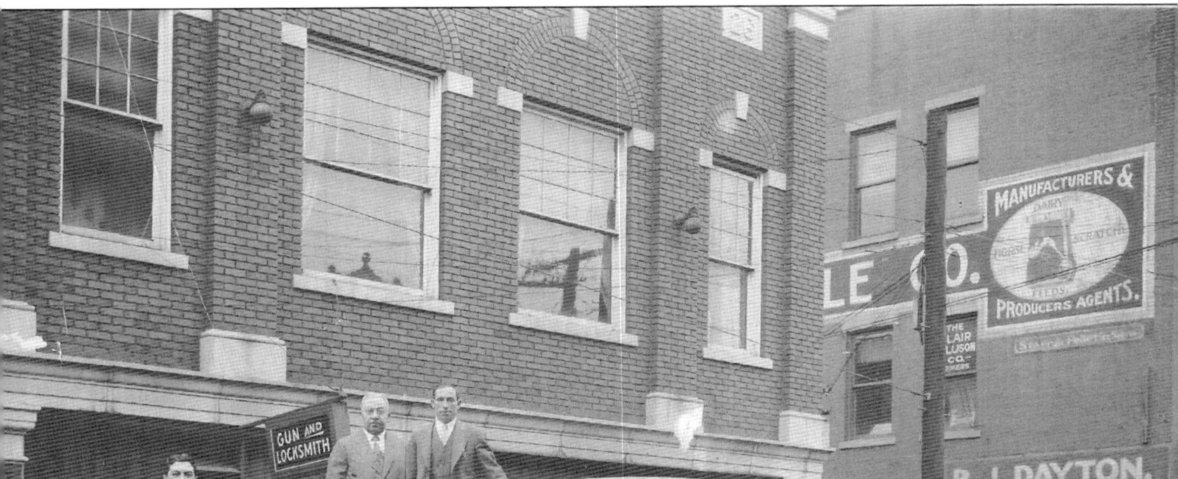

OSIA William Marconi Lodge No. 1140, Clarksburg, West Virginia, 1920s. This group photograph was taken in front of the original OSIA Building on North Fourth Street. Pictured are, from left to right, (first row) unidentified, Tony Romano, Mrs. Tony Romano, Rose Zannino, Parnasina Zannino, Rose Lopez, unidentified, Catherine D'Annunzio, Vincenza Basile, Josephine Adams, Michael Adams, Antonio Pettito, Joseph Martin, James Borgese, unidentified, Joe Delapa, Joe Gorgonio, and Joseph Crispino; (second row) Vincenzo (Jimmy) D'Annunzio, Prof. Frank Currano, Frank Angotti, Joseph Martino, Mr. Perri, unidentified, Mrs. Joseph Martino, two unidentified women, Bruno Marino, Antonio Basile, Dominick Ferise, and unidentified. Antonio Arena and Frank Lopez (leaning on the bus top) are standing on the bus. Parnasina Zannino-Biafore, pictured in the first row, is still living today. (Courtesy of John B. and Mary Ann Angotti.)

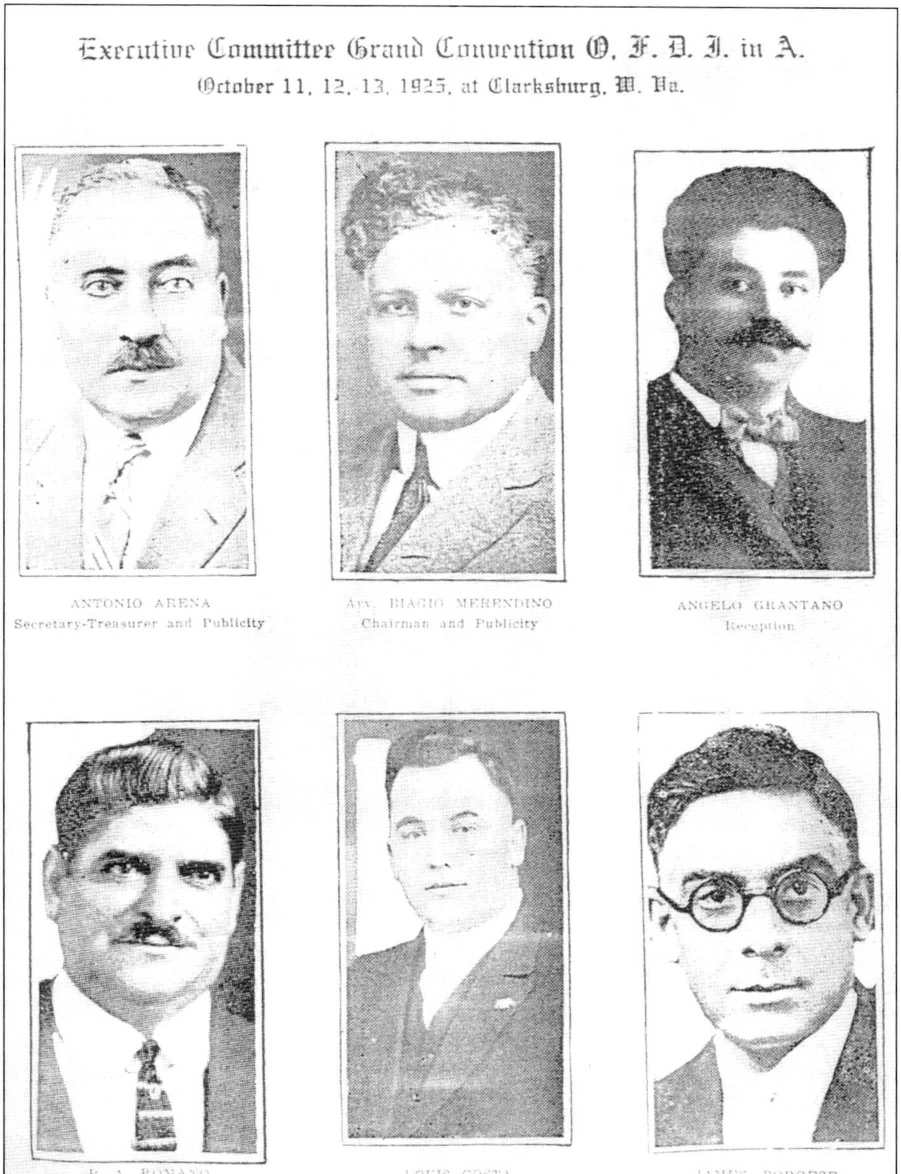

OSIA EXECUTIVE COMMITTEE, GRAND CONVENTION, CLARKSBURG, 1925. Members of the executive committee for the grand convention were Antonio Arena, secretary, treasurer, and publicist; Biagio Merendino, Esq., chairman and publicist; Angelo Grantano, reception; P.A. Roman, banquets and hotels; Louis Costa, banquets and hotels; and James Borgese, decoration and parades. The installation of the Grand Lodge of West Virginia was commemorated with a solemn ceremony on Sunday, April 29, 1923, and was officiated by the supreme venerable of the OSIA, Giovanni M. DiSilvestro, an attorney from Philadelphia. At the grand convention held in Clarksburg in 1925, fourteen lodges from throughout the state participated. (Courtesy of John B. and Mary Ann Angotti.)

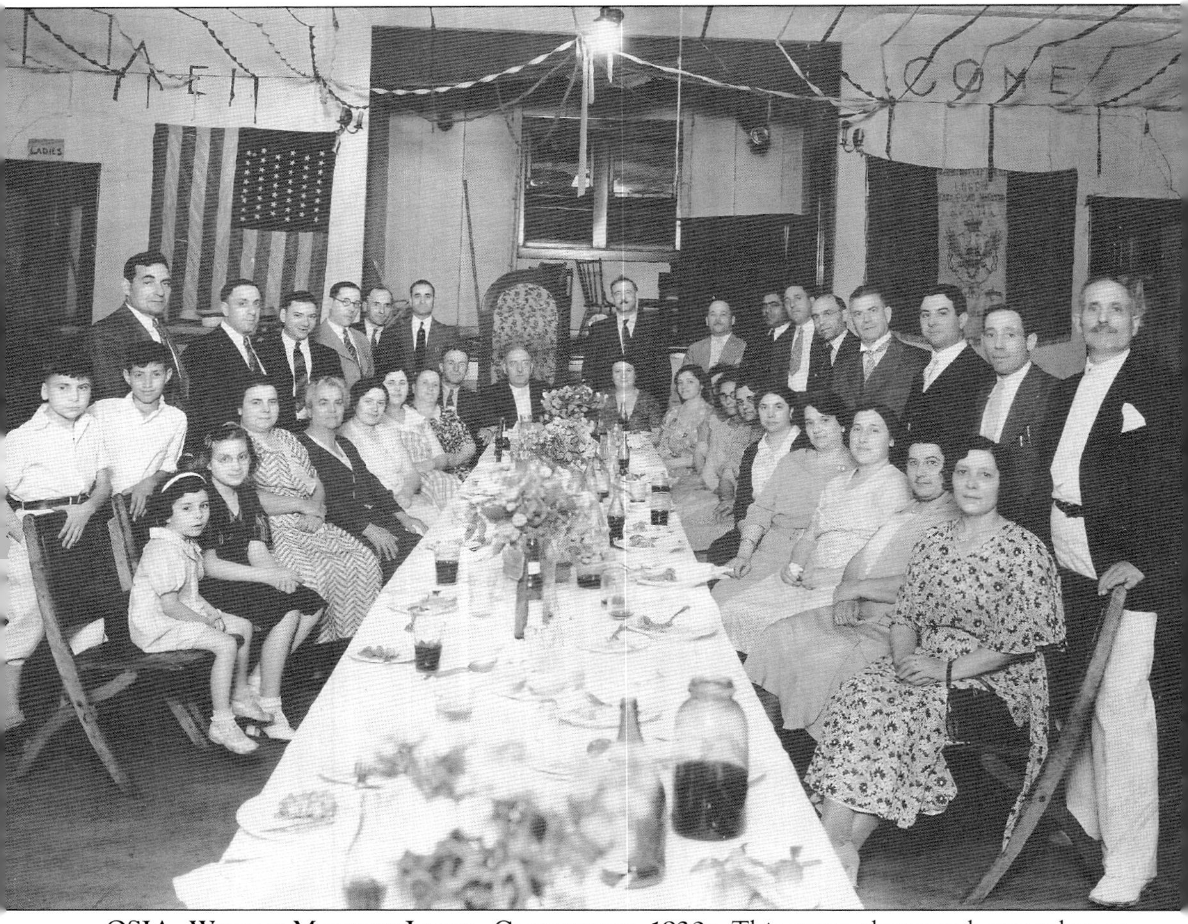

OSIA, William Marconi Lodge, Clarksburg, 1930s. This group photograph was taken at a Sunday afternoon gathering. The couples in the photograph are (from left to right) John and Frank Adams (children standing); Rose Marie Scalise and Flora Scornatelli (children seated); Sam Ferrise; Mr. and Mrs. Frank Angotti; May Ann Paladino (seated); Mr. and Mrs. Tom Adams; Mr. and Mrs. Michael Adams; Mr. Tony Romano (standing behind the Pettitos); Mr. Louie Vasile (standing behind the Pettitos); Mr. and Mrs. Angelo Pettito (seated); Mr. and Mrs. Antonio Arena (seated); Mr. and Mrs. Virgil Arena; Mr. and Mrs. Louie Costa; Mr. and Mrs. Dominick Ferrise; Mr. and Mrs. Antonio Basile; Mr. and Mrs. Dominick Ali; Mr. and Mrs. Joe Martin; Mr. and Mrs. Jim D'Annunzio; Mr. and Mrs. Frank Lopez; and Mr. and Mrs. Giuseppe Zannino. (Courtesy of John B. and Mary Ann Angotti.)

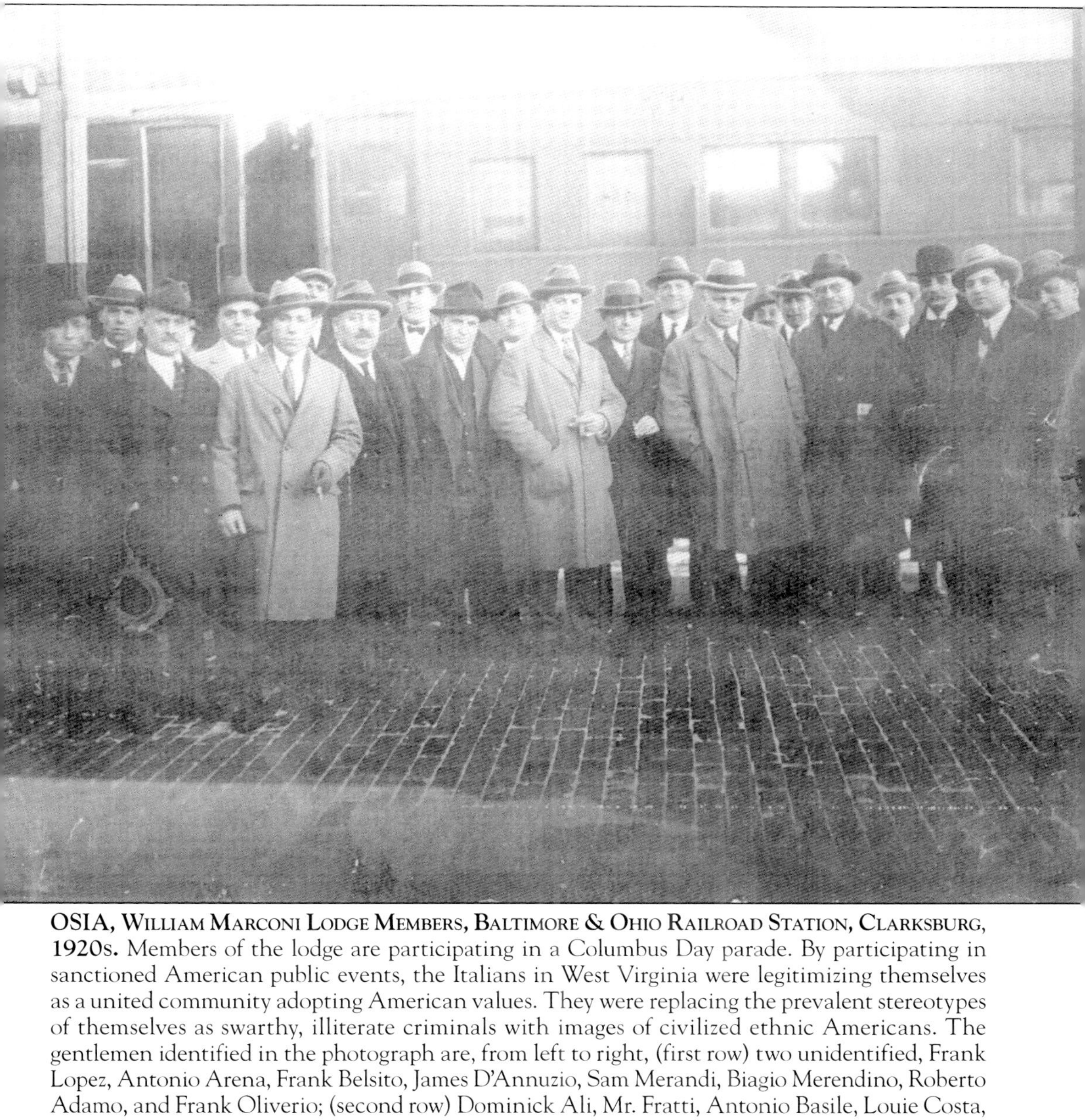

OSIA, WILLIAM MARCONI LODGE MEMBERS, BALTIMORE & OHIO RAILROAD STATION, CLARKSBURG, 1920s. Members of the lodge are participating in a Columbus Day parade. By participating in sanctioned American public events, the Italians in West Virginia were legitimizing themselves as a united community adopting American values. They were replacing the prevalent stereotypes of themselves as swarthy, illiterate criminals with images of civilized ethnic Americans. The gentlemen identified in the photograph are, from left to right, (first row) two unidentified, Frank Lopez, Antonio Arena, Frank Belsito, James D'Annuzio, Sam Merandi, Biagio Merendino, Roberto Adamo, and Frank Oliverio; (second row) Dominick Ali, Mr. Fratti, Antonio Basile, Louie Costa, Angelo Pettito, Sam Folio, John Folio, Vincenzo Procopio, and Mr. Angotti. (Courtesy of the Frank Oliverio family.)

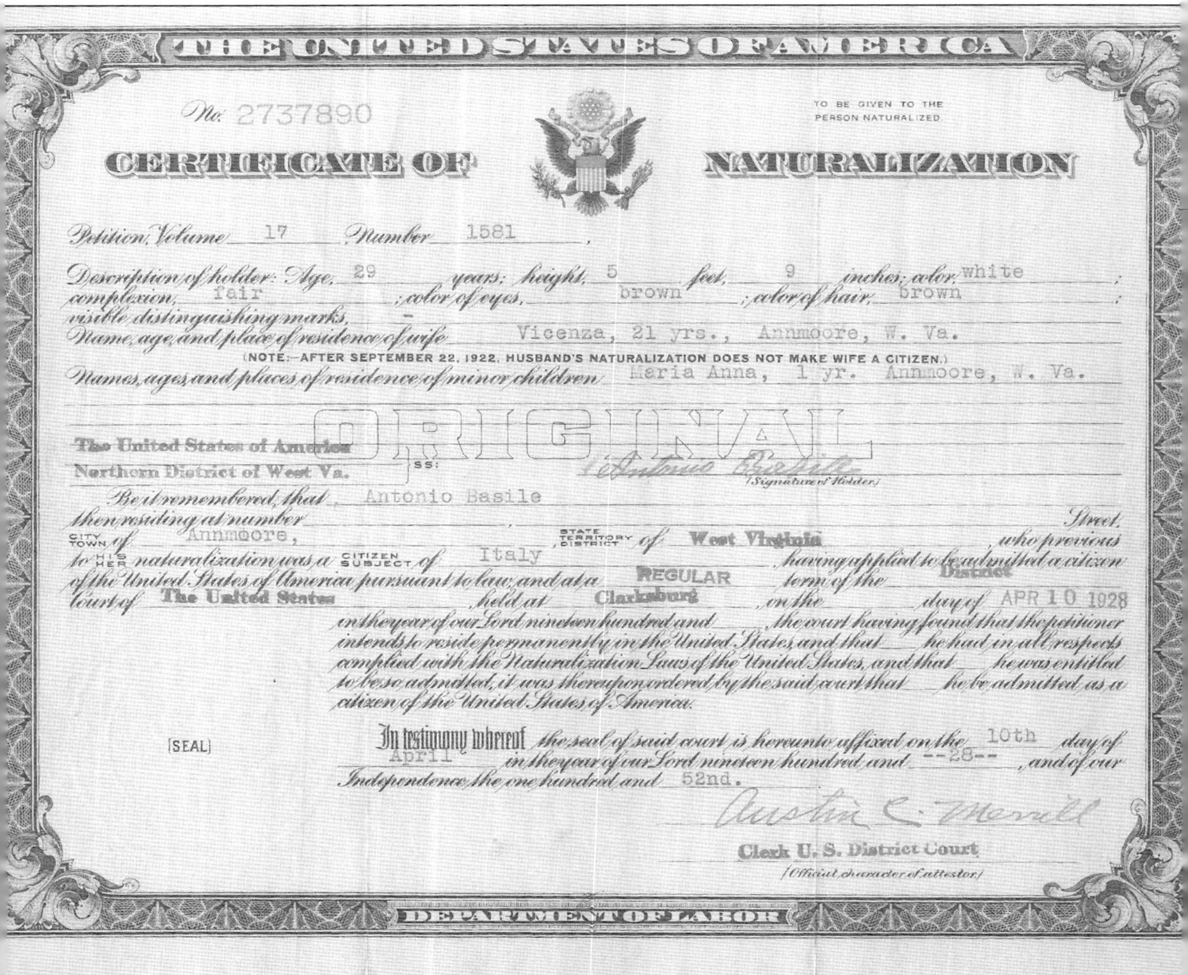

THE UNITED STATES OF AMERICA

No. 2737890

TO BE GIVEN TO THE PERSON NATURALIZED

CERTIFICATE OF NATURALIZATION

Petition Volume 17 Number 1581

Description of holder: Age 29 years; height 5 feet, 9 inches; color white; complexion fair; color of eyes brown; color of hair brown; visible distinguishing marks –

Name, age and place of residence of wife Vicenza, 21 yrs., Annmoore, W. Va.

(NOTE:—AFTER SEPTEMBER 22, 1922, HUSBAND'S NATURALIZATION DOES NOT MAKE WIFE A CITIZEN.)

Names, ages and places of residence of minor children Maria Anna, 1 yr. Annmoore, W. Va.

ORIGINAL

The United States of America
Northern District of West Va. } SS:

Antonio Basile
(Signature of Holder)

Be it remembered, that Antonio Basile then residing at number Street, city/town of Annmoore, state of West Virginia who previous to his naturalization was a subject of Italy having applied to be admitted a citizen of the United States of America pursuant to law, and at a REGULAR term of the District Court of The United States held at Clarksburg on the day of APR 10 1928 in the year of our Lord nineteen hundred and the court having found that the petitioner intends to reside permanently in the United States, and that he had in all respects complied with the Naturalization Laws of the United States, and that he was entitled to be so admitted, it was thereupon ordered by the said court that he be admitted as a citizen of the United States of America.

[SEAL]

In testimony whereof the seal of said court is hereunto affixed on the 10th day of April in the year of our Lord nineteen hundred and --28--, and of our Independence the one hundred and 52nd.

Austin C. Merrill
Clerk U. S. District Court
(Official character of attestor)

DEPARTMENT OF LABOR

ANTONIO BASILE'S CERTIFICATE OF NATURALIZATION, APRIL 10, 1928. The OSIA offered assistance to its members to become US citizens. Early naturalization certificates had indicated spaces for color and complexion. The government did not know how to categorize Italian immigrants; some had very dark complexions. In her book *Are Italians White?*, Jennifer Guglielmo and a group of Italian American writers discuss this issue. This book talks about how Italians dealt with America's views of race. Italians were not only discriminated against in America because they were olive-skinned foreigners from southern Europe; they were also discriminated against in Italy by northern Italians. Despite the prejudice in America, the federal government always considered Italians "white." So Italians were able to benefit in ways that blacks, Hispanics, and Asians could not in regards to housing, jobs, and the right to vote. They could marry whomever they wanted, own property, and become citizens. (Authors' collection.)

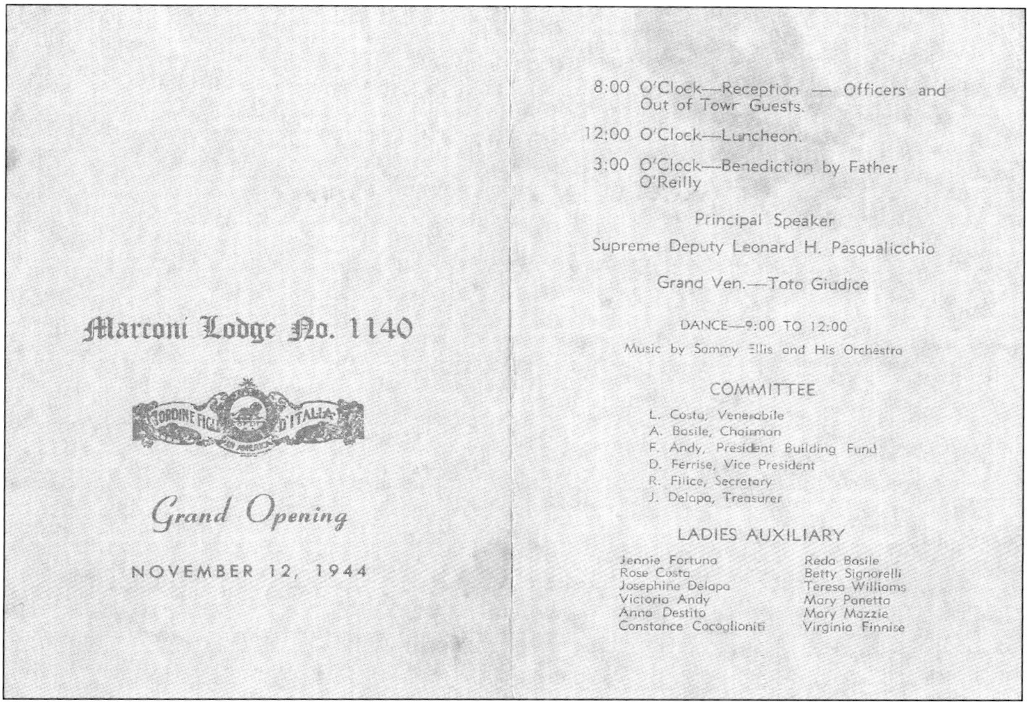
Marconi Lodge No. 1140

L'ORDINE FIGLI D'ITALIA IN AMERICA

Grand Opening

NOVEMBER 12, 1944

8:00 O'Clock—Reception — Officers and Out of Town Guests.

12:00 O'Clock—Luncheon.

3:00 O'Clock—Benediction by Father O'Reilly

Principal Speaker

Supreme Deputy Leonard H. Pasqualicchio

Grand Ven.—Toto Giudice

DANCE—9:00 TO 12:00

Music by Sammy Ellis and His Orchestra

COMMITTEE

L. Costa, Venerabile
A. Basile, Chairman
F. Andy, President Building Fund
D. Ferrise, Vice President
R. Filice, Secretary
J. Delapa, Treasurer

LADIES AUXILIARY

Jennie Fortuna
Rose Costa
Josephine Delapa
Victoria Andy
Anna Destito
Constance Cocoglioniti
Reda Basile
Betty Signorelli
Teresa Williams
Mary Panetto
Mary Mazzie
Virginia Finnise

WILLIAM MARCONI LODGE NO. 1140 GRAND OPENING, CLARKSBURG, 1944. After the lodge moved from Fourth Street to Baltimore Avenue, it had a grand opening luncheon followed by a dance party on November 12, 1944. The principal speakers for the luncheon were Leonard H. Pasqualicchio, supreme deputy, and Toto Giudice, the grand venerable of West Virginia. During the world wars, OSIA members bought war bonds and war stamps to support the war effort, and lodges competed with each other to contribute the most money to the Red Cross. (Above, Authors' collection; below, courtesy of John B. and Mary Ann Angotti.)

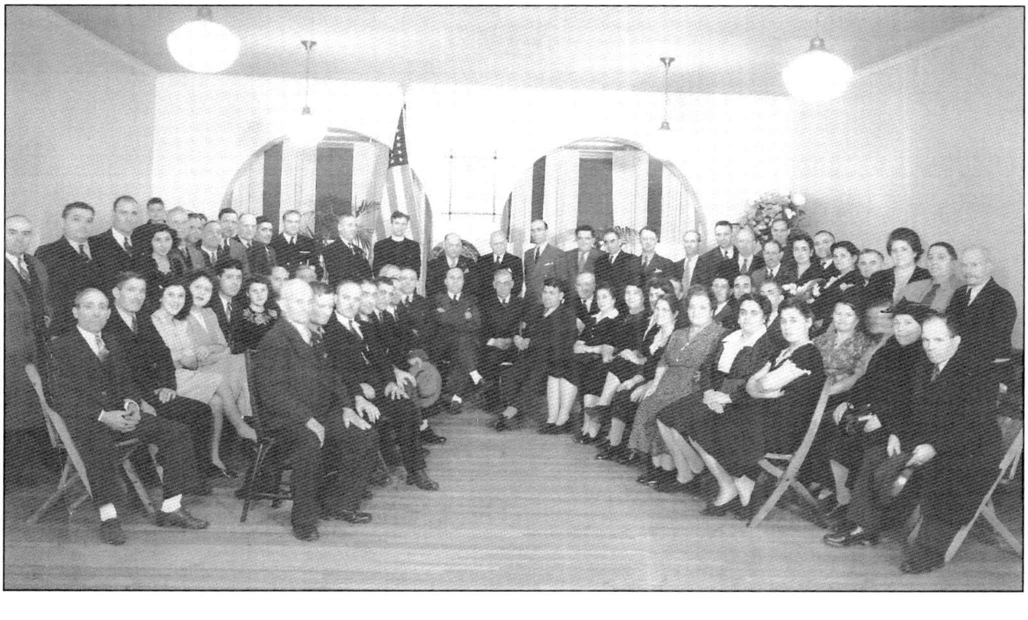

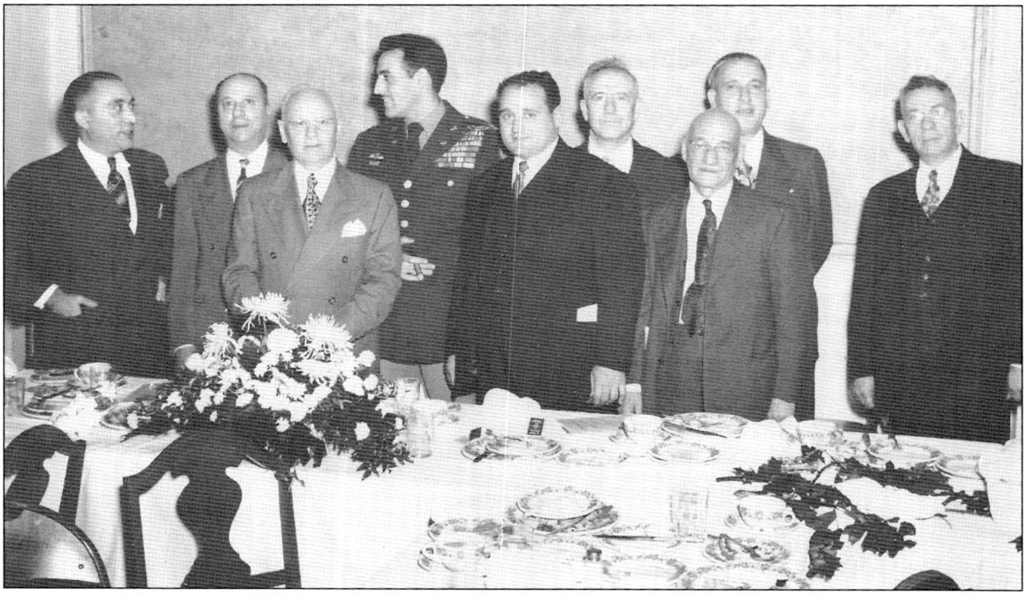

BANQUETS HONORING US MILITARY LEADER AND REV. COLOMBO BANDIERA, CLARKSBURG, 1950s. A banquet was held honoring a US military officer of Italian heritage at the Waldo Hotel. Standing in the photograph above are officers of the lodge and guests. From left to right are Toto Giudice, the Italian consul stationed in Charleston, West Virginia; the grand venerable of the OSIA in West Virginia, Angelo Vianni; Mr. Mallamo, the grand secretary; the unidentified military honoree; Anthony Folio, venerable of the William Marconi Lodge; Virgil Arena; unidentified; Antonio Basile; and Joseph Grogornio. In the photograph below, the OSIA William Marconi Lodge holds a welcoming banquet for Rev. Colombo Bandiera, who was appointed the pastor of St. John's Italian Catholic Church in 1954. (Both, courtesy of John B. and Mary Ann Angotti.)

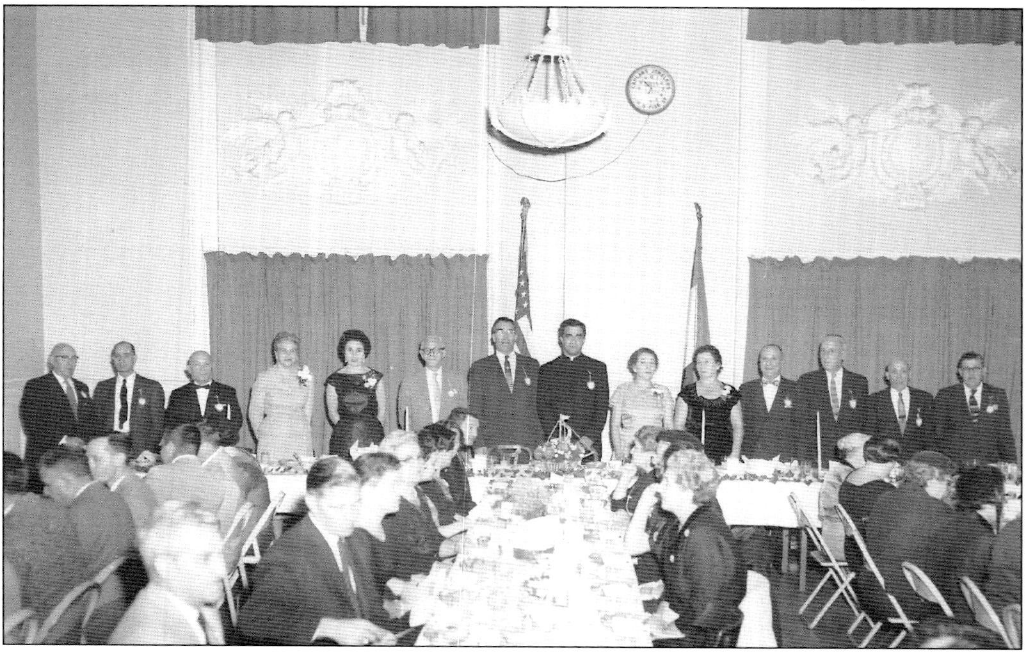

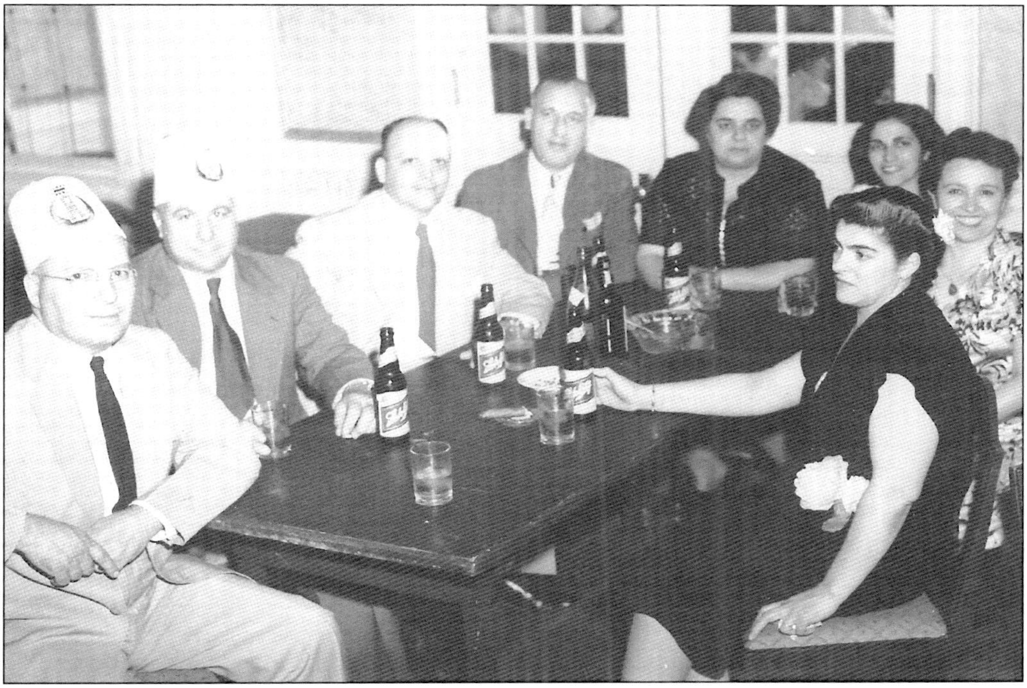

ALHAMBRA DINNER DANCE AND OSIA NATIONAL CONVENTION, TAMPA, FLORIDA, 1950S. First-generation Italian Americans began to branch out and form other social and cultural organizations. The Alhambra was an organization that promoted goodwill and neighborliness through planned group activities and social functions. It sponsored sporting events, travel, theater and the arts, social events, and interclub competitions. Pictured at the 1947 dinner dance at the Stonewall Jackson Hotel are, from left to right, Joseph Oliverio, John Barile, Sam Colombo, Antonio Basile, Vincenza Basile, Loretta Colombo, Anna Barile, and Angie Oliverio. Below, West Virginia representatives are pictured in the back left section of the photograph at the OSIA National Convention held at the Tampa Terrace Hotel in Tampa, Florida. (Both, courtesy of John B. and Mary Ann Angotti.)

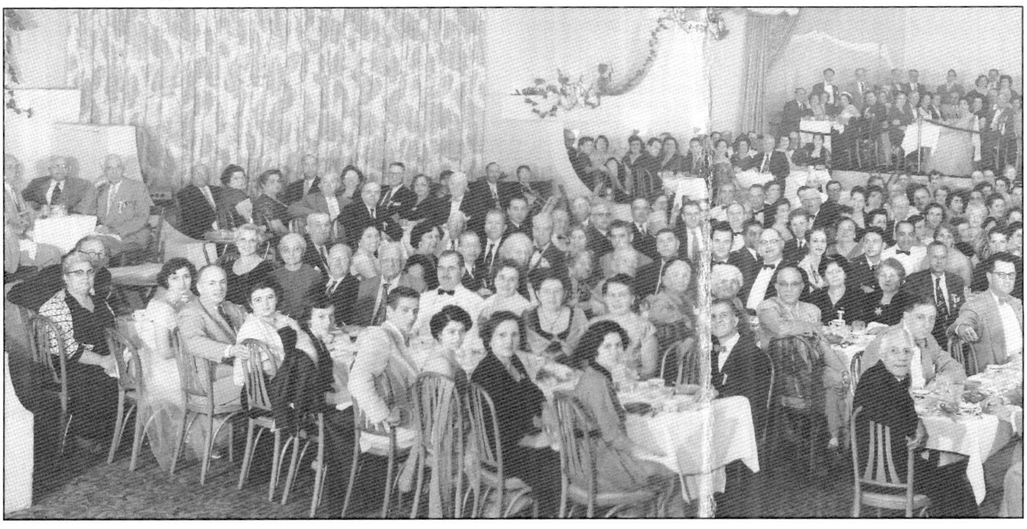

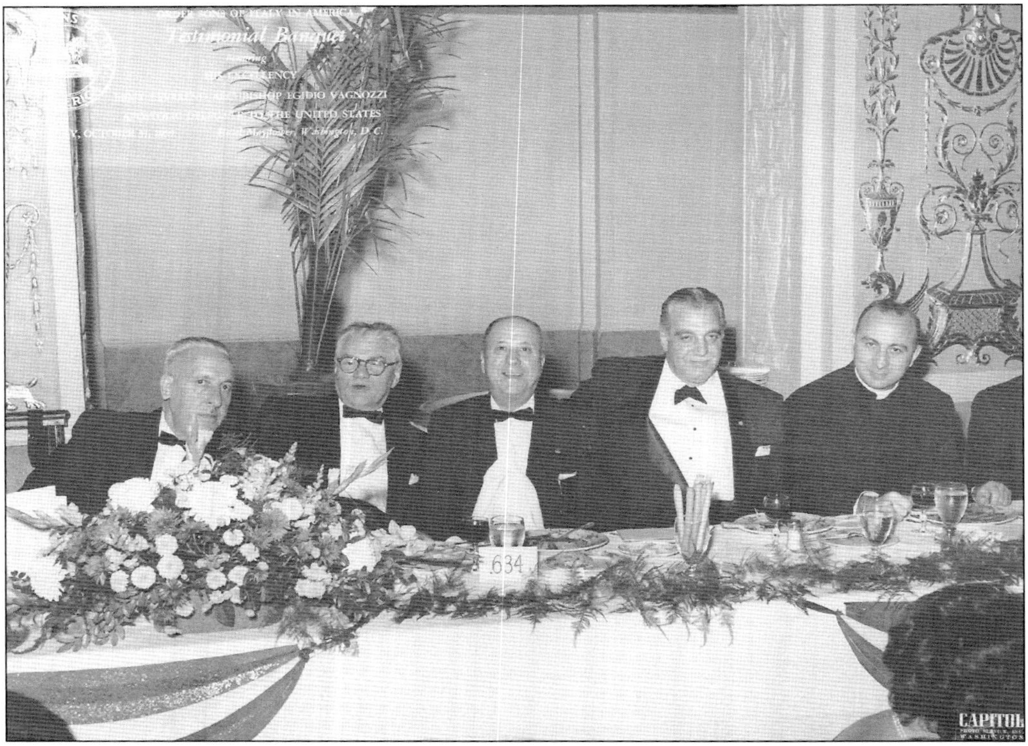

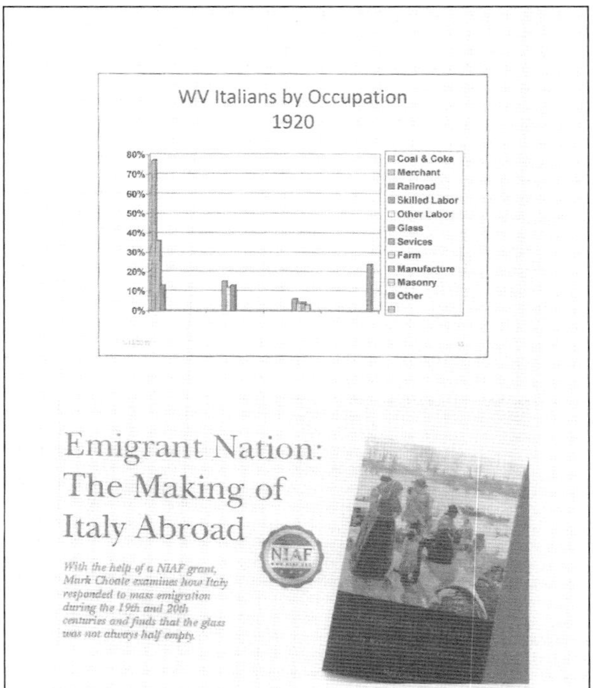

OSIA Testimonial Banquet and West Virginia Italians by Occupation. His Excellency the Most Reverend Archbishop Egidio Vagnozzi, apostolic delegate to the United States, was honored at this testimonial banquet held at the Mayflower Hotel in Washington, DC, on October 31, 1959. The apostolic delegate is the Vatican's official ambassador to the United States. The US Census of 1920 disclosed that the majority of the Italians in West Virginia worked in the coal and coke industries (approximately 70 percent); the second most common occupation for the Italians in the 1920s was merchant. In his book *Emigrant Nation: The Making of Italy Abroad*, Mark I. Choate states that expatriates who sold Italian goods became the natural leaders in developing Italian communities abroad. Promoting an Italian identity was in their economic interest. (Both, Authors' collection.)

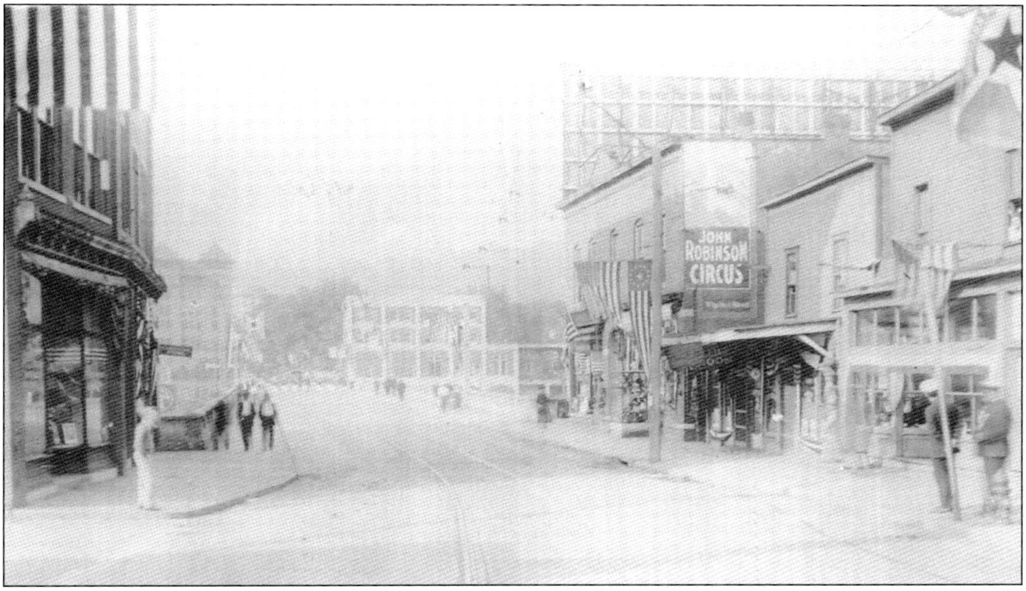

VIEW OF GLEN ELK SECTION AND THE FOURTH STREET BRIDGE, CLARKSBURG, 1920. Glen Elk eventually became the Little Italy of Clarksburg. North Fourth and Clark Streets were lined with Italian businesses, including corner stores, clothing stores, restaurants, saloons, pool halls, and hotels. There were also a number of barbershops, bakeries, and shoe repair shops. Baltimore Avenue, across from the Baltimore & Ohio Railroad Depot, was the wholesale section. In 1901, John Koblegard, an emigrant from Denmark, and his cousin Peter opened up a wholesale business of dry goods and notions known as Koblegard and Company. The wholesale houses catered to Italian businesses. The lower section of Sixth Street near the Sixth Street Bridge was residential. It consisted of a number of boardinghouses, row houses, and private residences. Seventh Street was also residential. (Both, courtesy of John B. and Mary Ann Angotti.)

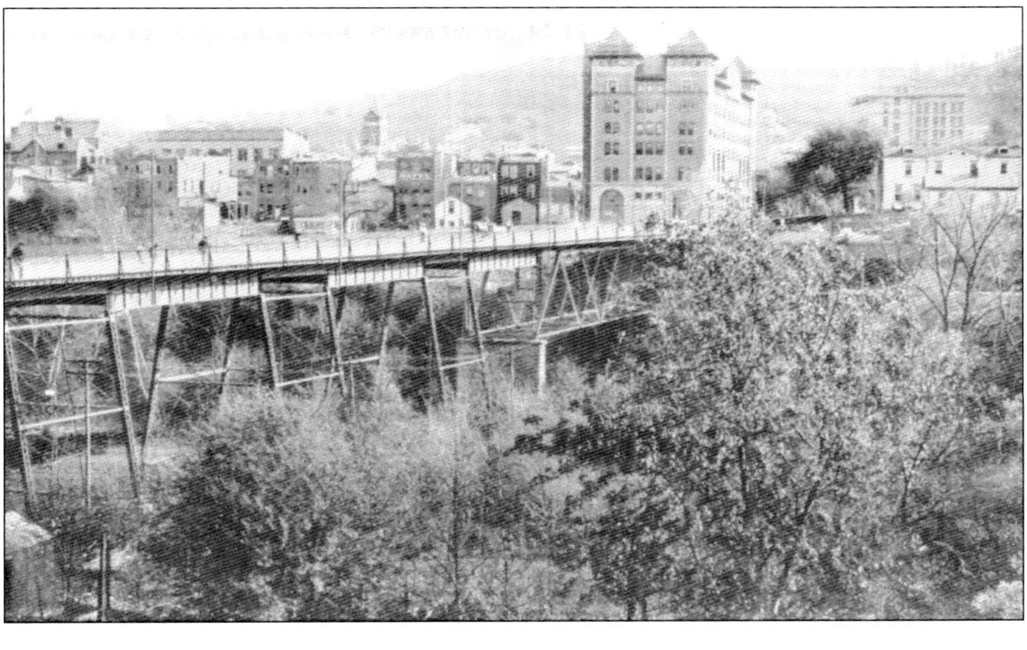

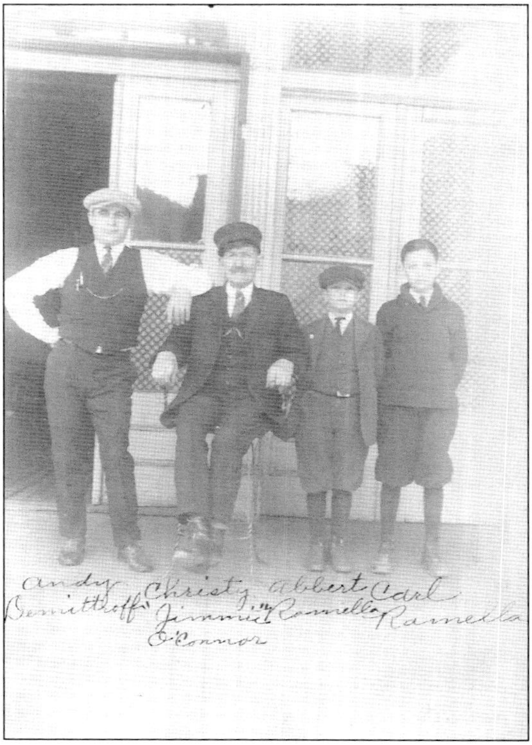

The Colonial Hotel Staff and Guests, Clarksburg, 1925. These photographs were taken in front of the Colonial Hotel, which was located at 412 North Fourth Street. Pictured at left from left to right are Andy Demittroff, Christy "Jimmie" O'Connor, Albert Ramella, and Carl Ramella. In the late 1920s the Colonial Hotel had a celebrity guest in residence, "Dutch" Schultz. Pictured below from left to right are Andy Demittroff, Albert Ramella, and Dutch Schultz in front of the Colonial Hotel. Dutch Schultz, Jewish American gangster, made his fortune in organized crime in the New York City area in the 1920s and 1930s. (Both, courtesy of John B. and Mary Ann Angotti.)

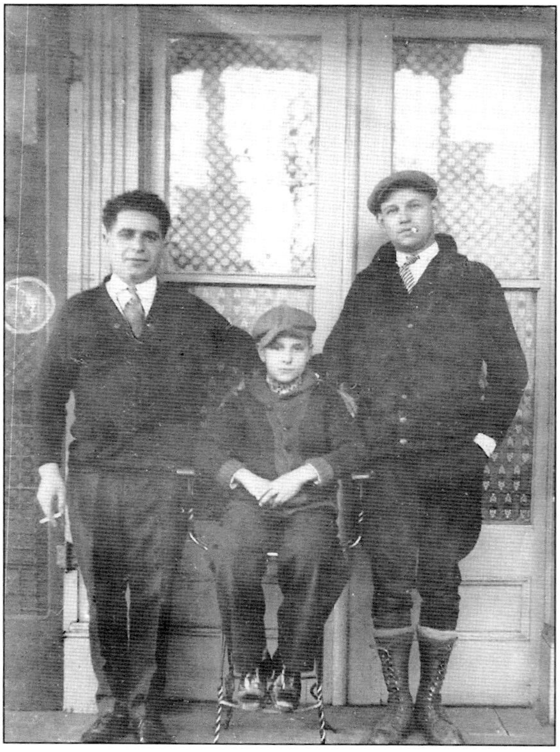

Boardinghouses and Dining Tents, West Virginia, 1910–1920. Boardinghouses and dining tents were needed for the mine workers and their families. Families that had immigrated earlier would take in the newly arrived immigrants as boarders to supplement the family income. There are a number of boardinghouse structures still standing in the Glen Elk section of Clarksburg. The discovery of oil and gas in Shinnston, West Virginia, strained its ability to deal with the influx of population. Doak's Dining Tent, below, provided workers at the Mudlick oil field a place to sit down to eat a hot meal. It grew up around a gristmill that Levi Shinn built in 1778 during the Revolutionary War; his home still stands. (Both, courtesy of West Virginia and Regional Collection, West Virginia University Libraries.)

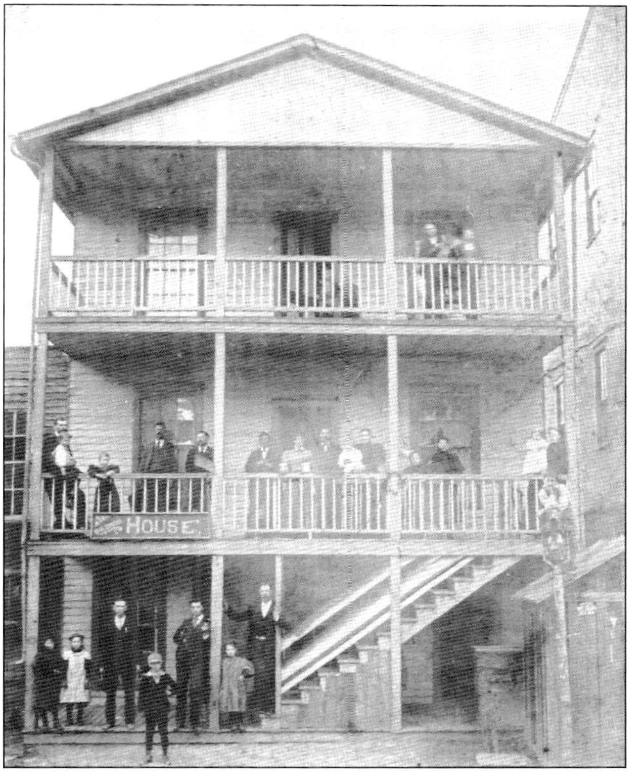

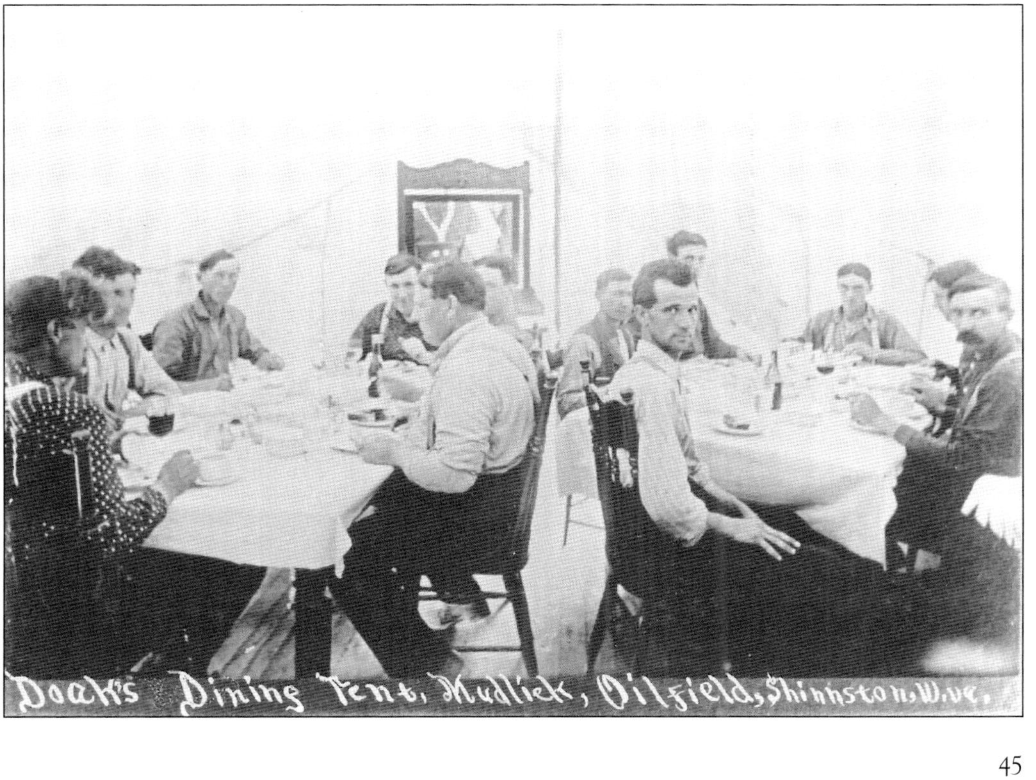

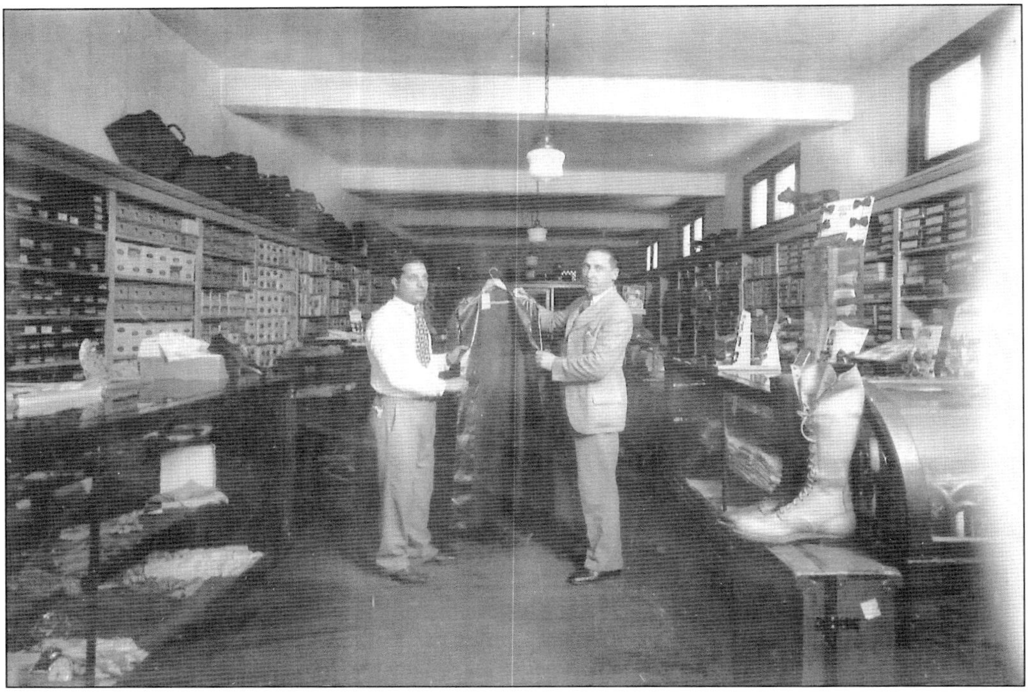

AB Clothing and Dry Goods Store and Oliverio's Grocery Store, Clarksburg, 1924. This well-stocked Italian clothing store was located at the corner of North Fourth Street and Clark Street. Pictured above Roberto Adamo (left) and Antonio Basile. Most stores at the time had a long, narrow aisle with the merchandise displayed on both sides of it. This technique was used so that the merchandise would appear well stocked and endless. Oliverio's storefront grocery store was on Clark Street. Pictured are Mr. and Mrs. Frank Oliverio and their daughter, Frances. The store is still in operation and managed by two of the daughters, Angela and Frances. Frank Anthony branched out and opened a food products company that specializes in canned Italian peppers. (Above, courtesy of John B. and Mary Ann Angotti; below, courtesy of Angela and Frances Oliverio.)

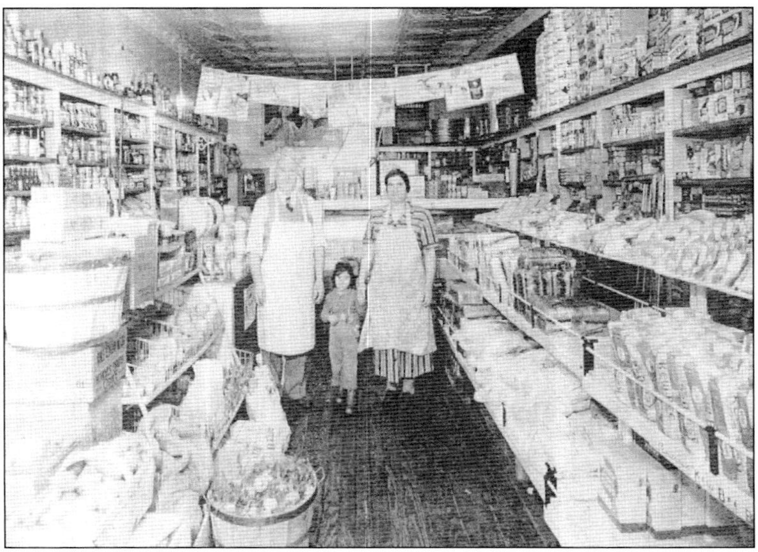

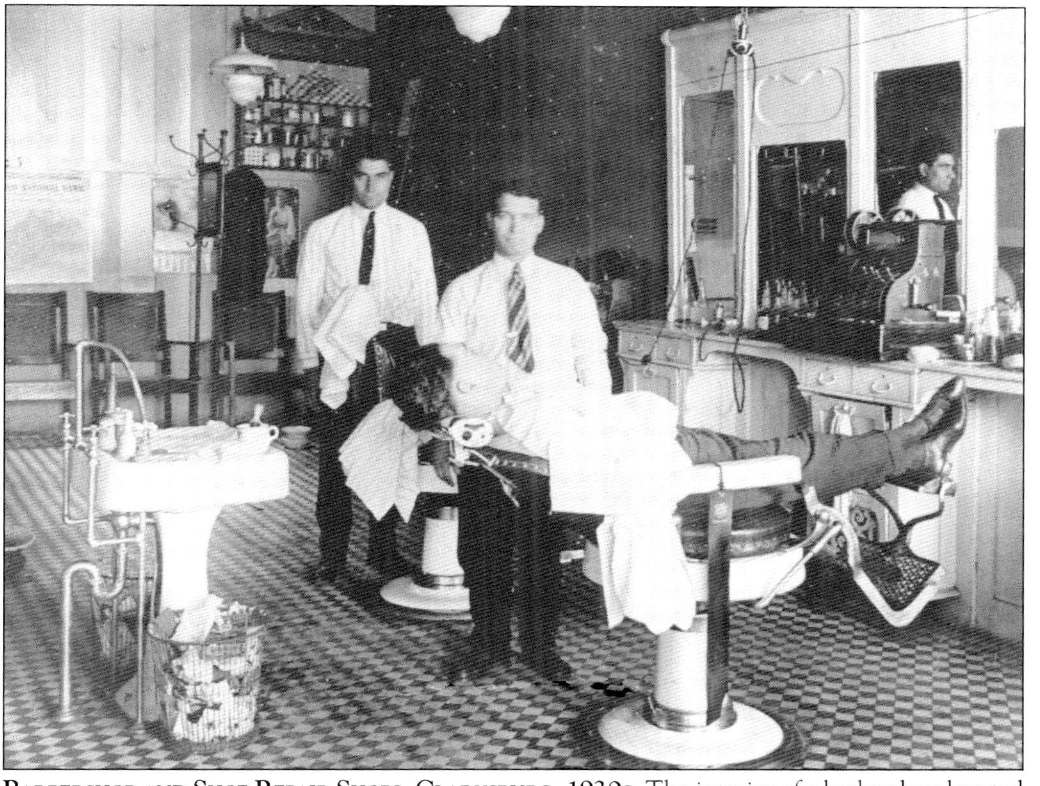

BARBERSHOP AND SHOE REPAIR SHOPS, CLARKSBURG, 1930S. The interior of a barbershop located next door to the Annex Hotel on Fifth Street is pictured above. The Annex Hotel was owned by H.L. Panetta; it had a European plan, running water, and rooms for $1 and $1.50 in 1925. Jim Lacaria and Sam Talerico were the barbers in the shop. Barbering and shoe repairing were popular occupations for Italian males. These shops were not only centers for hair grooming and shoe repairing, they were also popular shops for exchanging daily news and gossip. The 1925 West Virginia OSIA State Convention Brochure listed a number of shoe shops: Pike Shoe Repair, Progressive Shoe Shop, Champion Shoe Shop, and Rago's Shoe Repair. (Above, courtesy of the Talerico family; below, courtesy of the Library of Congress.)

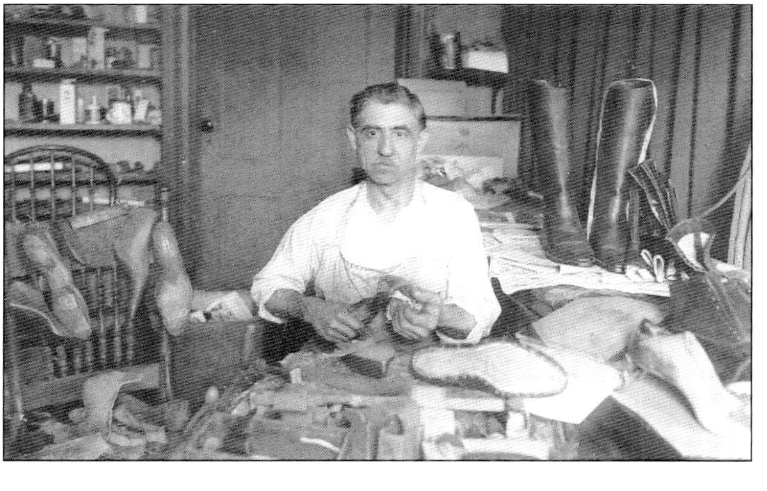

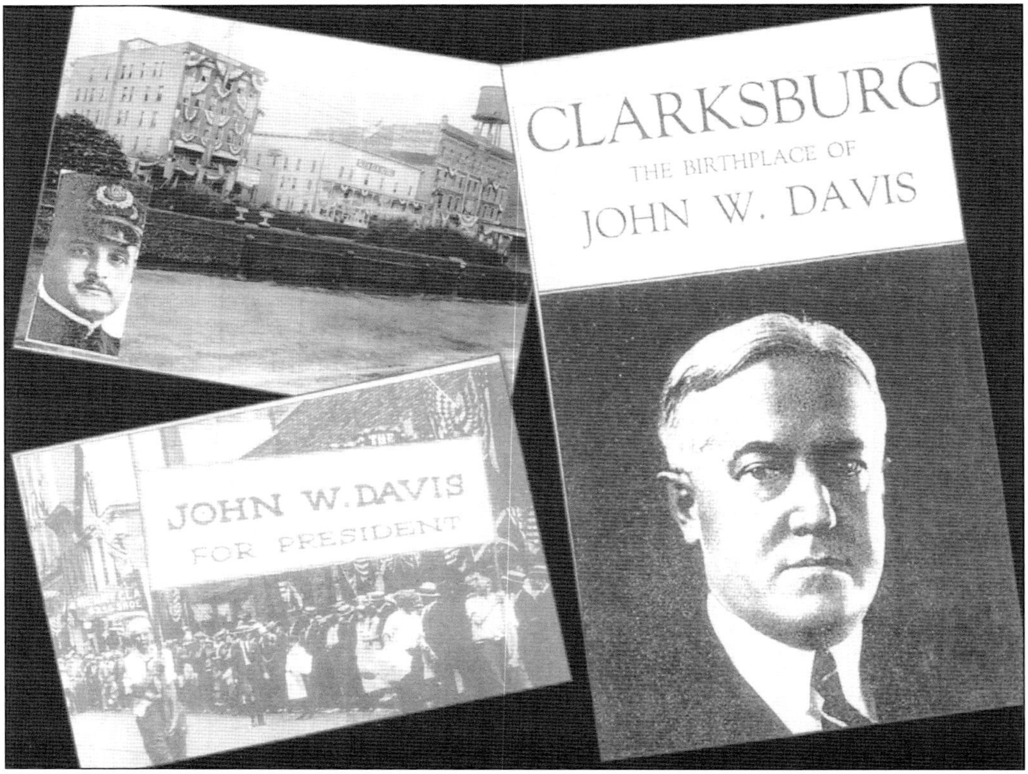

JOHN W. DAVIS, PRESIDENTIAL CANDIDATE, AND GLEN ELK SECTION WELCOME, 1924. Glen Elk District, the "Little Italy" section of Clarksburg, West Virginia, gave a grand welcoming-home reception to John W. Davis, a native of Clarksburg, after he won the Democratic nomination for president in 1924. John William Davis (1873–1955) was an American diplomat and lawyer. He served as the US solicitor general and ambassador to the United Kingdom under Pres. Woodrow Wilson. Italian Americans were very supportive of the 1924 presidential candidate because he argued in a court case that no man should be deprived of the right to vote because of color. Italians favored his presidential platform because many had dark complexions and had been discriminated against by white groups. (Both, courtesy of Robert F. Stealey.)

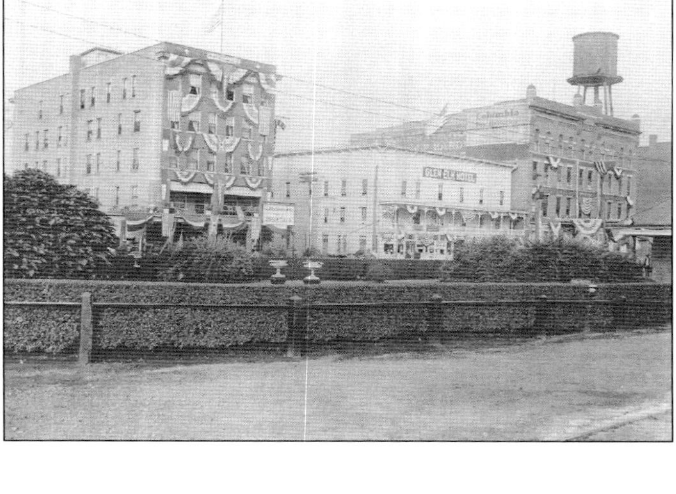

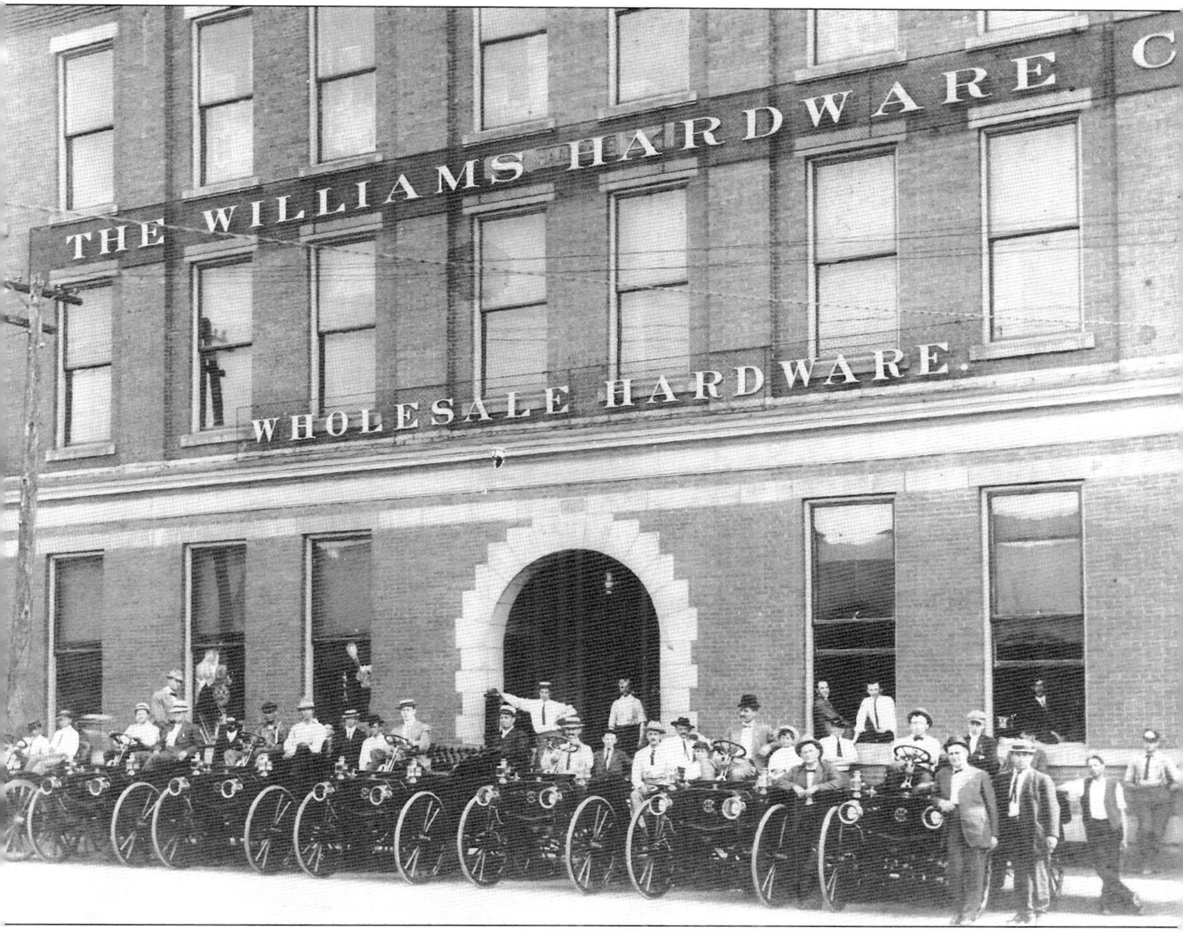

Parade Automobile Line Up, Clarksburg, 1924. These automobiles are lined up in front of the Baltimore & Ohio Railroad Station for the homecoming parade of John W. Davis. The crowd eventually increased, and the citizens of Clarksburg welcomed their hometown presidential candidate with a grand parade that was routed through the main streets of the city. Two huge stages were set up on East Main Street in Goff Plaza on the evening of Monday, August 11, 1924, for the presidential nominee to deliver his acceptance address. The largest crowd in Clarksburg's history assembled for this event. (Courtesy of John B. and Mary Ann Angotti.)

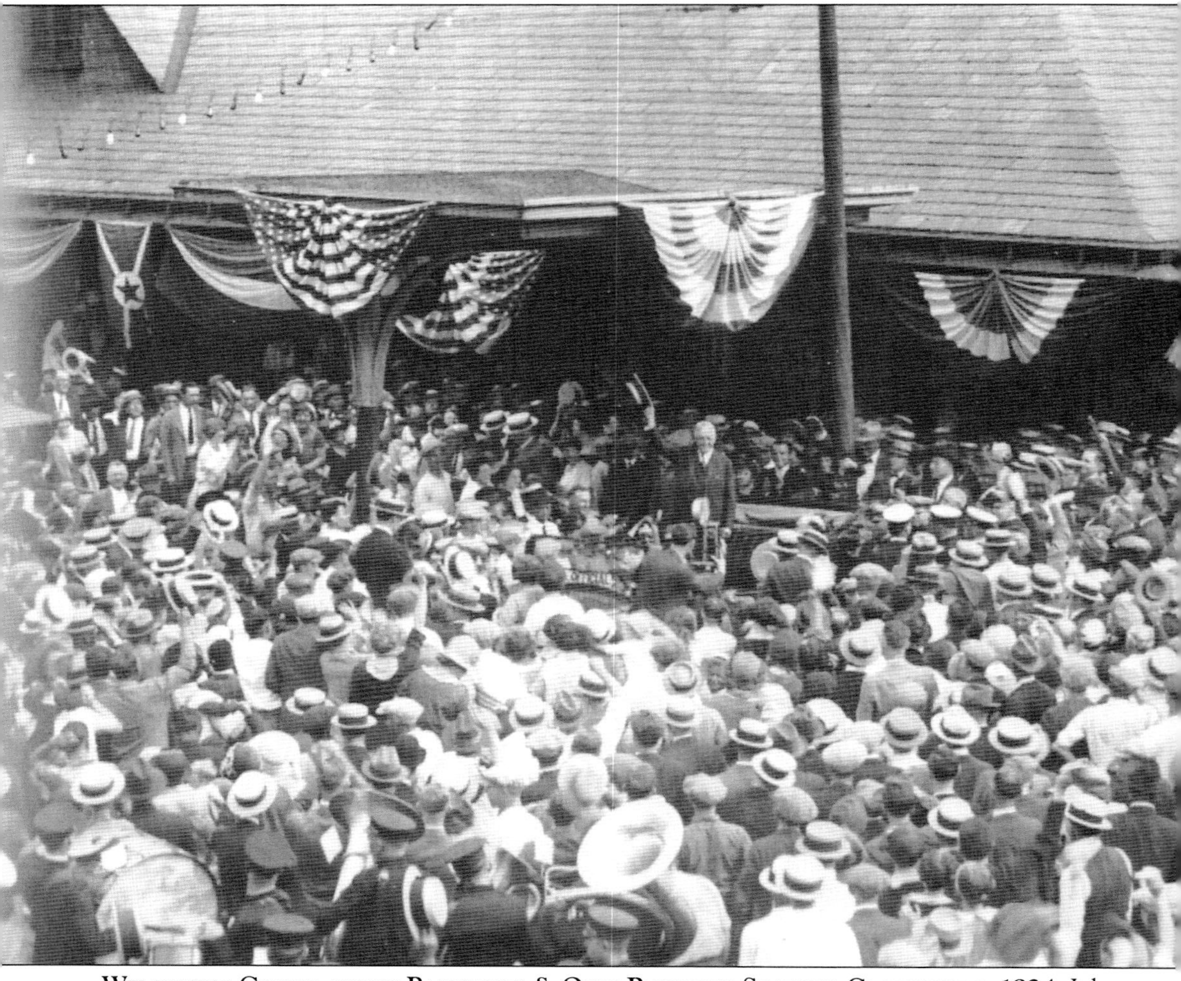

Welcoming Crowd at the Baltimore & Ohio Railroad Station, Clarksburg, 1924. John W. Davis was a compromise candidate for the Democratic nomination for president in 1924. As solicitor general under Woodrow Wilson, he denounced the Ku Klux Klan and advocated for black voting rights. Both of these issues cost him votes in the South and among conservative Democrats. He lost to the incumbent, Calvin Coolidge, in a landslide. (Courtesy of West Virginia and Regional Collection, West Virginia University Libraries.)

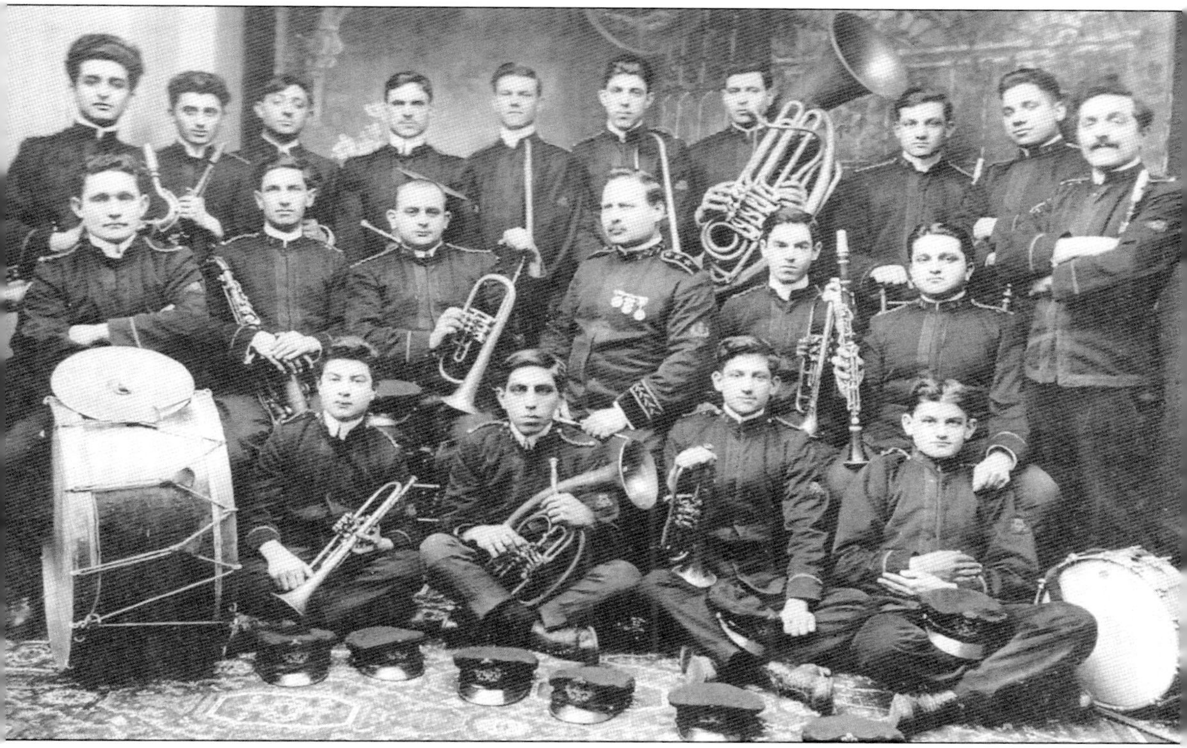

Order of Sons of Italy in America (OSIA) Bands, 1924. The OSIA bands participated in presidential candidates' parades. The OSIA band in Clarksburg, under the direction of Prof. Fran Currrado, had 30 trained musicians. It had a complete musical repertoire befitting any occasion. The uniforms consisted of dark-blue coats and gray-blue trousers with red stripes. In an advertisement in the OSIA West Virginia Convention Bulletin of 1925, the band claimed to have the most attractive band uniforms in the state and presented a very fine appearance. The Clarksburg band was joined by hundreds of Italian spectators on the parade route cheering their support for the West Virginian John W. Davis, who was campaigning for president. (Courtesy of the Balch Institute for Ethnic Studies, Philadelphia.)

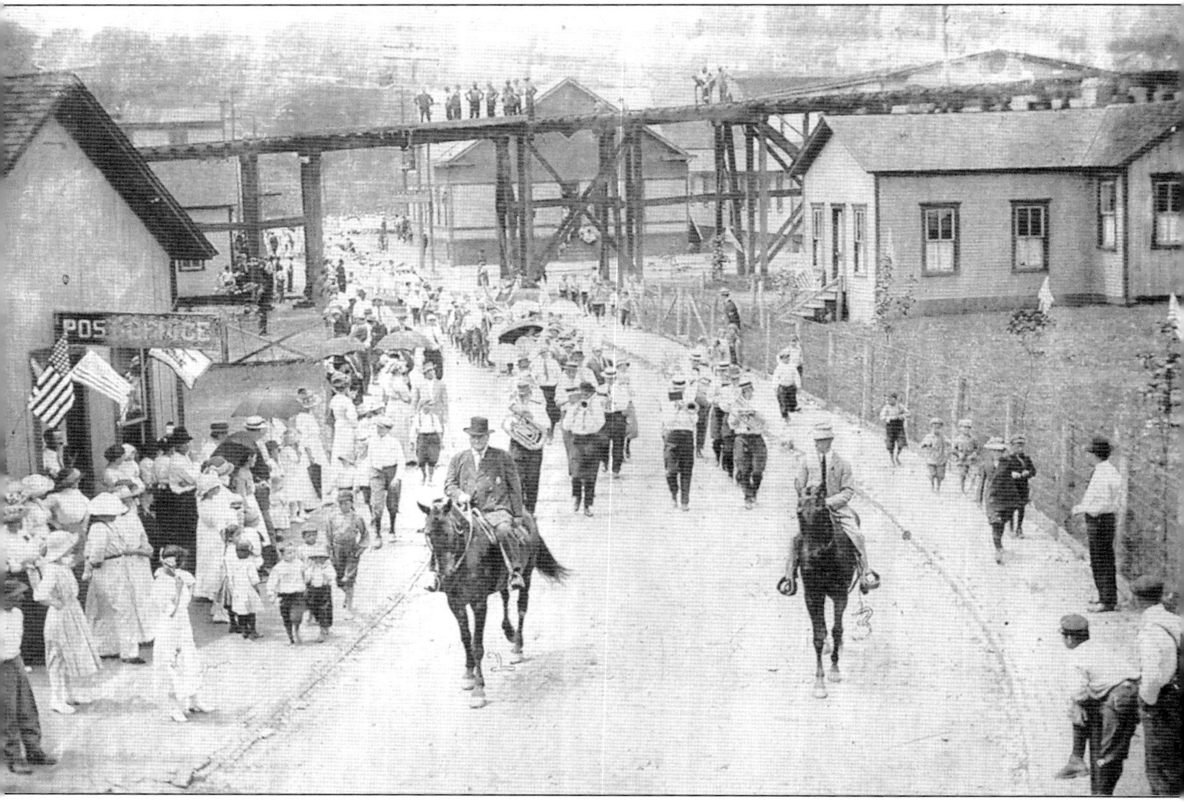

Parade in Marion County, 1915. Most Italians endorsed a closely linked agenda of patriotism and Americanization. The John W. Davis celebration message was clear: the city's Italians had taken up the task of Americanization and were worthy of joining the city's sober, law-abiding middle class. However, this type of celebration did not resonate well with all Italians. A few years earlier, between 300 and 600 Italian, Polish, Russian, and Croatian mine workers congregated and marched along the dirt roads of Marion County with an American flag and a red socialist flag. These miners carried a banner that read, "United We Stand. Divided We Fall. Give Us Justice, Or Nothing At All." Radicals politicized Italian ethnicity and made it an integral part of their militancy so that the subversives historically stood squarely against Americanization and in defense of the cultural rights of the entire community. (Courtesy of the West Virginia and Regional Collection, West Virginia University Libraries.)

Four

Leisure, Travel, and Ethnic Advancement

On weekends, Italians would gather for festive affairs that were characterized by Italian food, language, and music. Italian clubs provided a place where Italian men gathered to play card games, bocce, and morra. Leisure for women was centered in the home and the community. On occasion, they would gather in their church or club kitchens to exchange recipes and plan the food for a feast day or a spaghetti and meatball fundraising dinner. In the summertime, women joined their husbands in their backyards and planted gardens. They would harvest and can tomatoes, mushrooms, and wild greens and share them with neighbors and friends.

In the 1900s, local travel among cities was enhanced with the introduction of rail passenger service and the Ford Model T automobile. People became more mobile. They toured the West Virginia countryside and traveled to nearby metropolitan cities and eastern seashore resort destinations. For male members of the first and second generations, sports became an important avenue for assimilation. Italians males gravitated to the sports of football, basketball, and baseball. Sports provided not only a form of entertainment but also a chance for advancement. Through athletic scholarships and the GI Bill, first-generation Italian males were able to move forward in education, business, politics, and governmental positions. Early immigrant women had to struggle to learn English. Some attended citizenship and English classes. Basically, they stayed indoors; they sewed, knitted, quilted, and embroidered in groups; at these sessions, they exchanged and communicated their values. At home, they would train other members of the family in these folk crafts. Women tended to advance in food preparation, handicrafts, and music. They tended to be more literate than men, especially those who were fortunate enough to receive a secondary school education and attend commercial colleges. Music was a common leisure activity in the community. Coal towns had municipal bands in which many Italian Americans participated. Local Italian clubs would stage dramatic farces and comedies that included Italian dances and folksongs. Music was the catalytic element that promoted and preserved the festive lifestyle of the Italians in West Virginia.

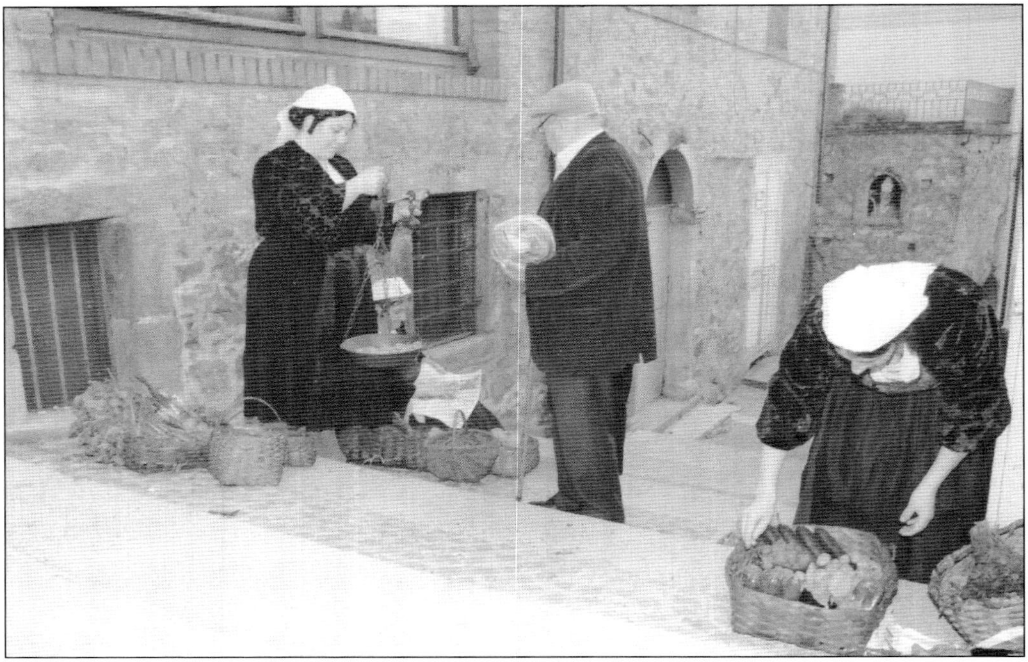

Calabrian Women Selling Vegetables and Sewing in the Square, San Giovanni in Fiore, Italy. Calabrian cuisine was influenced by military invasions and visitors. The Arabs brought oranges, lemons, raisins, artichokes, and eggplants. Cistercian monks introduced new agricultural practices, hearty green vegetables, and dairy products. French rule, along with Spanish influence, affected the language and culinary skills. Macaroni-type pasta is widely used in regional dishes, often served with goat, beef, or pork sauce and salty ricotta. Women were well trained in the art of embroidery; they would gather in the square and appraise each other's craft. (Both, courtesy of Sal Olivito.)

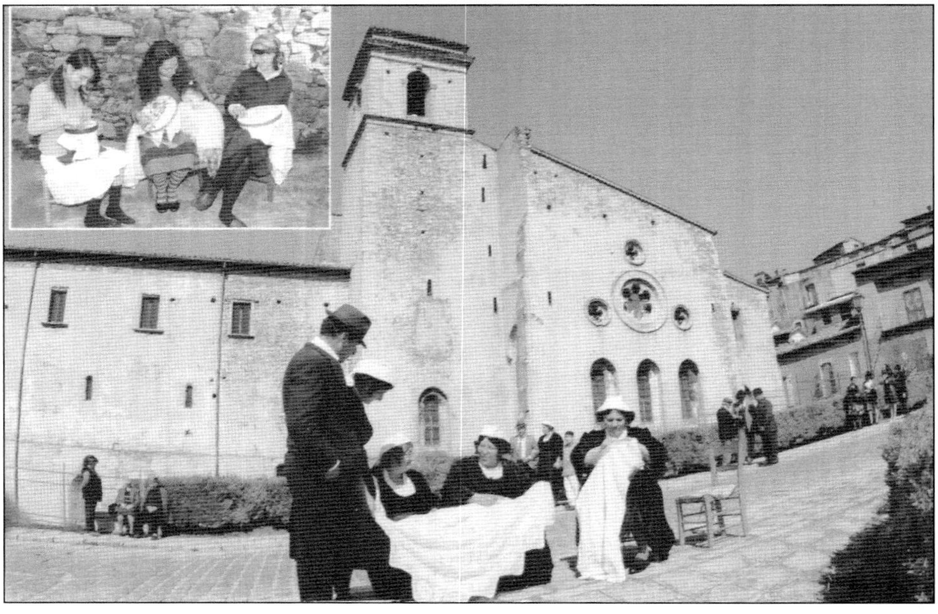

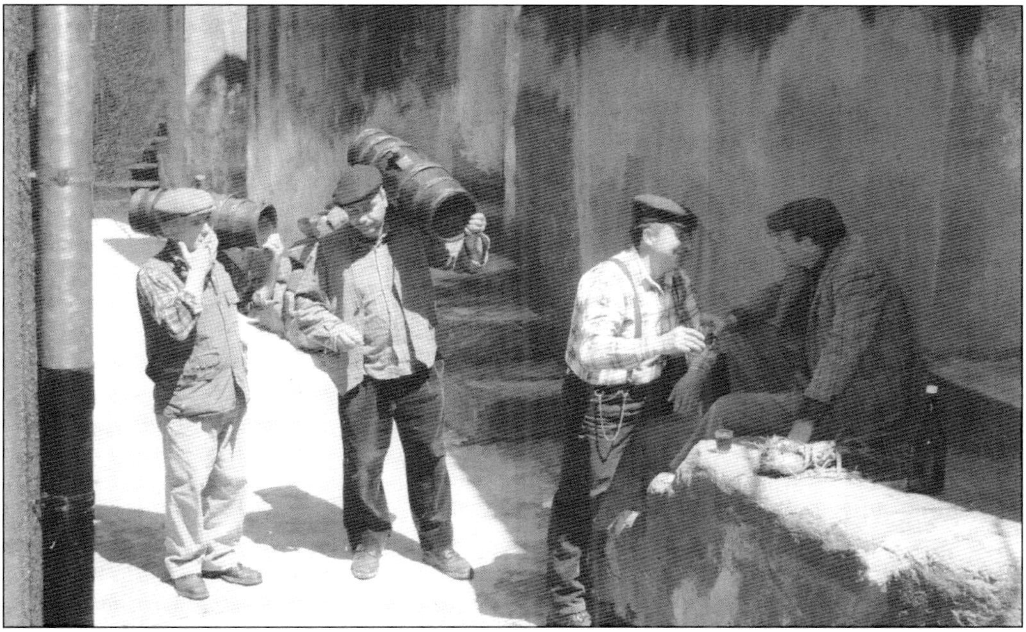

Calabrian Men Enjoying their Wine and Celebrating the Feast of St. John the Baptist. Calabria was cultivated by the Greeks and was part of Magna Graecia. Most of the towns in Calabria were built on hilltops to defend against invaders and escape the malaria that attacked the lowlands. The hearty red wine Ciro rossa is the noted wine of the region. Tradition has it that the wine is still made in the same way today as it was in the time of the Greeks. In many Mediterranean countries, the summer solstice is dedicated to St. John the Baptist. Festivals are held around his feast day, June 25. (Both, courtesy of Sal Olivito.)

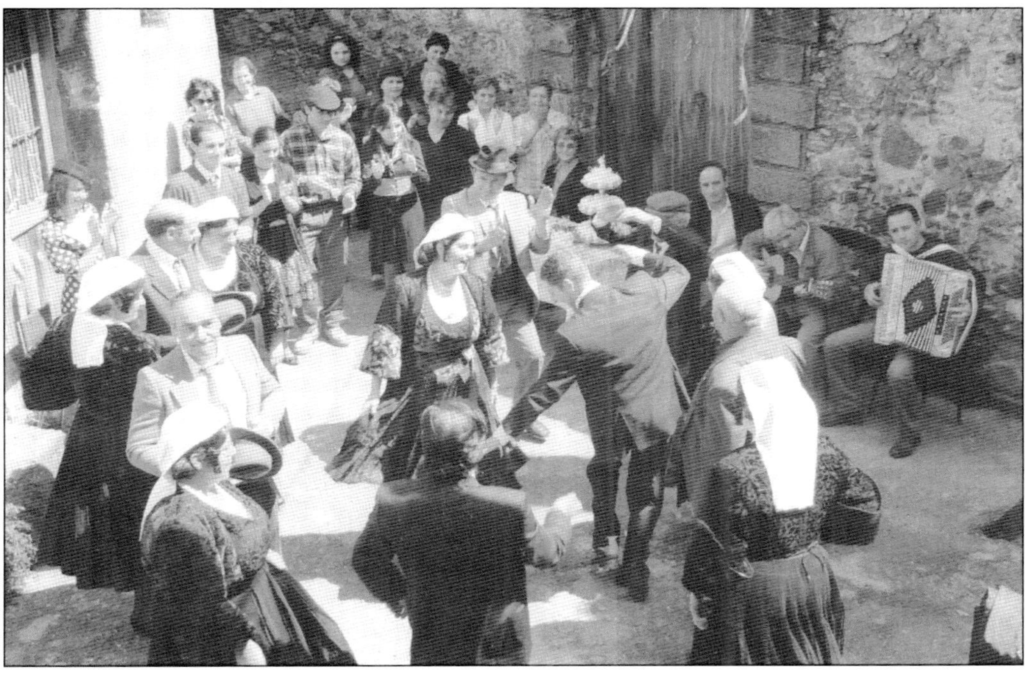

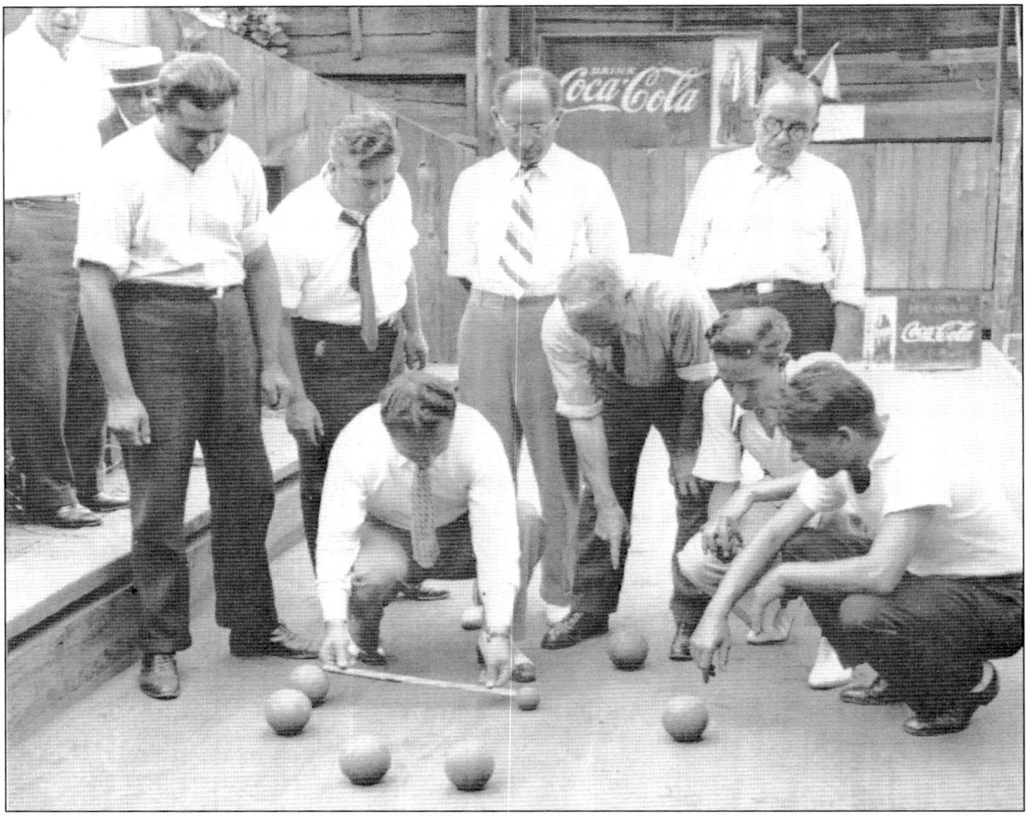

WEST VIRGINIA MEN PLAYING BOCCE AND CARDS AT THEIR LOCAL CLUBS. On weekends, men would gather to play bocce, morra, and cards at their local Italian clubs. Bocce is an Italian version of lawn bowling; Morra is a betting game using fingers in which players simultaneously shout out guesses at the joint total. Pinochle and poker were also popular with Italian American men. Pinochle is played in groups of two, three, or four players and uses a 48-card deck. (Both, courtesy of Rocco Muriale.)

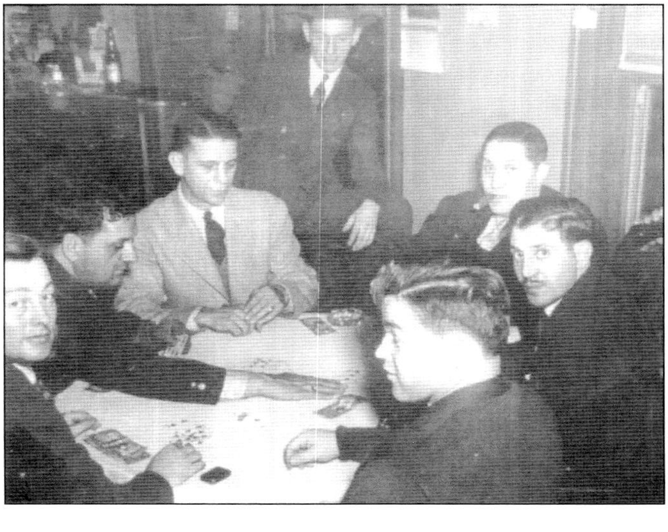

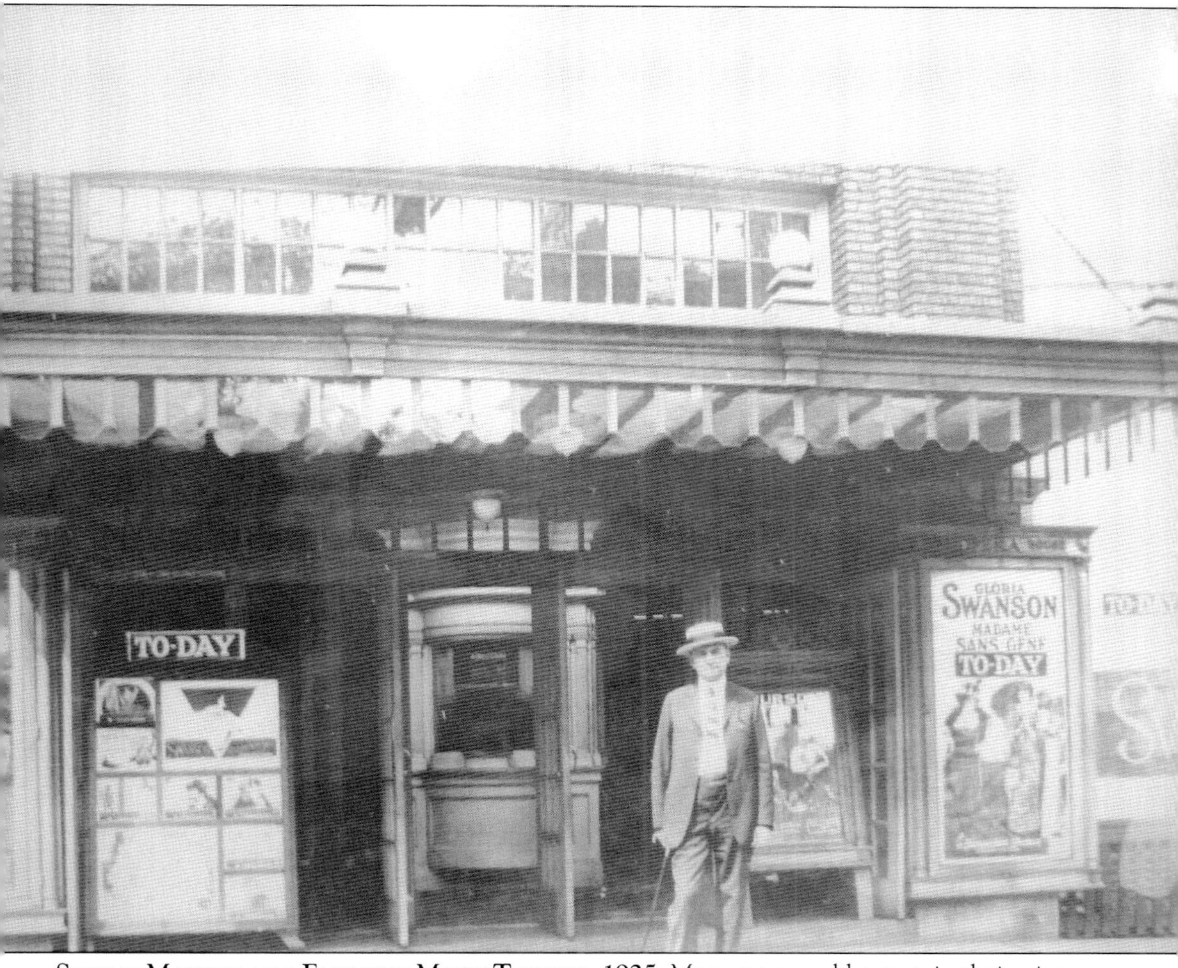

Sunday Matinee at a Fairmont Movie Theater, 1925. Many men would entertain their wives and children by taking them to a Sunday afternoon matinee. The feature at this downtown Fairmont movie theater is *Madame Sans-Gene* (released in 1925). Gloria Swanson is the star featured in this silent romantic comedy. She was popular during the silent-film era as both an actress and a fashion icon. Today she is best remembered for her role as Norman Desmond in the film *Sunset Boulevard* (1950), for which she received an Academy Award. (Courtesy of Rocco Muriale.)

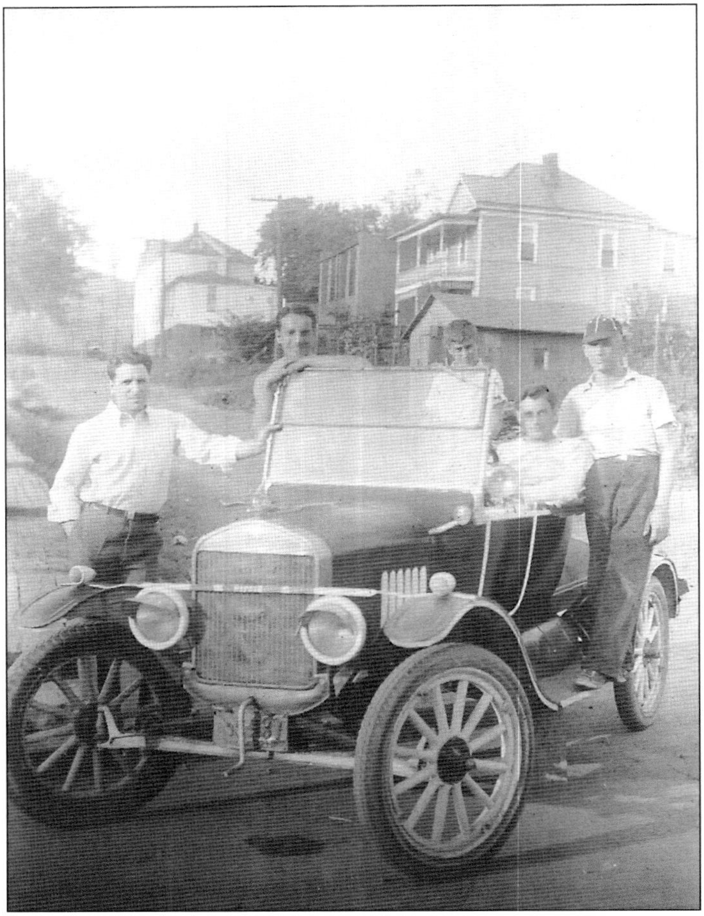

RAMELLA'S EARLY-MODEL AUTOMOBILES, 1900s. The Ford Model T was produced from 1908 through 1927. It is generally regarded as the first affordable automobile and the car that opened travel to middle-class Americans. Henry Ford said, "the vehicle will be so low in price that no man making a good salary will be unable to own one and enjoy with his family the blessings of God's great open spaces." The introduction of the Ford Model T and later-model automobiles allowed Italians to become more mobile. They began to enjoy the romantic landscape of the West Virginia countryside. (Both, courtesy of John B. and Mary Ann Angotti.)

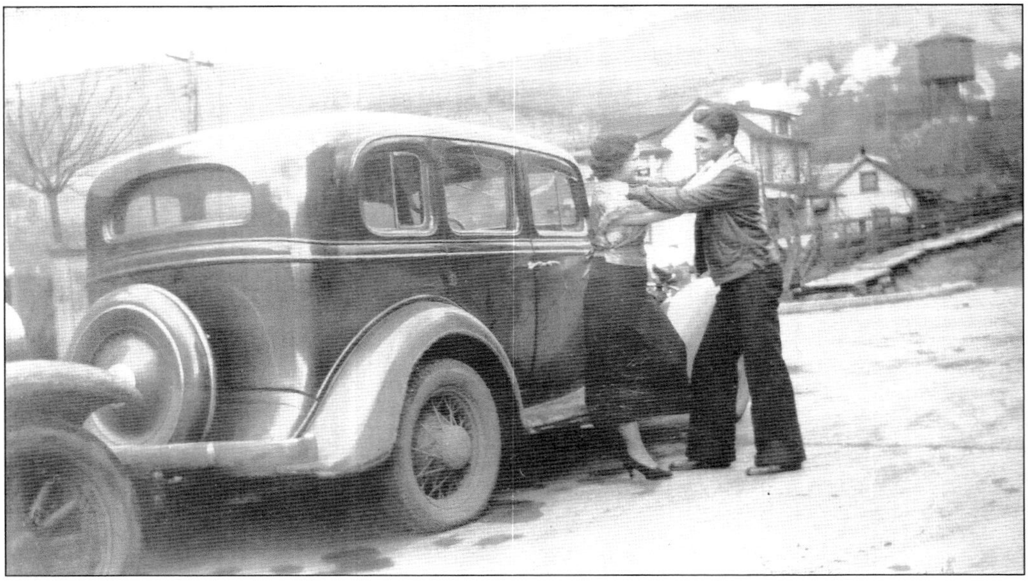

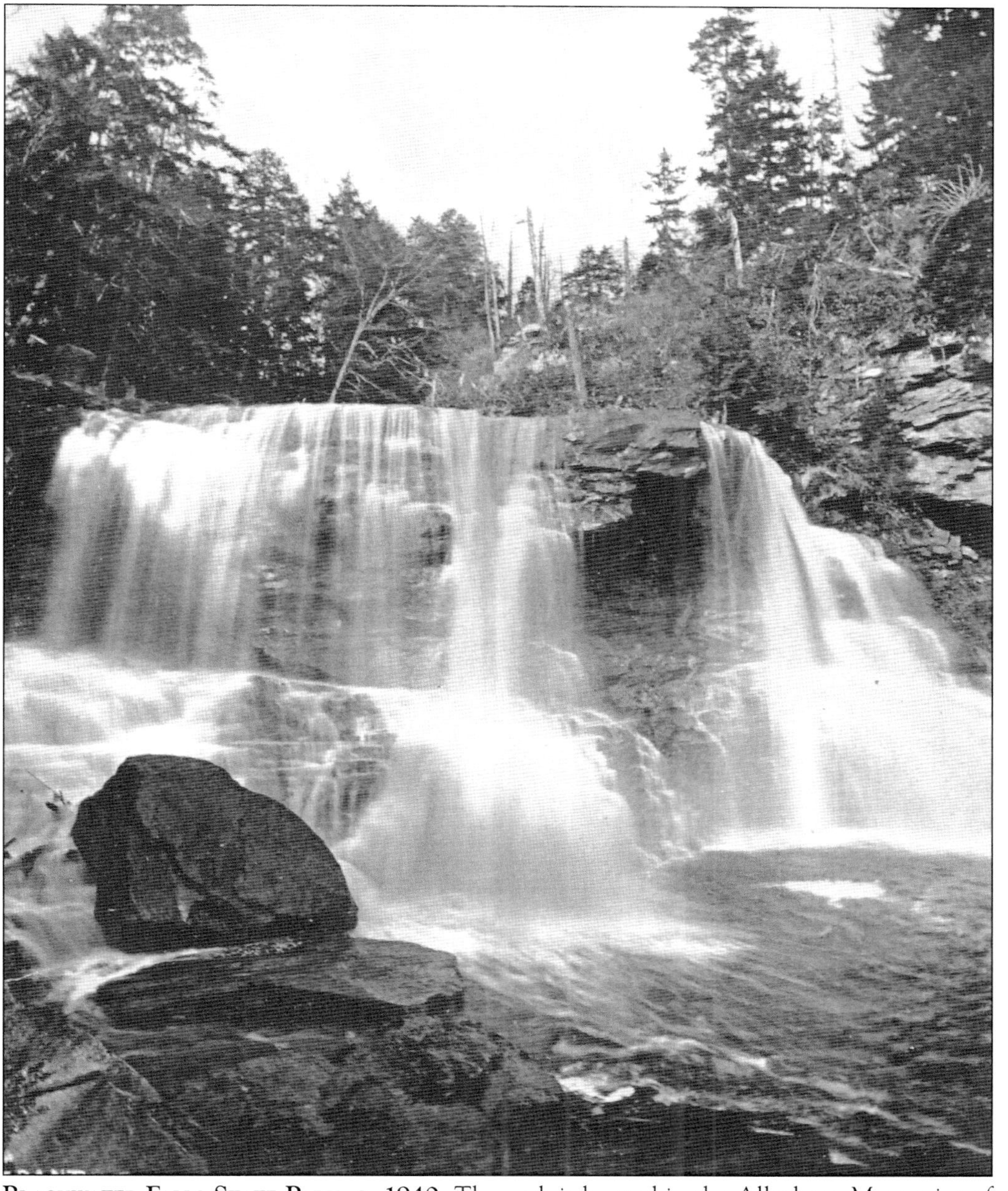

BLACKWATER FALLS STATE PARK, C. 1940. The park is located in the Allegheny Mountains of Tucker County, West Virginia. This particular park was special to the Italian Americans, because its romantic landscape was very reminiscent of the Sila Mountains of Calabria, Italy. Blackwater Falls State Park was a popular recreational area for Italian American summer outings of hiking, fishing, camping, picnicking, and swimming. The centerpiece of the park is Blackwater Falls, a 62-foot cascade. (Courtesy of West Virginia and Regional History Collection, West Virginia University Libraries.)

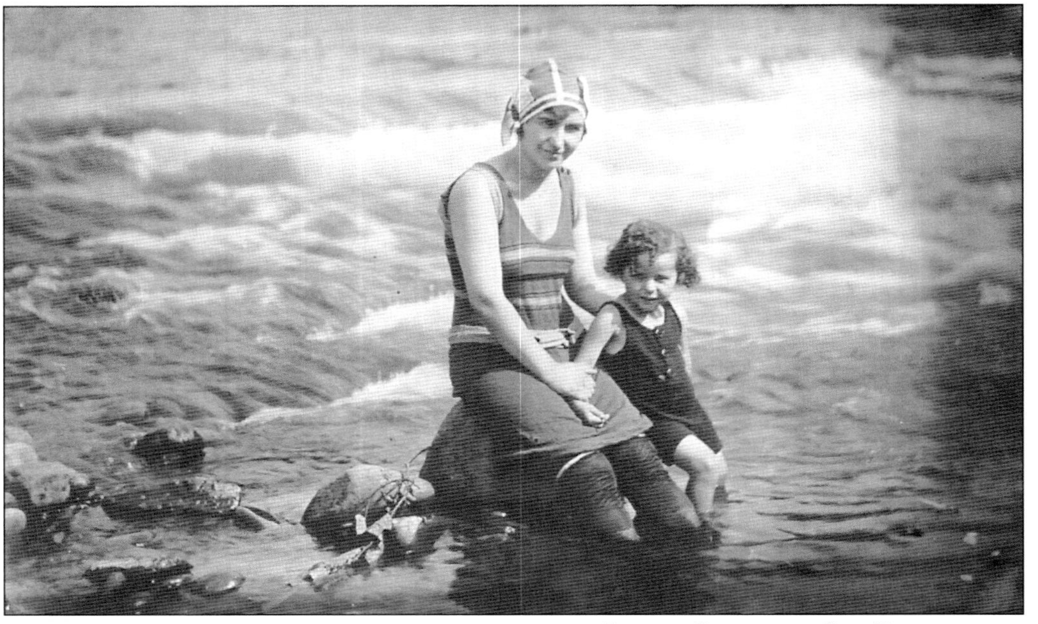

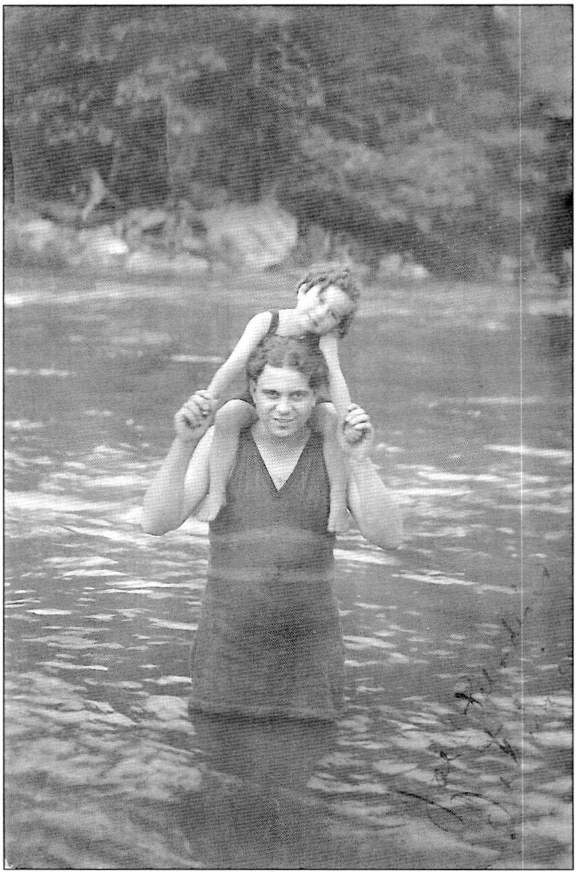

LOUISA COSTA AND SAM PALLADINO WITH JOHN B. ANGOTTI ENJOYING THE WEST VIRGINIA STATE PARKS, 1920s. The introduction of the automobile in the 1920s made it possible for residents of West Virginia to become more mobile and travel to the many recreational areas and parks located in the state. Louisa Costa and Sam Palladino are enjoying an afternoon outing with "Little" John B. Angotti. West Virginia parks provided a safe environment for citizens and their young family members, giving the opportunity to enjoy outdoor activities and to learn how to swim. Family values were nurtured through quality time spent together in outdoor recreational activities. (Both, courtesy of John B. and Mary Ann Angotti.)

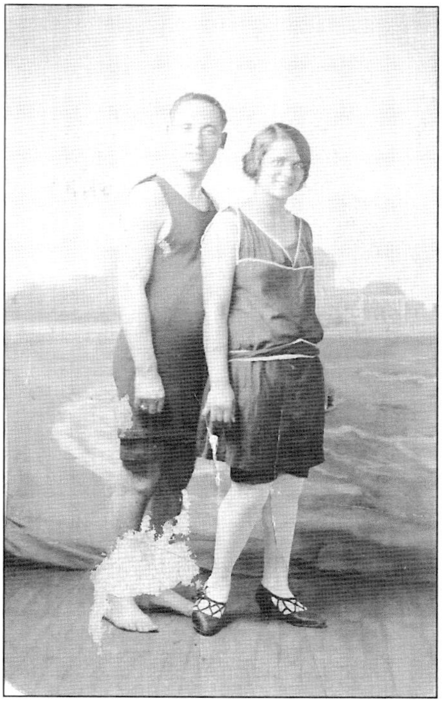

BALTIMORE & OHIO RAILROAD STATION AND ANTONIO AND VINCENZA BASILE IN ATLANTIC CITY, NEW JERSEY, 1920S. The Baltimore & Ohio Railroad introduced better passenger services in the 1920s. Residents of West Virginia began to travel to nearby metropolitan cities and eastern seashore resort destinations. Antonio and Vincenza Basile, who were married in 1924, were able to enjoy their honeymoon in Atlantic City, New Jersey. (Both, Authors' collection.)

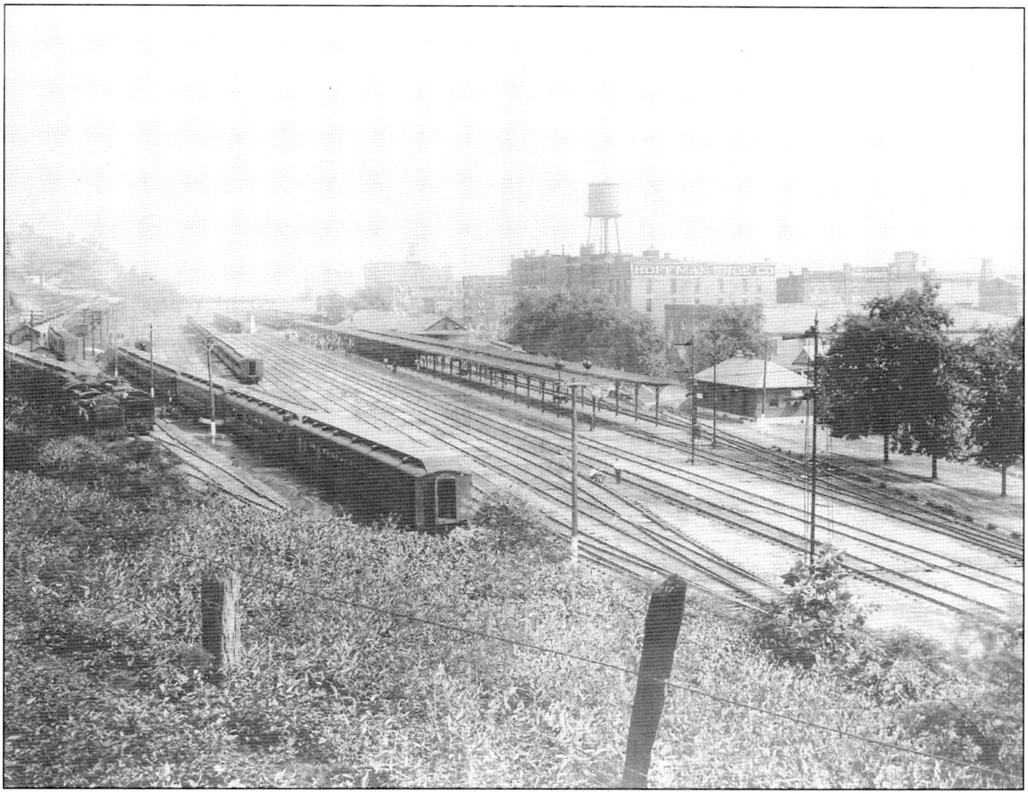

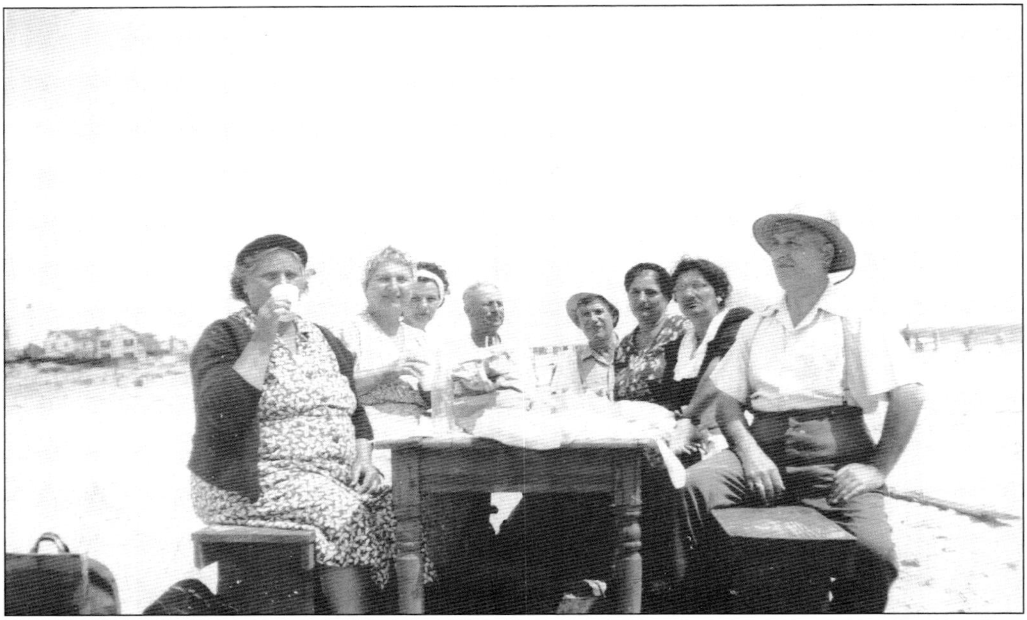

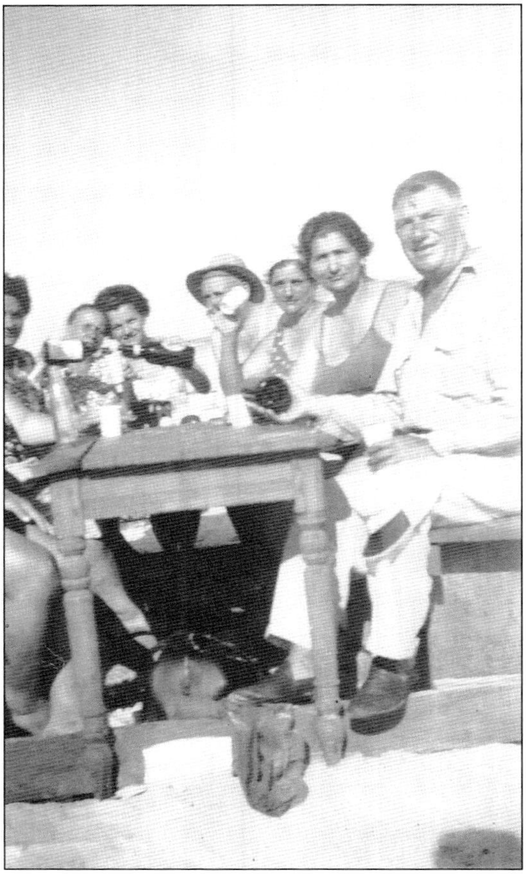

West Virginia Italians Enjoying the Beaches of Atlantic City, 1940s. Atlantic City was a renowned resort city with extensive beaches. It was very popular with Italian Americans from the 1920 to the 1950s. Many would spent their summer vacations (15 August–1 September) at this resort destination. This eastern seashore resort became a very popular summer vacation destination for Italians in West Virginia, as it was closest to the state. It was also popular with Italian Americans from the metropolitan areas of Baltimore and Philadelphia. In the 1880s, the Philadelphia–Atlantic City Railroad was constructed to transport tourists; it connected with the Baltimore & Ohio Railroad, which ran through West Virginia. Italians would stay in rooming houses operated by fellow Italian Americans and spent one to two weeks enjoying the beaches by day and the boardwalk by night. (Both, Authors' collection.)

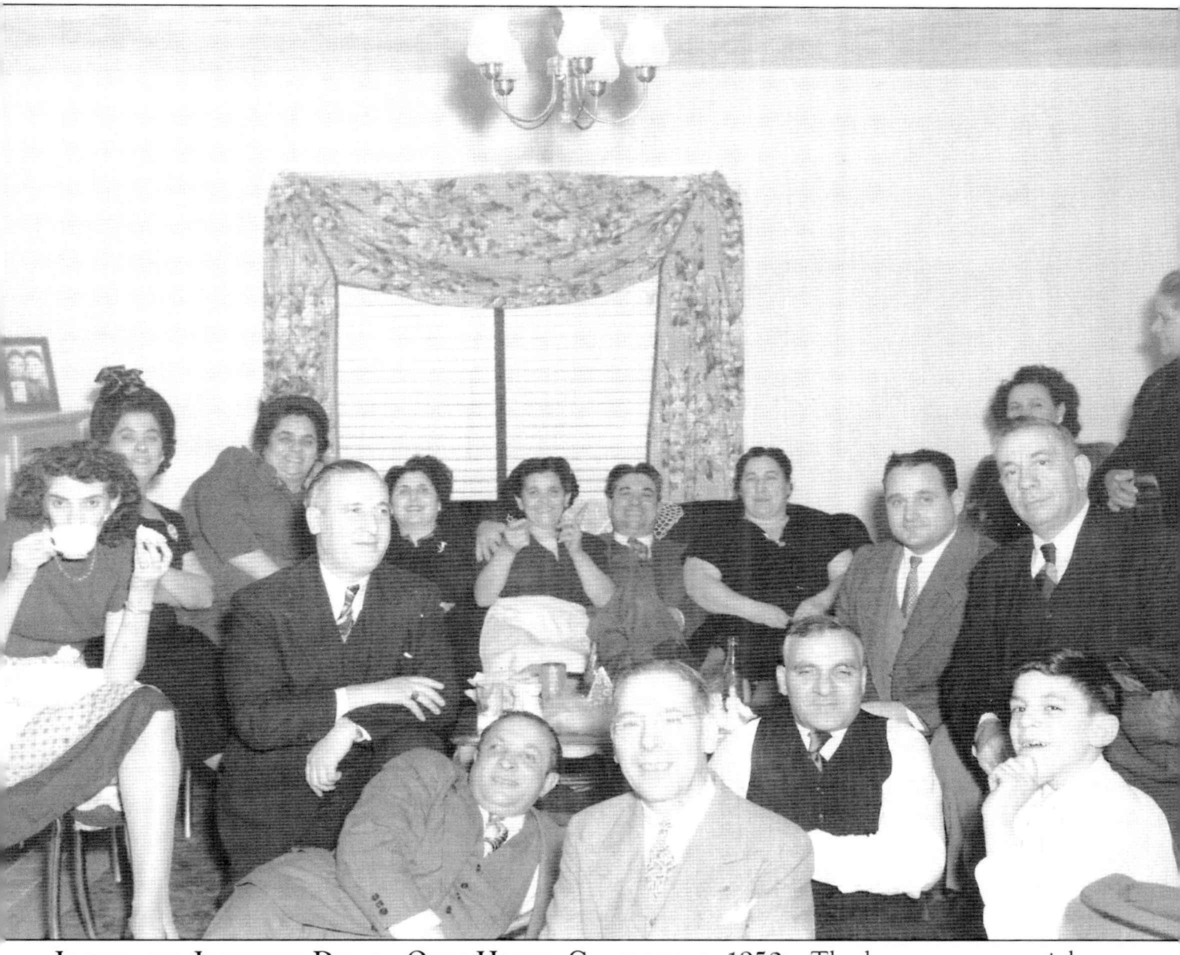

Joseph and Josephine Delapa Open House, Clarksburg, 1950s. The home was a special place in the Italian community. "Joe" Delapa had a shoe repair shop in the Broadway section of Clarksburg. Every Saturday afternoon, he had the Metropolitan Opera broadcast playing on his radio. He and Josephine's new house was built across the street from the shoe shop. Pictured is a group of Italian American family and friends enjoying and celebrating the newly constructed home at a housewarming party. (Courtesy of the John B. and Mary Ann Angotti.)

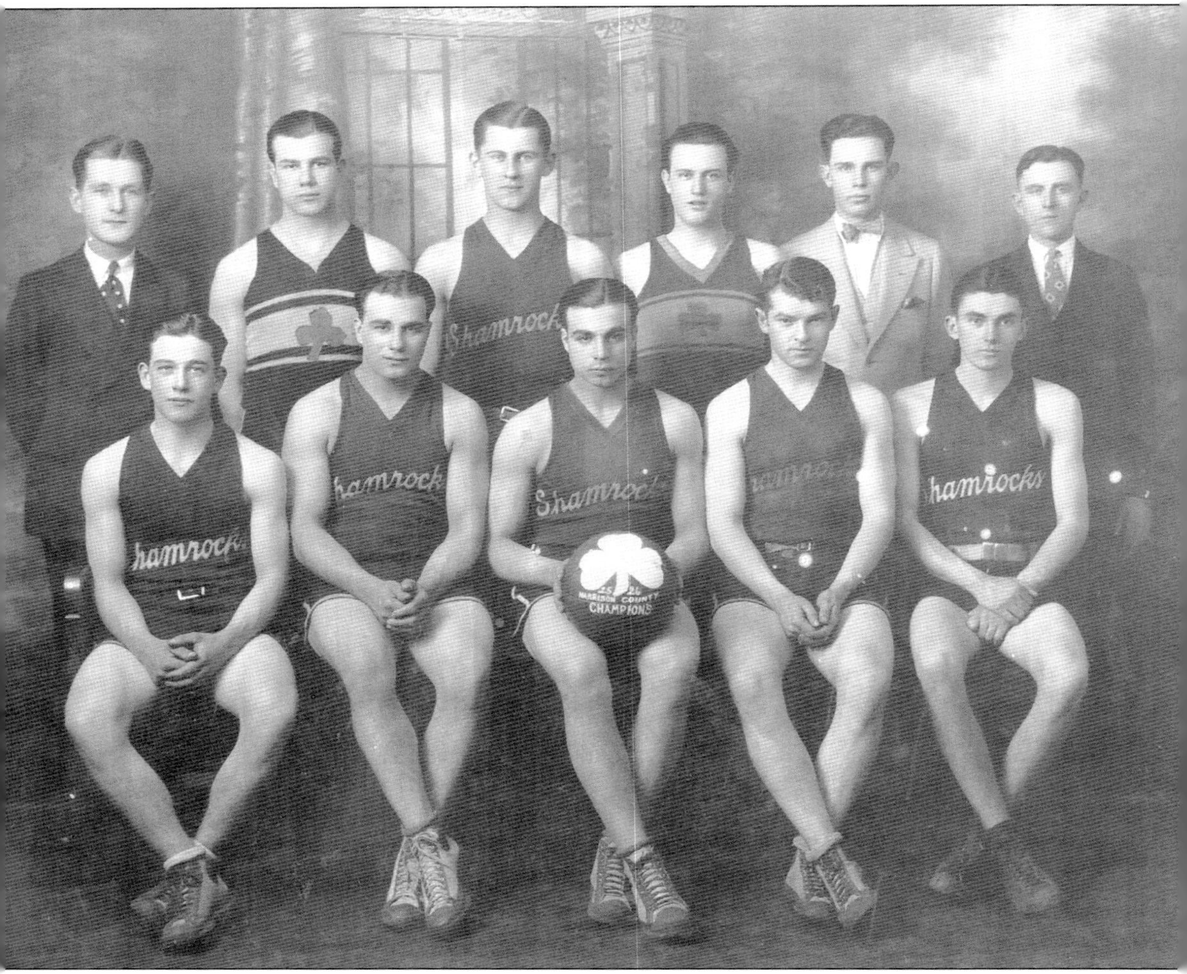

Shamrocks, Harrison County Champs, 1925–1926. The Shamrocks were Harrison County Independent Basketball champions in the 1925–1926 season. There were many teams playing basketball in the county at that time, and winning the championship was a great achievement. Pictured are, from left to right, (first row) Brad Reynolds, John Paladino, Jim Paladino, Mac McConloque, and Ralph Judge; (second row) Bill Coughlin, Sam Paladino, Andy Faron, Don Wilson, Harry Rogan, and Spot Ward. The Paladino brothers were first-generation Italians; through team sports, such as basketball, they were able to advance in business, government positions, and higher education. (Courtesy of Thomas and Louise Cavallaro-Martin.)

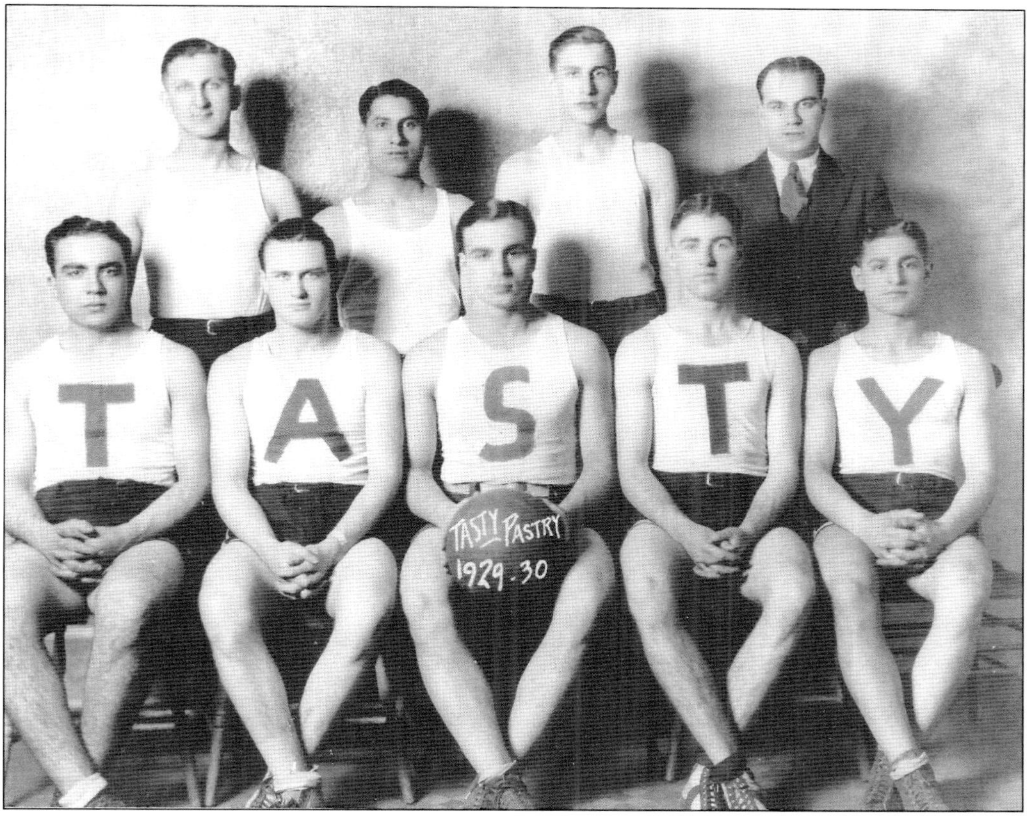

TASTY PASTRY BASKETBALL TEAMS AND DELIVERY TRUCK, 1929–1930. Because of their athletic ability, the Paladino brothers became spokesmen for their family's business, Tasty-Cakes Bakery. They organized a basketball team called "Tasty Pastry" and became the city league's basketball champs in 1929–1930. Pictured are, from left to right, (first row) Frank "Toot" Paladino, Don Wilson, Jimmy Paladino, Bud Coyne, and Phil Herrick; (second row) Johnny Ferron, Pat Abruzzino, unidentified, and John Paladino. Below, John B. Angotti is driving the 1929 delivery truck. The family's truck was bought by Joe Paladino in Elmira, New York. (Both, courtesy of John B. and Mary Ann Angotti.)

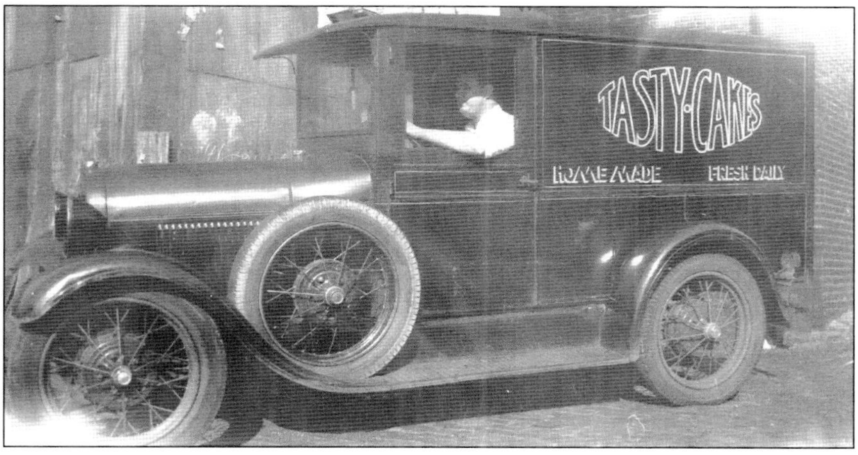

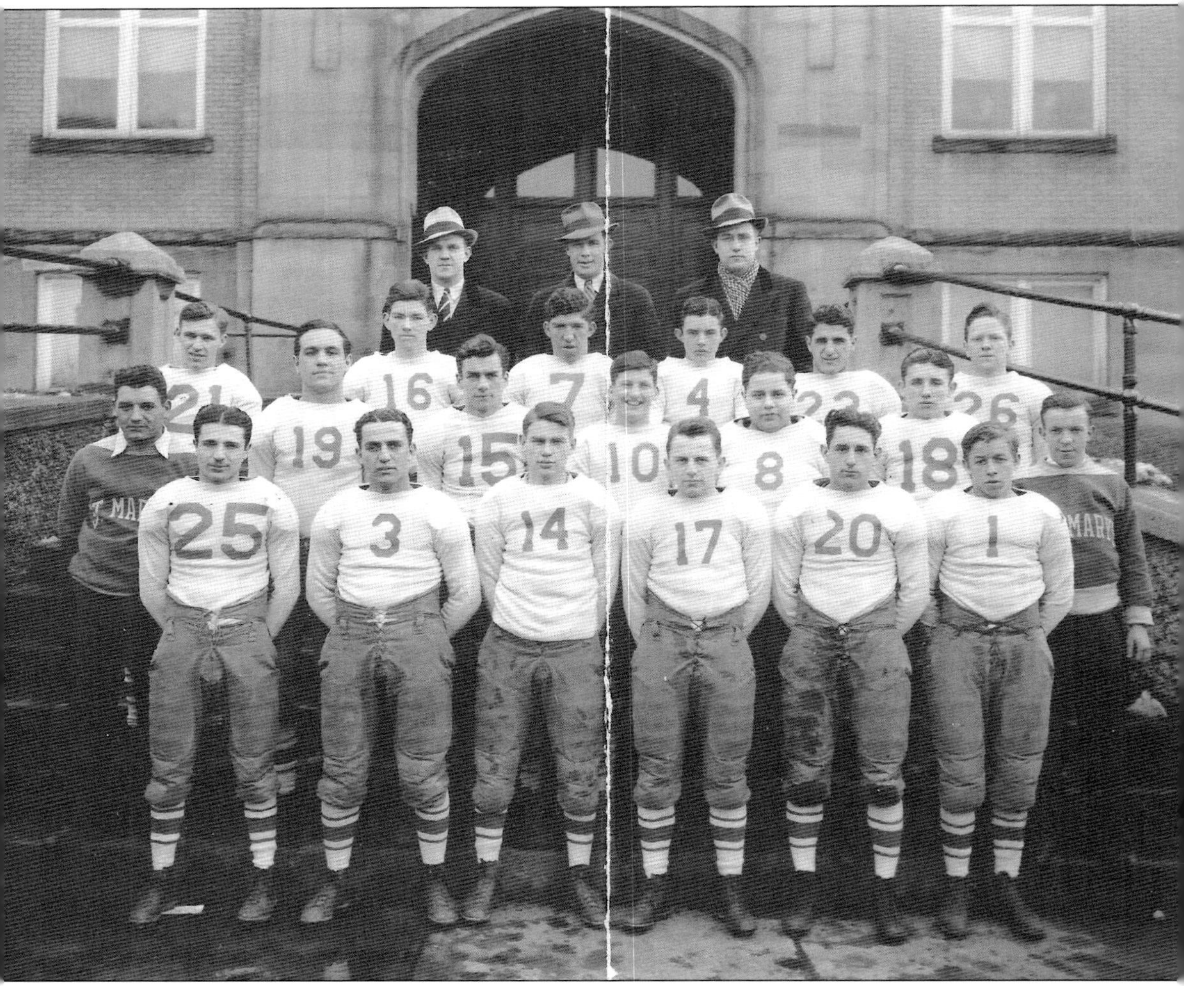

ST. MARY'S HIGH SCHOOL FOOTBALL TEAM, CLARKSBURG, 1936. At the urging of the student body, St. Mary's High School in 1936 decided to field a football team. Although totally inexperienced, the Stripers compiled a 3-3-1 record as a first-year team. The members and coaches of that first squad were, from left to right, (first row) Tony Oliverio, Bill Fredrick, Emmett Malloy, Al McGuire, Joe Gonzalez, and John Kichak; (second row) John Scott, Floyd Perri, Albert Trecost, Alfred Manson, John Angotti, Jim Dolan, and Bob Farrell; (third row) Bill Lynch, Louie Coughlin, John Bueno, Dan Mulheran, Sam Veltri, and Joe Bailey; (fourth row) coaches Carl Hageman, Harry Rogan, and John Keeley. (Courtesy of Thomas and Louise Cavallaro-Martin.)

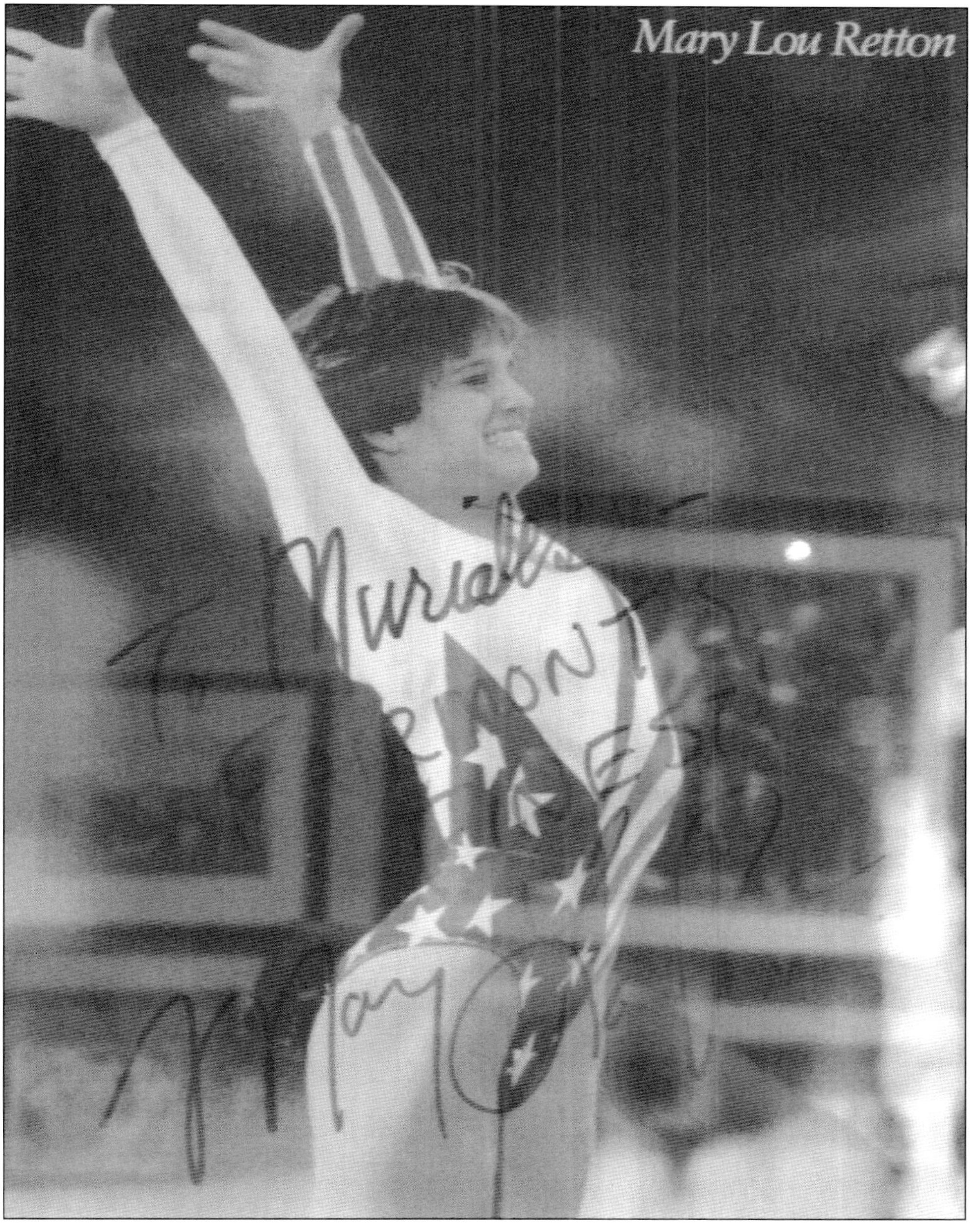

Mary Lou Retton, an Italian American Gymnast Born in Fairmont in 1968. The Olympic Gold medalist and Italian American Mary Lou Retton captured the hearts of Americans in the 1984 Olympics. Her father, Ronnie, operated a business specializing in transportation equipment for the coal industry. She attended Fairmont Senior High School and began competing in the Olympic Games during her sophomore year. She won the American Cup in 1983 and was the first female gymnast from outside of Eastern Europe to win the Olympic all-around title. In 1984, she was a designated honoree of the West Virginia Italian Heritage Festival. The Retton family returned to West Virginia in 2009. Her husband, Shannon Kelley, works for the Fairmont State University Athletic Department, and they have four daughters. (Courtesy of Rocco Muriale.)

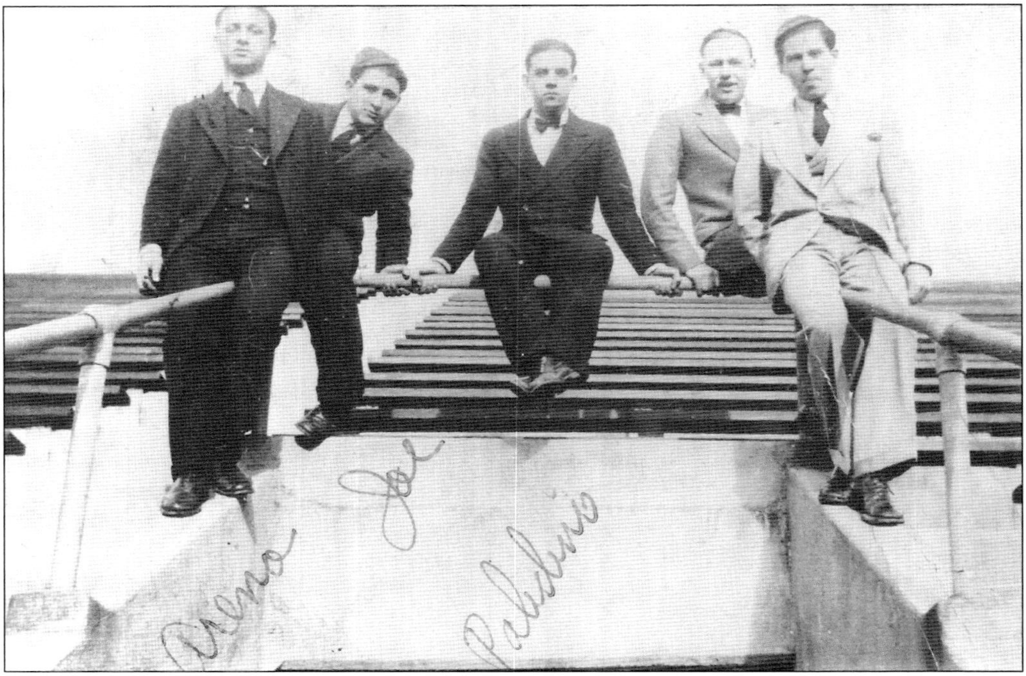

First-Generation Males at West Virginia University and Washington Irving High School, 1930s. Photographed at West Virginia Football Stadium are Pat Arena, Joe Oliverio, and Benjamin Paladino; the two males on the right are unidentified. Arena became a civil engineer, Oliverio a pharmacist, and Paladino an electrical engineer. For males of the first and second Italian American generations, sports became a vehicle for assimilation. Sports provided not only a form of entertainment but also a chance for advancement. Through athletic scholarships and later the GI Bill, first-generation Italian American males were able to move forward in higher education, business, politics, and governmental positions. There are several Italian American males in the graduation photograph below, taken in front of Washington Irving High School. (Both, courtesy of John B. and Mary Ann Angotti.)

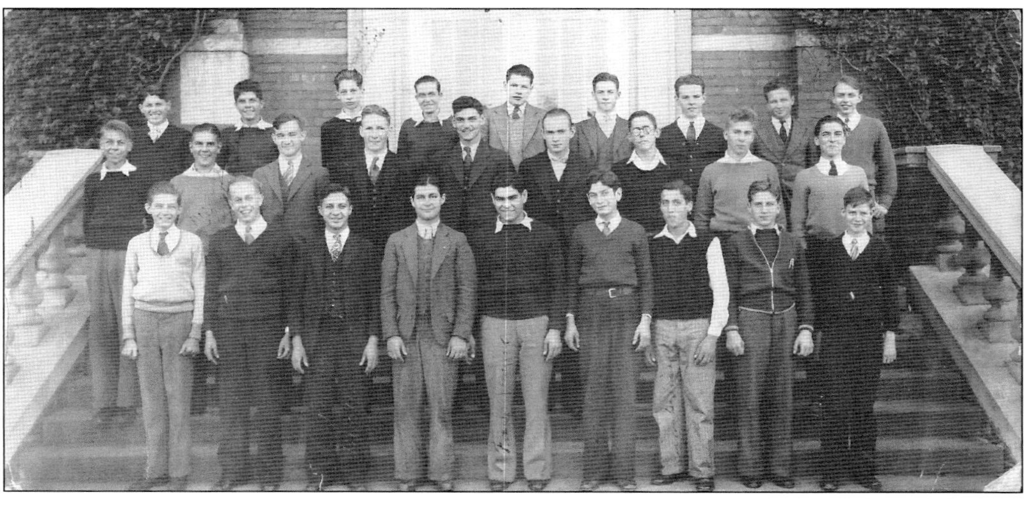

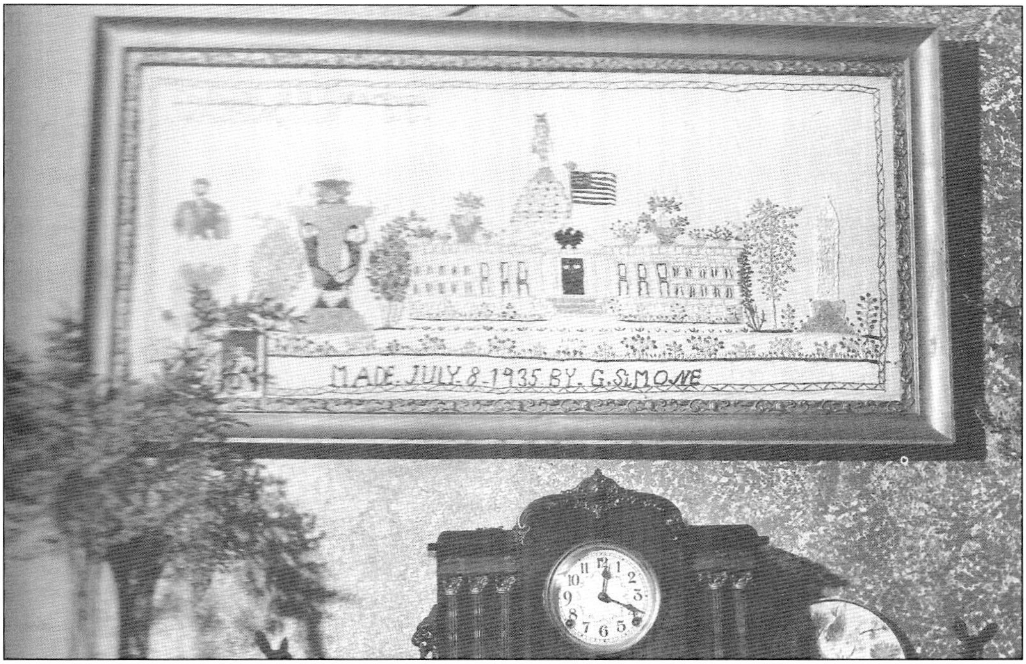

EMBROIDERY BY G. SIMONE AND WOMEN LEARNING ENGLISH. Early immigrant women had to struggle to learn English. Some attended citizenship and English classes (below). Basically, they stayed indoors, reared the children, and took care of the domestic affairs of the home. However, they sewed, knitted, quilted, and embroidered in groups; at these sessions, they communicated and exchanged values with other women and their children. Their daughters, especially those who were fortunate enough to receive a primary and secondary education, tended to be more literate. A few first-generation women had the benefits of attending commercial and academic colleges. Above is a memorable embroidery by G. Simone, an early immigrant. It expresses her love for the United States and familiarity with the English language. (Both, courtesy of the Library of Congress.)

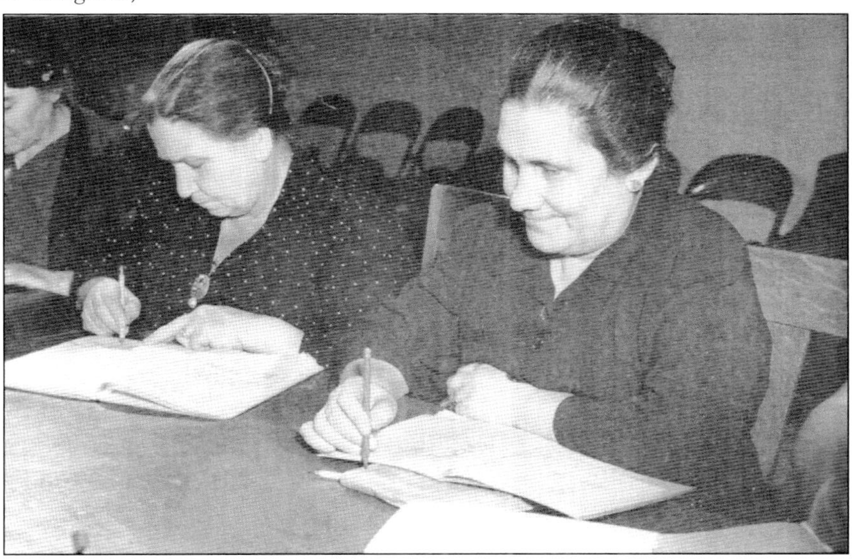

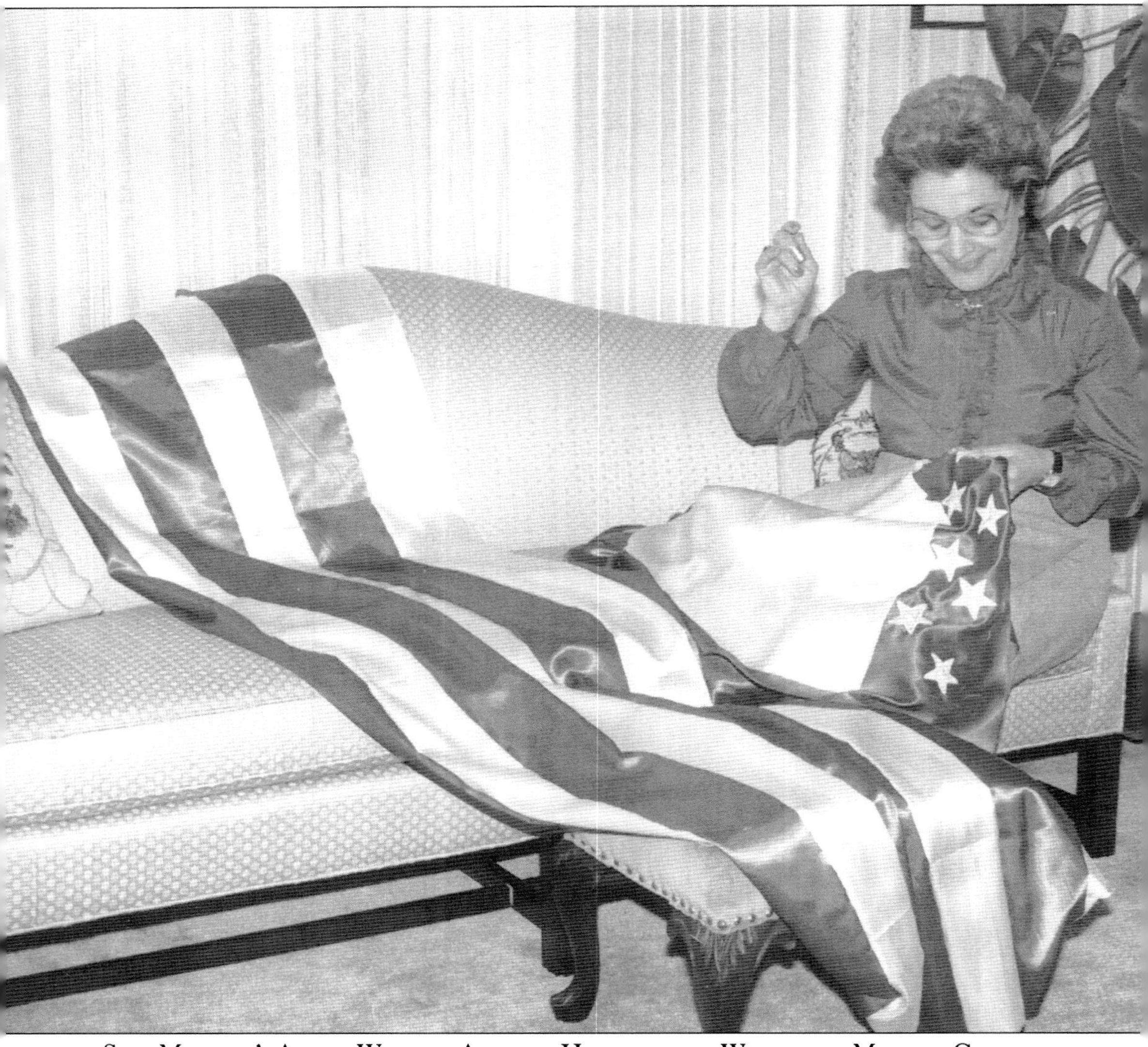

SERA MERANDI'S AWARD-WINNING ARTISTRY HOUSED IN THE WALDOMORE MUSEUM, CLARKSBURG. Sera Merandi, a post–World War II immigrant, has received several statewide awards for the West Virginia Women's Club. She received citations from both Gov. Jay Rockefeller and Sen. Jennings Randolph for her outstanding artistry. Here, she is sewing an American flag that is housed in the Waldomore Museum in Clarksburg. Both she and her husband, Frank, have been executive committee members of the WVIHF. A member of the Clarksburg Women's Club, Merandi resides in Clarksburg with her husband. (Courtesy of Frank and Sera Merandi.)

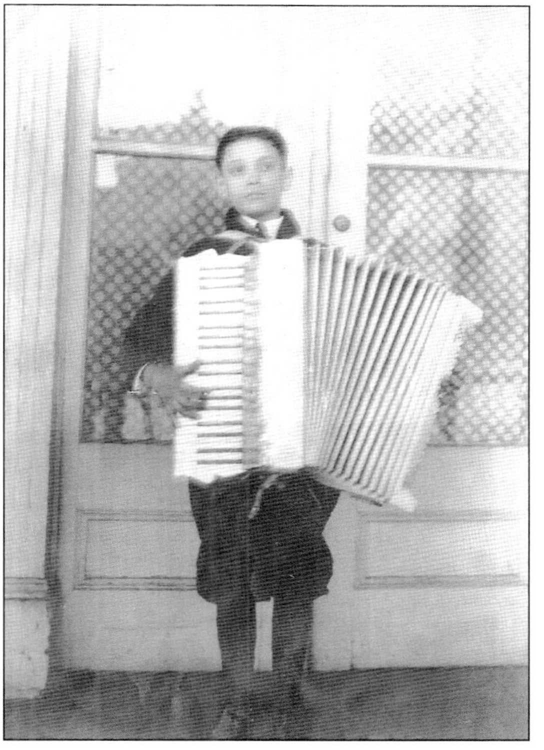

Carl Ramella with His Accordion and St. Mary's Drum and Bugle Corps, Clarksburg, 1924. Music has always been a popular form of entertainment in the Italian community. Pictured is Carl Ramella playing his 120-bass accordion in front of the Colonial Hotel. The accordion was the instrument for folk music; it was transported to North and South America by immigrants. From a historical perspective, immigrants' music had the three following traits: it was transmitted through an oral tradition, it was related to national culture, and it tended to commemorate historical and personal events. Eventually, talented Italian American musicians joined municipal, high school, and jazz bands. (Right, courtesy of John B. and Mary Ann Angotti; below, Thomas and Louise Cavallaro-Martin.)

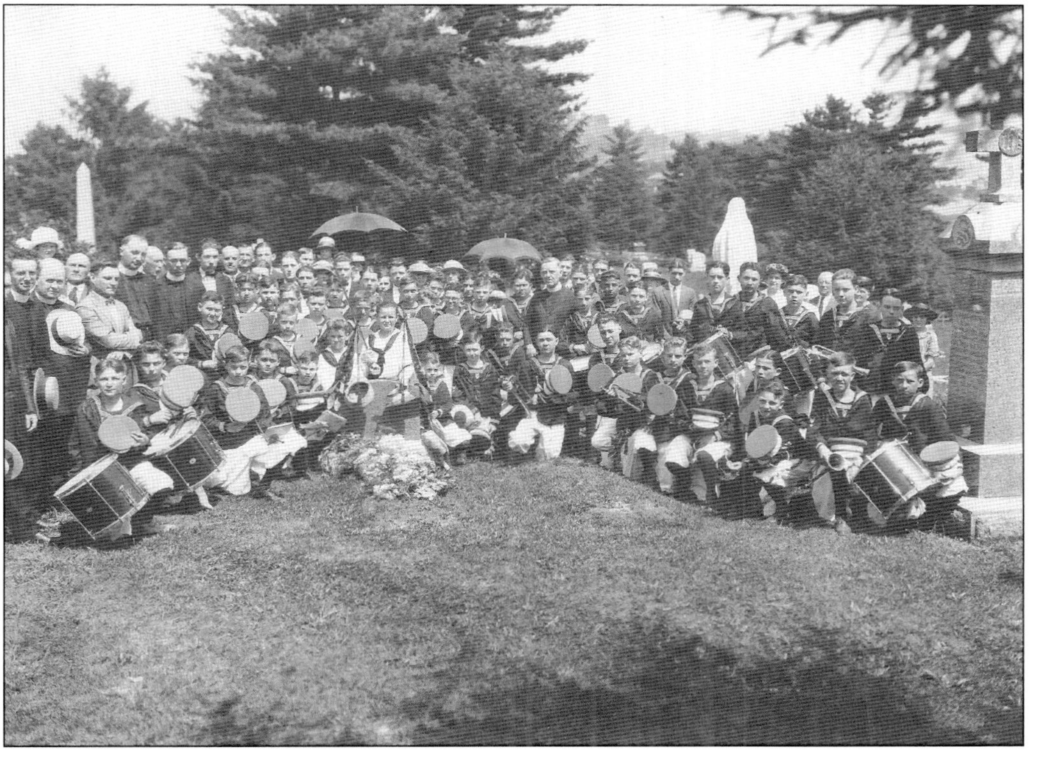

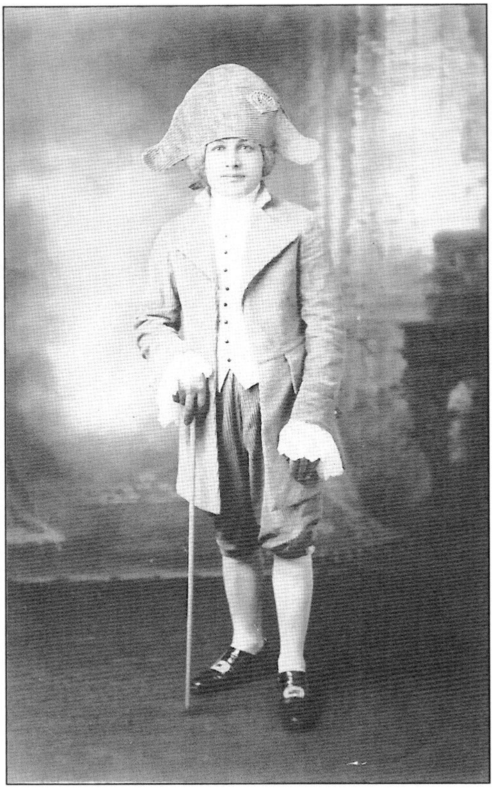

SAM MERANDI AND VINCENZA BASILE IN THEATRICAL COSTUMES, 1930S. The local Sons of Italy lodges would sometimes stage theatrical comedies based on the commedia dell'arte. This form of theater began in Italy and was characterized with masked "types" that performed improvised sketches and scenarios. Modern TV sitcoms are based on this type of comedy—for example, the "I Love Lucy Show." In these photographs, Sam Merandi is dressed as a captain and Vincenza Basile is a Spanish serving maid. The staging of these farces would take place in Italy during Carnival (the period between Epiphany and Ash Wednesday). (Both, Authors' collection.)

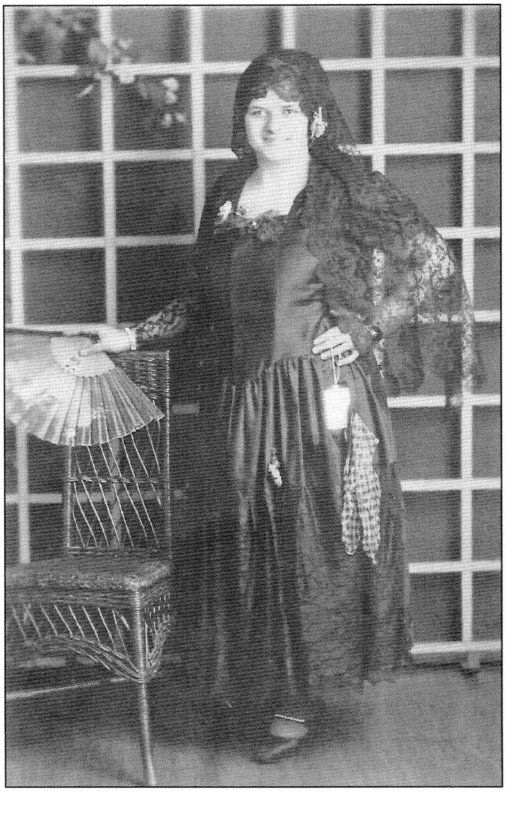

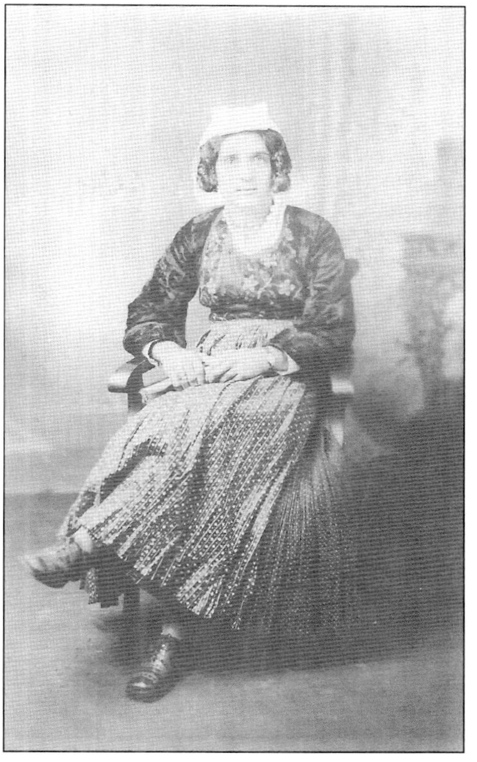

Roberto Adamo and Warrior Women in Costume, 1930s. By the end of the 16th century, prelates of the Church attempted to ban female performers. Church documents opposed courtesan roles because of their scanty attire and promiscuous lifestyle. Prelates felt that the scanty costumes would corrupt young men or at least infuse them with carnal desire. On occasion, male characters would assume the female roles in some of the scenarios. Roberto Adamo is photographed as a peasant woman substituting for an actress in a production. From left to right below, Vincenza Basile and Angela and Minnie Raschella are dressed in warrior outfits with spears and flags. In Italy, commedia masks and plots found their way into the opera buffa and the plots of Rossini, Verdi, and Puccini. (Both, Authors' collection.)

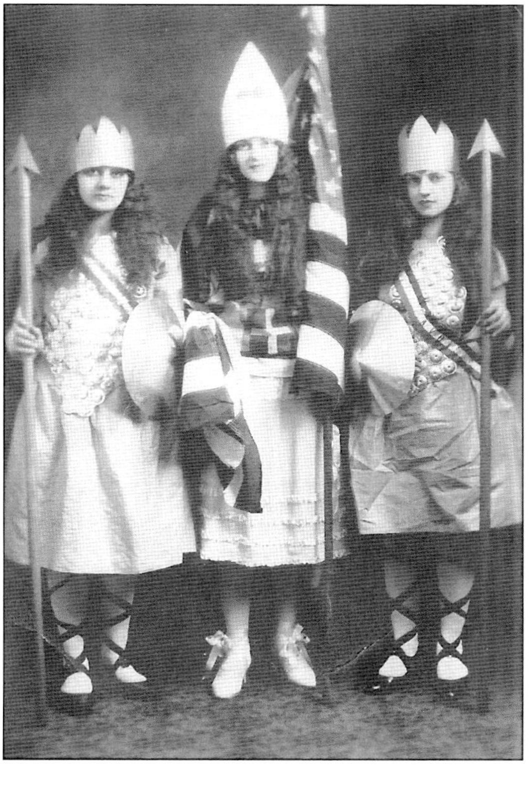

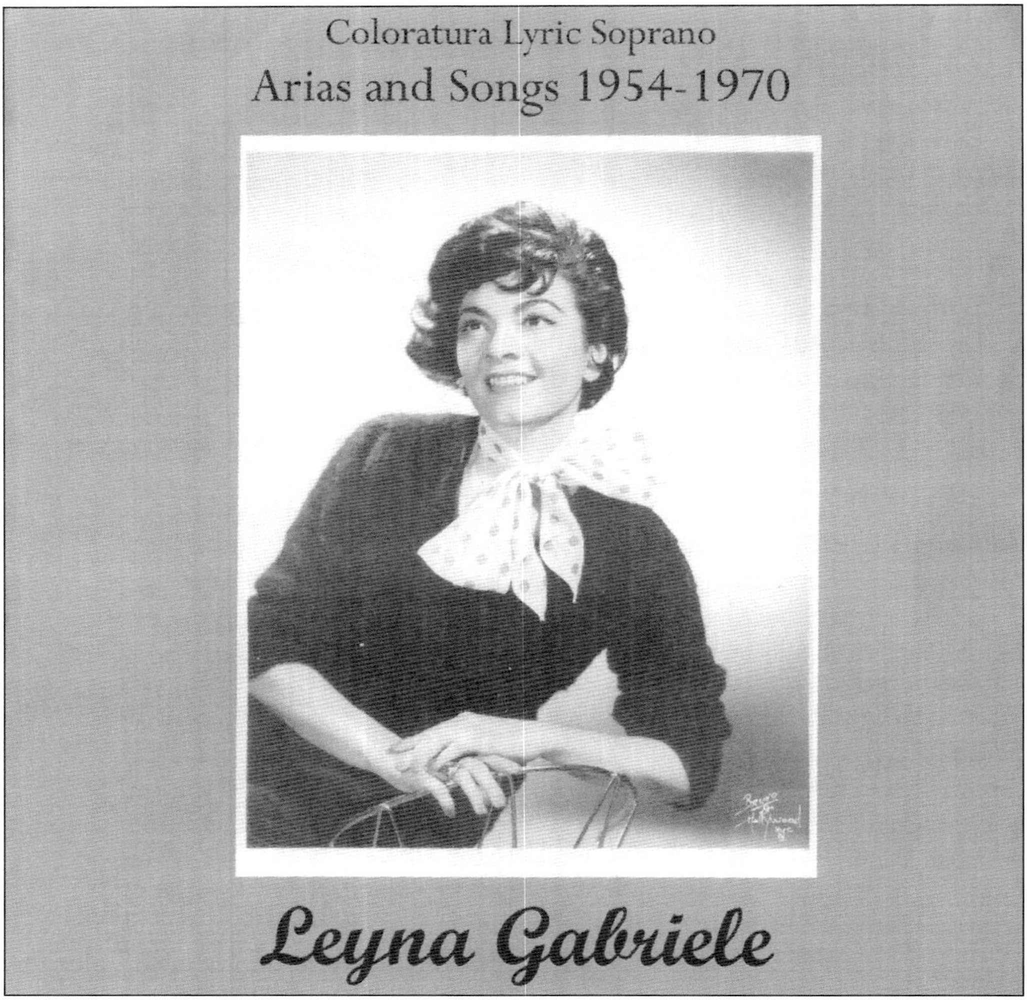

Leyna Gabriele, Opera Diva, Fairmont. Leyna Gabriele, a graduate of Fairmont State University, began her artistic training in West Virginia. She studied with Ruby Marshall Scott, a vocal coach who had an opera workshop studio in Clarksburg. In the 1940s, Scott and Leyna's father accompanied her to New York City to study with an opera impresario. In 1950, the Fulbright Foundation sent her to Milan, Italy, where she made her debut as Oscar in *Un Ballo in Maschera*. Following her debut in Italy, she returned to West Virginia to perform leading roles in the Clarksburg Opera Company's productions of *La Traviata* and *La Bohème*. She then took a job at Chez Vito in New York and married the owner, Vito Pisa, in 1954. The club reopened in a more elegant space at 30 East Sixtieth Street. Strolling violinists and a quartet of Metropolitan Opera singers serenaded the diners at candlelit tables with opera, Continental favorites, and show tunes. She was Italian American Women of the Year at the 2005 West Virginia Italian Heritage Festival. (Courtesy of Leyna Gabriele.)

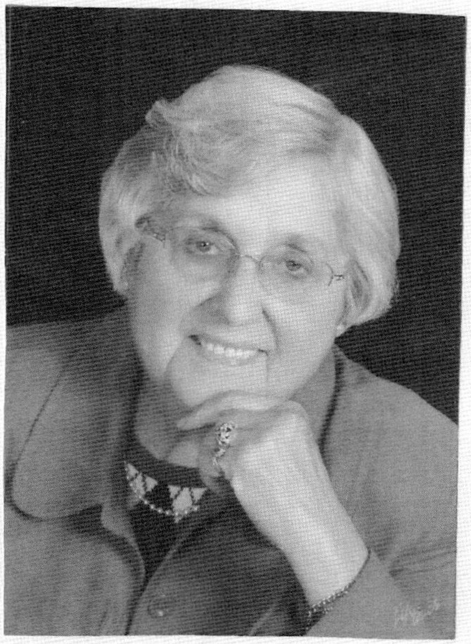

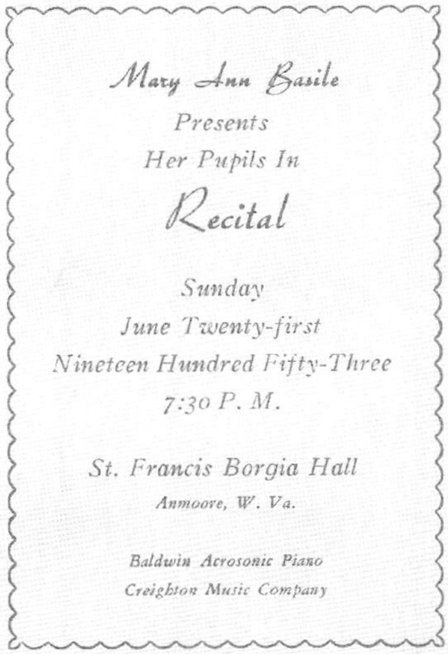

Mary Ann Basile
Presents
Her Pupils In
Recital

Sunday
June Twenty-first
Nineteen Hundred Fifty-Three
7:30 P. M.

St. Francis Borgia Hall
Anmoore, W. Va.

Baldwin Acrosonic Piano
Creighton Music Company

MARY ANN BASILE-ANGOTTI, PIANO INSTRUCTOR AND LITURGICAL MUSICIAN. In 1984, Mary Ann Basile-Angotti was honored as the Italian American Woman of the Year. She received her early musical training with Mary Garantano and later with the Sisters of St. Joseph. She made her musical debut singing the folk song "La Spagnola" on the stage at the Sons of Italy William Marconi Lodge. After graduating from St. Mary's High School, she began performing with local jazz orchestras and instructing piano students. She has been part of the music ministry at the Immaculate Conception Parish in Clarksburg for more than 70 years. In the 1990s, she received papal blessings from both Pope John Paul and Pope Benedict for her contributions to liturgical music. She attended Manhattanville College in New York and graduated from Fairmont State University. Many of her students have been awarded musical scholarships and have become professional musicians and church organists. Her son John B. Angotti Jr., a composer and vocalist, had a Carnegie Hall debut on January 14, 2011. (Courtesy of Mary Ann Basile-Angotti.)

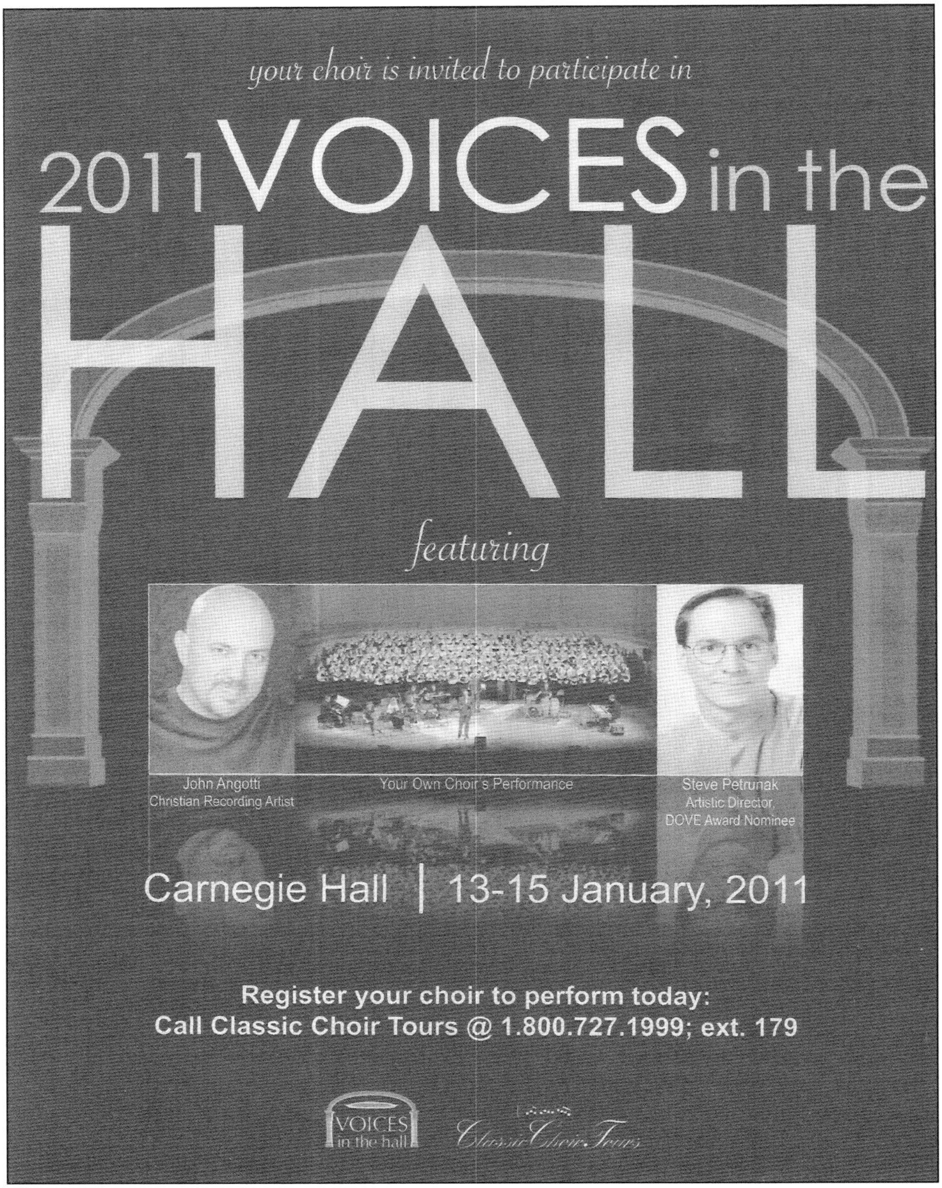

JOHN ANGOTTI AND THE VOICES IN THE HALL FESTIVAL CHORUS PERFORM IN CARNEGIE HALL, 2011. *Extraordinary Love*, an amazing and uplifting musical concert, was performed by the John Angotti Music Mission; 350 voices from across the United States sang his musical composition at Carnegie Hall on January 14, 2011. John Angotti's music brought a message of hope and love with which his audience might meet today's challenges. Through the performance of *Extraordinary Love*, Angotti accomplishes a masterful expression of the redeeming love at work in the lives of those living in the 21st century. His music has a timely spiritual relevance. The concert touched the hearts and inspired the lives of a record audience. John began his music training with his mother, Mary Ann Basile-Angotti; early on, he was a featured performer at the WVIHF. He is a graduate of West Virginia University, and he also attended the US Military School of Music. Angotti was a member of the US Navy Band, in which he was a lead vocalist. (Courtesy of John Angotti.)

Five

FAMILY

The home was a special space in an Italian community, and the family was the sacred unit that occupied the home. The Italian family was a *domus*-centered unit. (Domus is the Latin term meaning house or home.) In Italian families, the father was the symbolic head and usually the sole breadwinner. The mother was responsible for rearing and disciplining the children and caring for the domestic affairs of the home. Members of the family were expected to behave respectfully and somewhat formally in the home. The southern Italian immigrants did not know an Italian nation; they knew only the domus-centered family and its role within the community. When Italians immigrated, they brought not only the family (*la famiglia*, they also recruited their countrymen (*i paesani*). In the early years of immigration, many families invited recently arrived family members to reside in their homes. In such cases, the family unit became larger. These extended-family households were particularly common in coal-mining communities. Other Italian families housed young, single Italian men as boarders. By housing boarders, families could help recent arrivals and at the same time earn extra income for the household.

The Italian family helped to preserve many aspects of the old-world culture and ways of life. In the home, immigrants and their children commonly conversed in their regional dialect. The home also provided a place where immigrants could continue to practice old-world traditions. The kitchen, the theater in which the value-enforcing drama occurred, was the most important room of the house. The family would gather and eat together in the evenings. After dinner, they sat around the fireplace and talked over the events of the day. Some would gather around musical instruments and sing nostalgic songs of their glorious Italy. On being elected governor of New York in 1983, Mario Cuomo, a prominent Italian American politician, stated, "I am just moving on from a smaller family to a larger family—the State of New York."

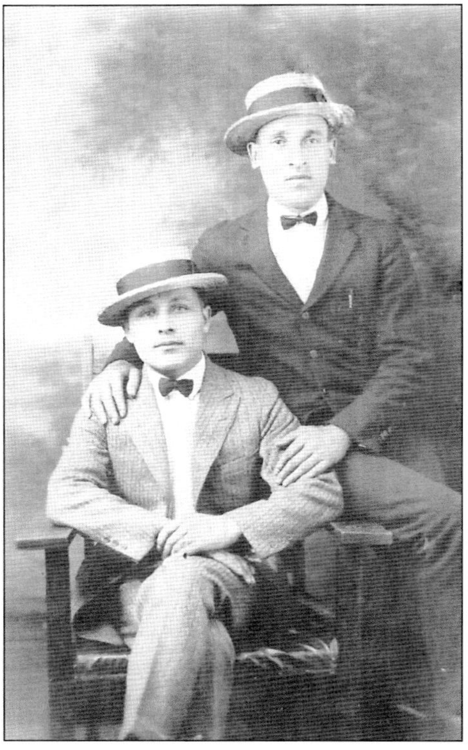

The Transition of Italian Families from Emigrants to American Ethnics, 1920s. Antonio Basile (sitting on the arm of the chair) joined his brother Angelo in West Virginia in 1922. He originally immigrated to the United States to work in the mines; however, he found that type of work too dangerous. Shortly after his arrival, he was photographed with friend Sam Merandi, who emigrated with him from Italy. Both of the men had been trained as tailors in Italy and began work in Clarksburg clothing stores. While the two stylish men were attending a social function at St. John's Italian Catholic Church, they encountered the fashionable Vincenza (Reda) Perri, a earlier immigrant who spoke English, Italian, and Spanish fluently. Shortly after, Antonio became engaged to Vincenza. (Both, Authors' collection.)

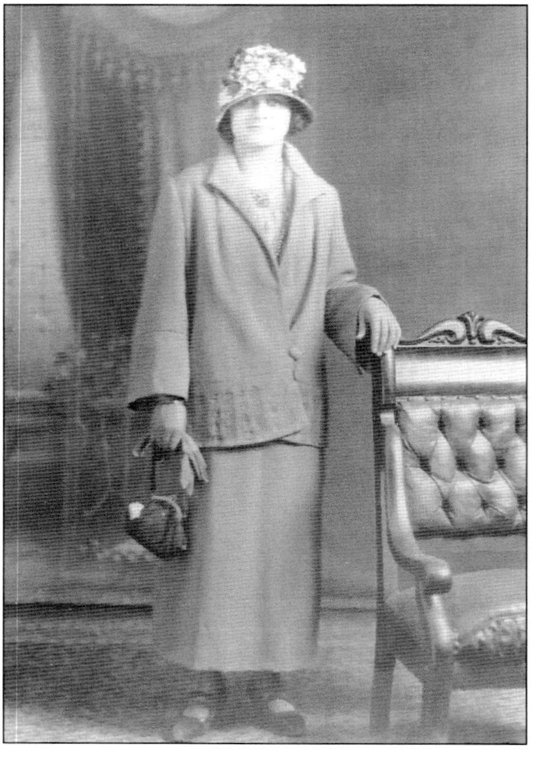

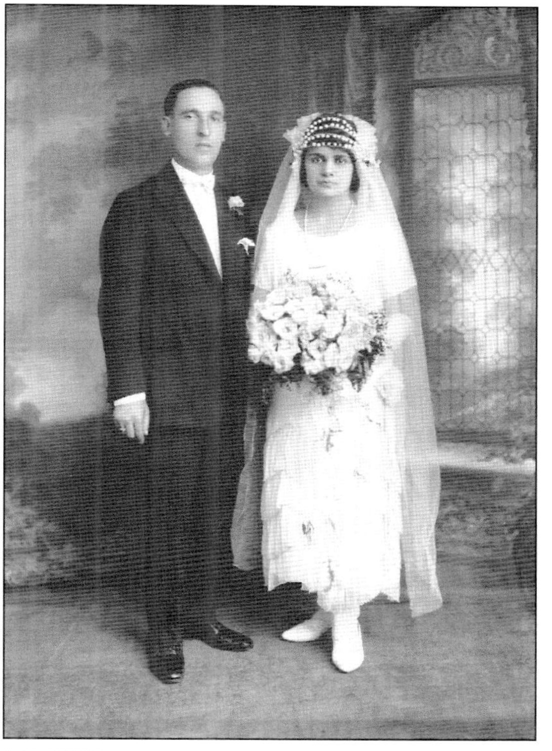

THE TRANSITION OF ITALIAN FAMILIES FROM EMIGRANTS TO AMERICAN ETHNICS, 1924–1958. Antonio Basile married Vincenza Perri in 1924 at St. Francis Borgia Church in Anmoore. After marriage, the couple worked for Angelo Grantano in his clothing and grocery stores; eventually, they bought his business. Antonio had a clothing store in Glen Elk, and Vincenza opened a grocery store in Anmoore. Their American family with Italian ethnicity is pictured below approximately one year after the birth of their younger son, Victor. They are, from left to right, Mary Ann (daughter), Anthony Jr. (oldest son), Vincenza (mother) holding infant Victor, and Antonio Basile (father). (Both, Authors' collection.)

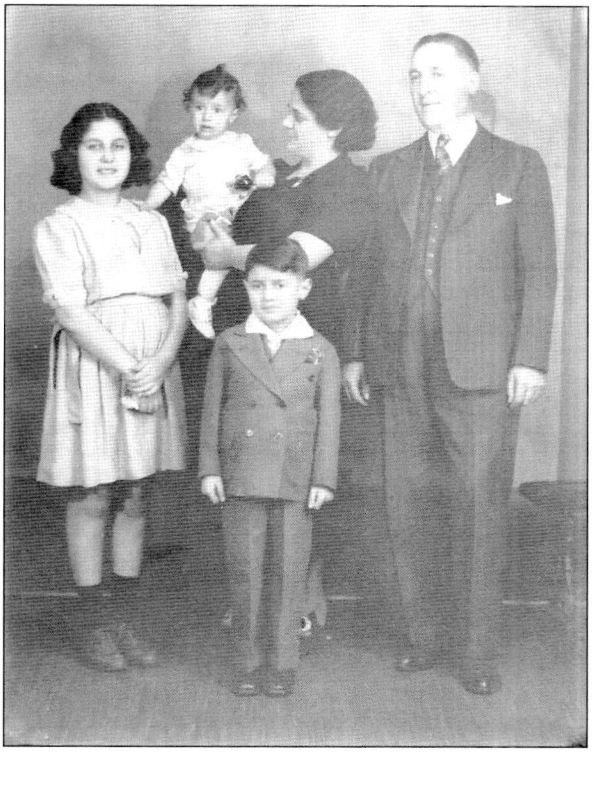

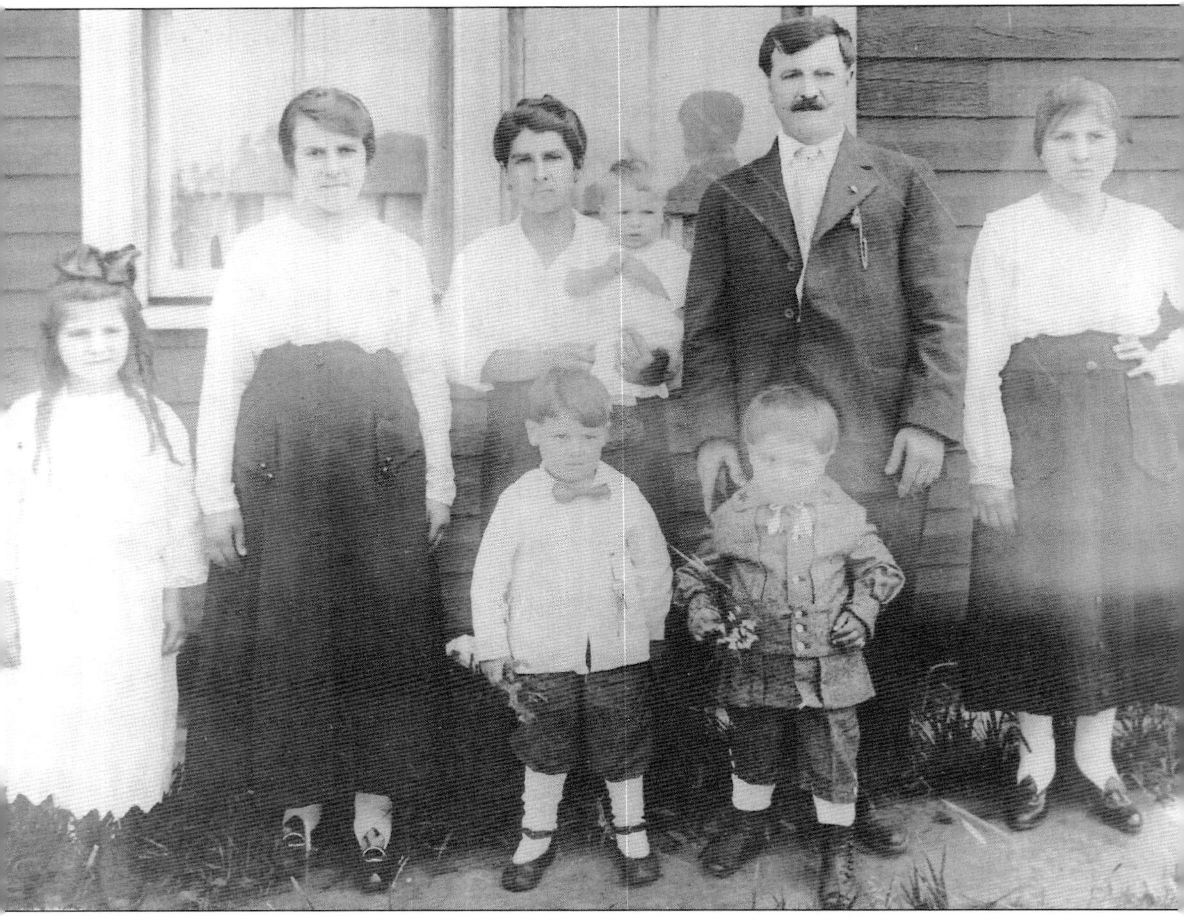

The Domus-Centered Italian Family, West Virginia, c. 1920s. The authors selected this photograph to illustrate the structure of an Italian domus-centered family. Italians believed that a family should be harmonious, sympathetic, united, and lovable, and that this type of family structure supported just government and religious foundations. (Courtesy of John B. and Mary Ann Angotti.)

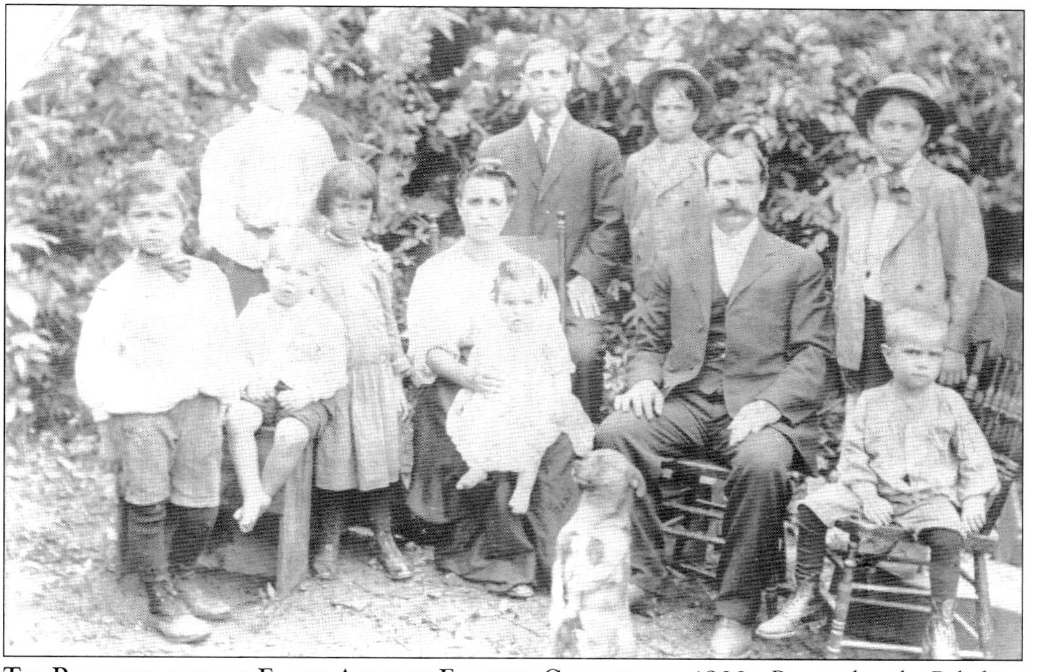

THE PALADINO AND THE FRANK ANGOTTI FAMILIES, CLARKSBURG, 1900S. Pictured in the Paladino family photograph are, from left to right, (standing) Jimmy Paladino (son in bow tie), Dominica "Minnie" Paladino-Angotti (daughter), Elizabeth Paladino-Delagatti (daughter), Frank Angotti (Dominica's husband), Joe Paladino (son), and John Paladino (son); (seated) Ben Paladino (son), Mary Ann Paladino (mother), Lily (infant), Antonio Paladino (father), and Sam Paladino (son). The dog's name is Judy. The Paladino family was one of the first to immigrate to West Virginia. This first wave of immigrants migrated to West Virginia to work on the railroads. The Paladinos were from Potenza in the province of Basilicata. Frank Angotti married Dominica Paladino in the early 1900s. Pictured in the Angotti family photograph below are, from left to right, Dominica "Minnie" Paladino-Angotti (wife), Maria Angotti Secret (daughter), John B. Angotti (son), Frank Angotti (husband), and Flora Angotti (daughter). (Both, courtesy of John B. and Mary Ann Angotti.)

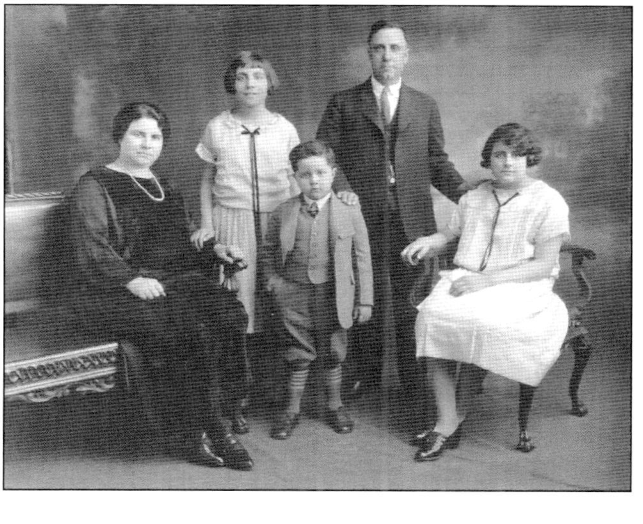

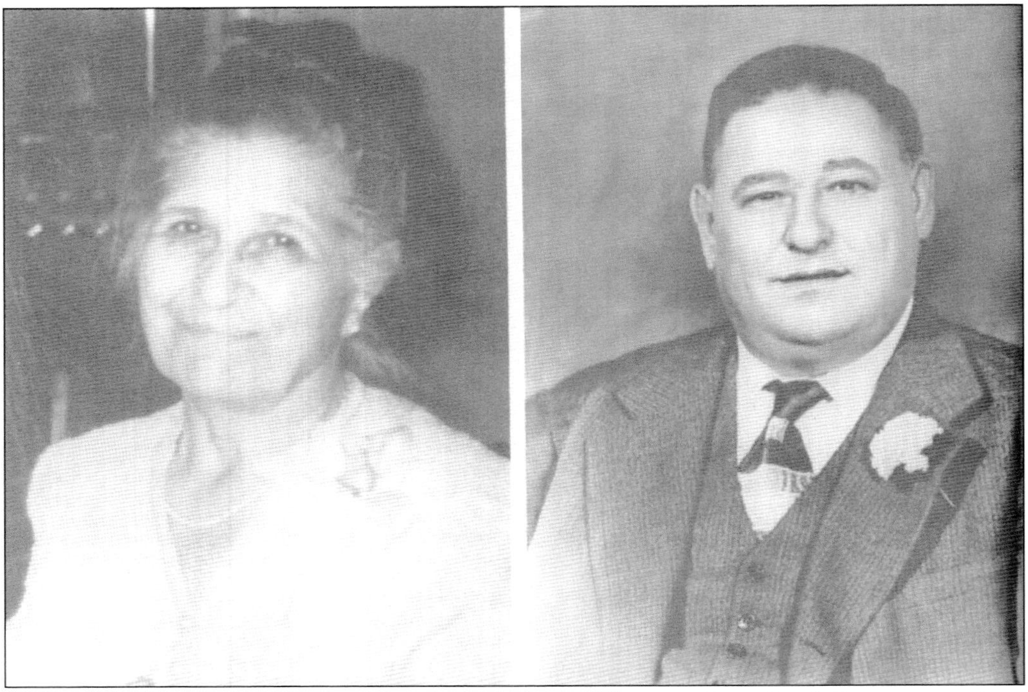

JOSEPHINE AUDIA AND FRANCESCO (FRANK) BONASSO, WYATT, 1920S. Frank Bonasso was from San Giovanni in Fiore and immigrated to America in 1914. He joined his brother Pietro in West Virginia and worked at the Hutchinson Coal Company's mine. In 1918, Frank and his brother opened up a modest grocery store catering to immigrant miners. In 1921, he married Josephine Audia. In 1922, their first son, Russell F. Bonasso, was born; four males and one female followed—Samuel, Jack, Peter, Lucille, and William. Russell became a community leader for the West Virginia Italian American experience. He wrote two books, *Casa Allegro* and *Fire in the Hole*, and was the major organizer for the Monongah Mine Disaster Centennial Observance held on December 7, 2007. (Above, courtesy of WVIHF; below, courtesy of Ron Rittenhouse.)

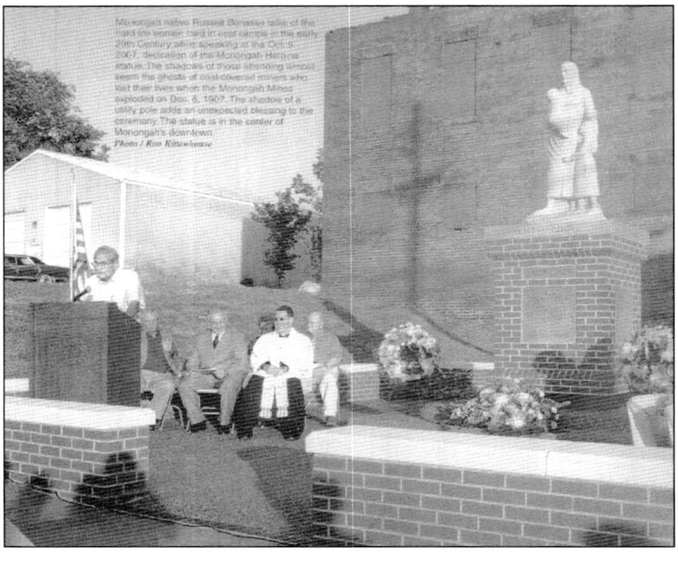

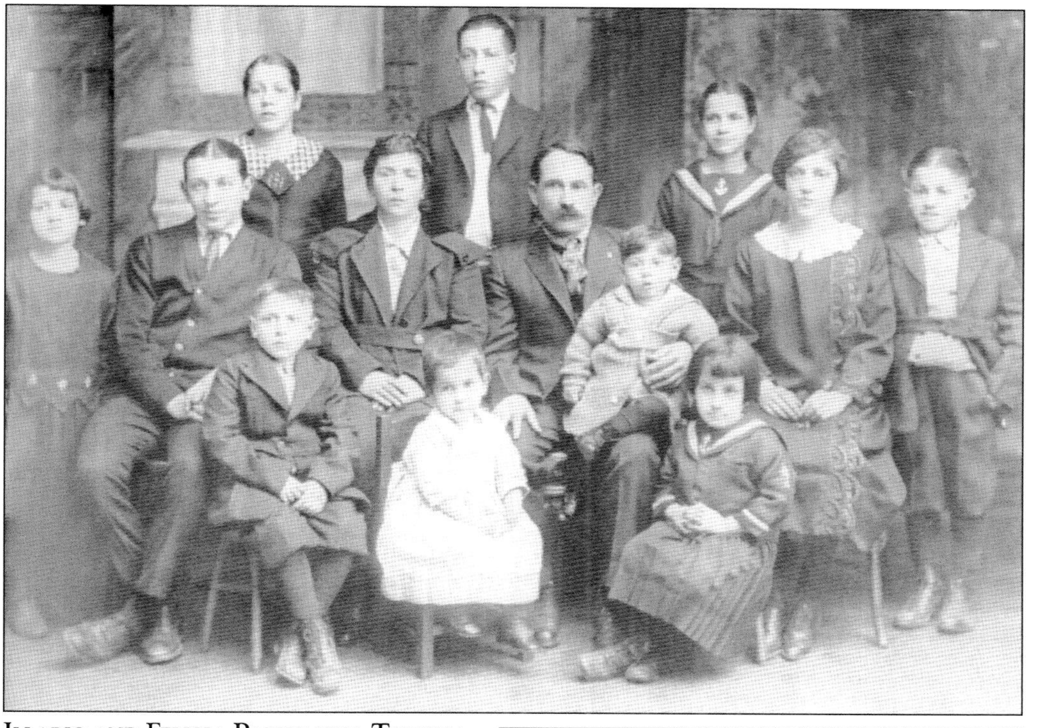

Illario and Felicia Pasqualina Torchia Candido (Cann) Family, Clarksburg, c. 1920s. Illario came to West Virginia as a young man to work in the mines. On arrival in Monongah, Illario's surname was changed from Candido to Cann. In 1899, Illario married Felicia Torchia. After their marriage, they moved to a building on Water Street in Clarksburg. On the ground floor, they had a grocery store; upstairs, they had a boardinghouse. James, their eldest son, worked at the Tin Plate Mill to get through college. In 1924, he received his law degree from Georgetown University, an unusual accomplishment for the son of immigrants. On the right, James is pictured with his wife, Antoinette, at the ordination of their son, Hilarion (Larry) Cann, in Rome. (Above, courtesy of the WVIHF; right, courtesy of Rev. Hilarion Cann.)

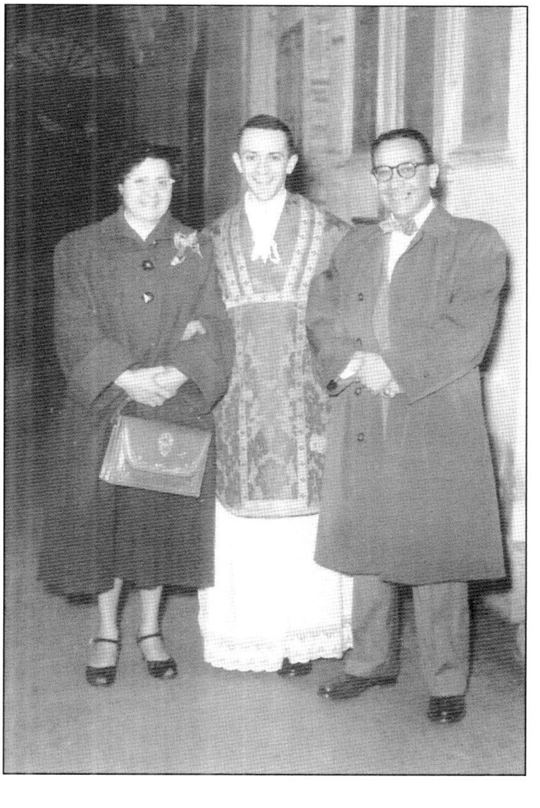

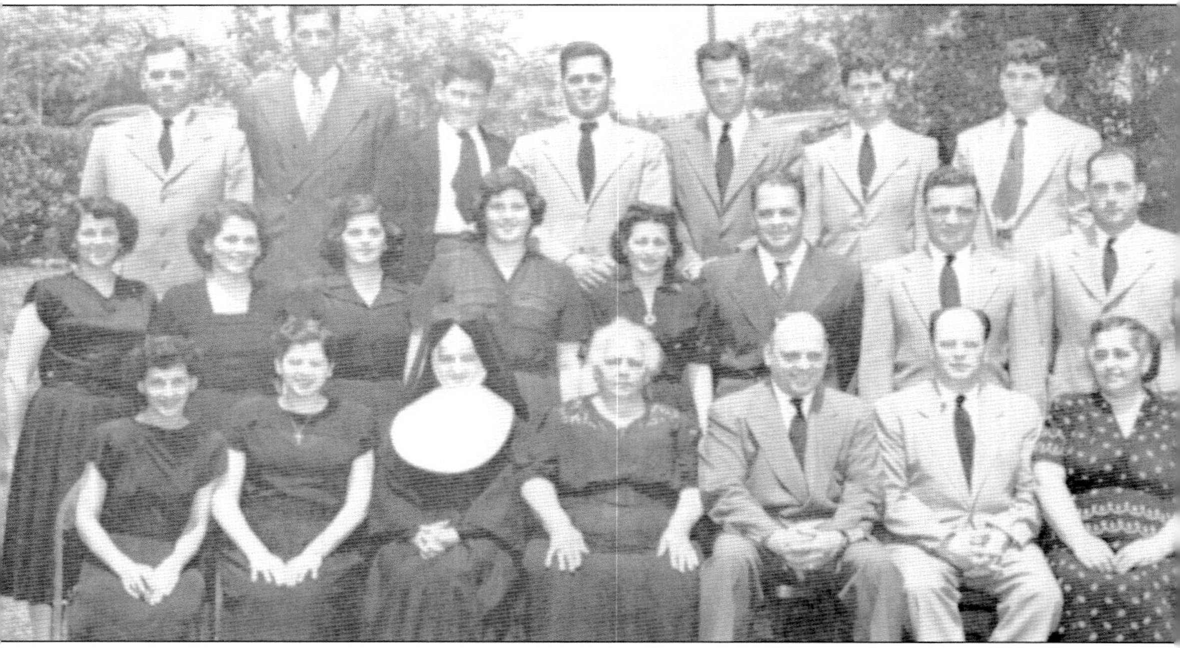

THE FAMILY OF BATTISTA AND ANTONIA TIANO COLOMBO, CLARKSBURG, 1950. Battista and Antonia were both emigrants from San Giovanni in Fiore. They met in Junior, West Virginia, and they were married on August 21, 1903. The Colombo family has always been well known in West Virginia; they had 21 children. This photograph was taken on July 29, 1950, at the family residence in Stonewood, West Virginia, following Battista Colombo's death. Family members are, from left to right, (first row) Teresa Colombo Chuckler, Margaret Colombo Lopez, Sister Frances Cabrini (Mary) Colombo, SSJ, Antonia Tiano Colombo, Samuel Colombo, Dr. J.N. Colombo, and Rose Colombo Barberio; (second row) Angela Colombo, Velma Colombo, Josephine Colombo Quinn, Sister Jean Colombo, SSJ, Pasquelina Colombo, James Colombo, Sam Colombo Guzzi, and Anthony Colombo; (third row) Louis Colombo, Frank Colombo, Rudolph Colombo, Russell Colombo, Raymond Colombo, Dr. Armando Colombo, and Orlando Colombo. (Courtesy of the Congregation of St. Joseph's, Wheeling Center Archives.)

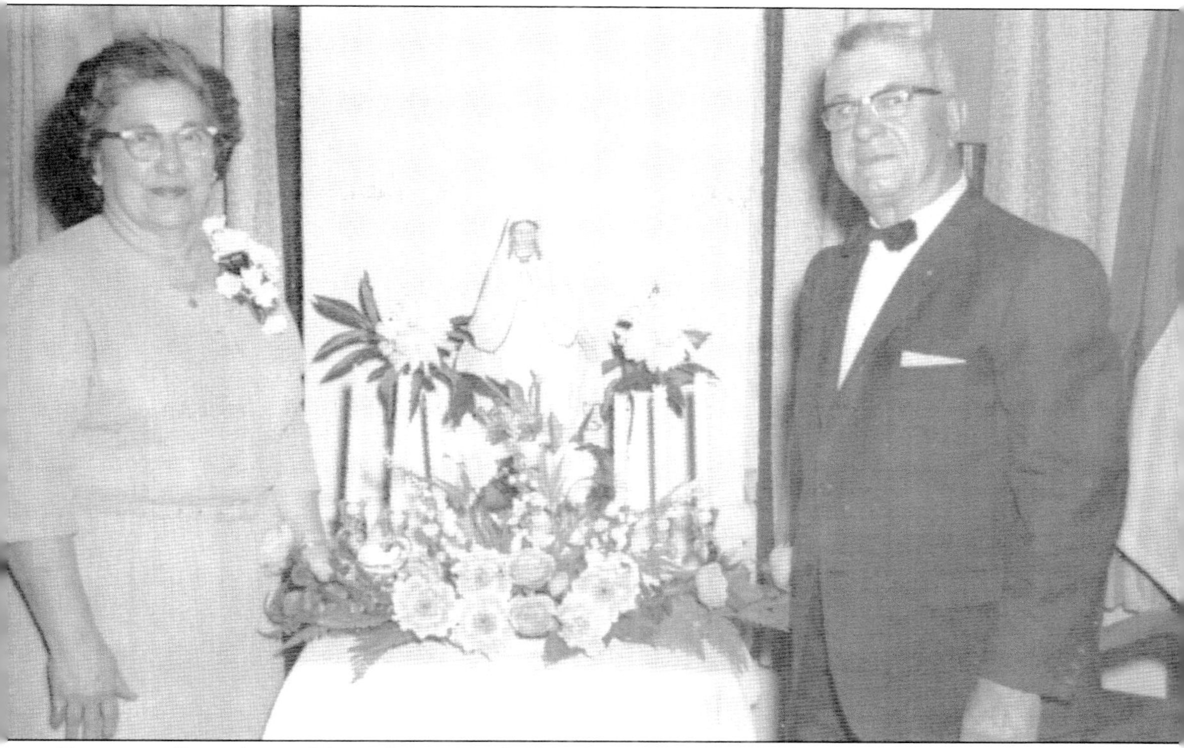

VINCENZO (JIMMY) AND MARY CATHERINE IAQUINTA D'ANNUNZIO, CLARKSBURG, MAY 19, 1968. Jimmy was born in the town of San Giovanni in Fiore, Italy, in 1895. At a young age, he became an apprentice to a local carpenter and immigrated with the master carpenter to São Paulo, Brazil, in 1911. He returned to Italy and served in World War I. After his military duty, he immigrated to the United States and founded the West Virginia Contractors Corporation with Frank Lopez. This corporation helped to build the Northview Junior High School, the Harrison County Courthouse, and the post office in Clarksburg, West Virginia. In 1925, Jimmy married Mary Catherine (Katie) Iaquinta. The D'Annunzios had three children—Gloria, Sam, and Benny. Jimmy served as an officer of the OSIA and helped build the OSIA Building in Glen Elk in 1925. He also encouraged people to participate in the organization; he believed that "with strength comes unity." *Compari* Jimmy passed away in 1986 at the age of 91. (Courtesy of WVIHF.)

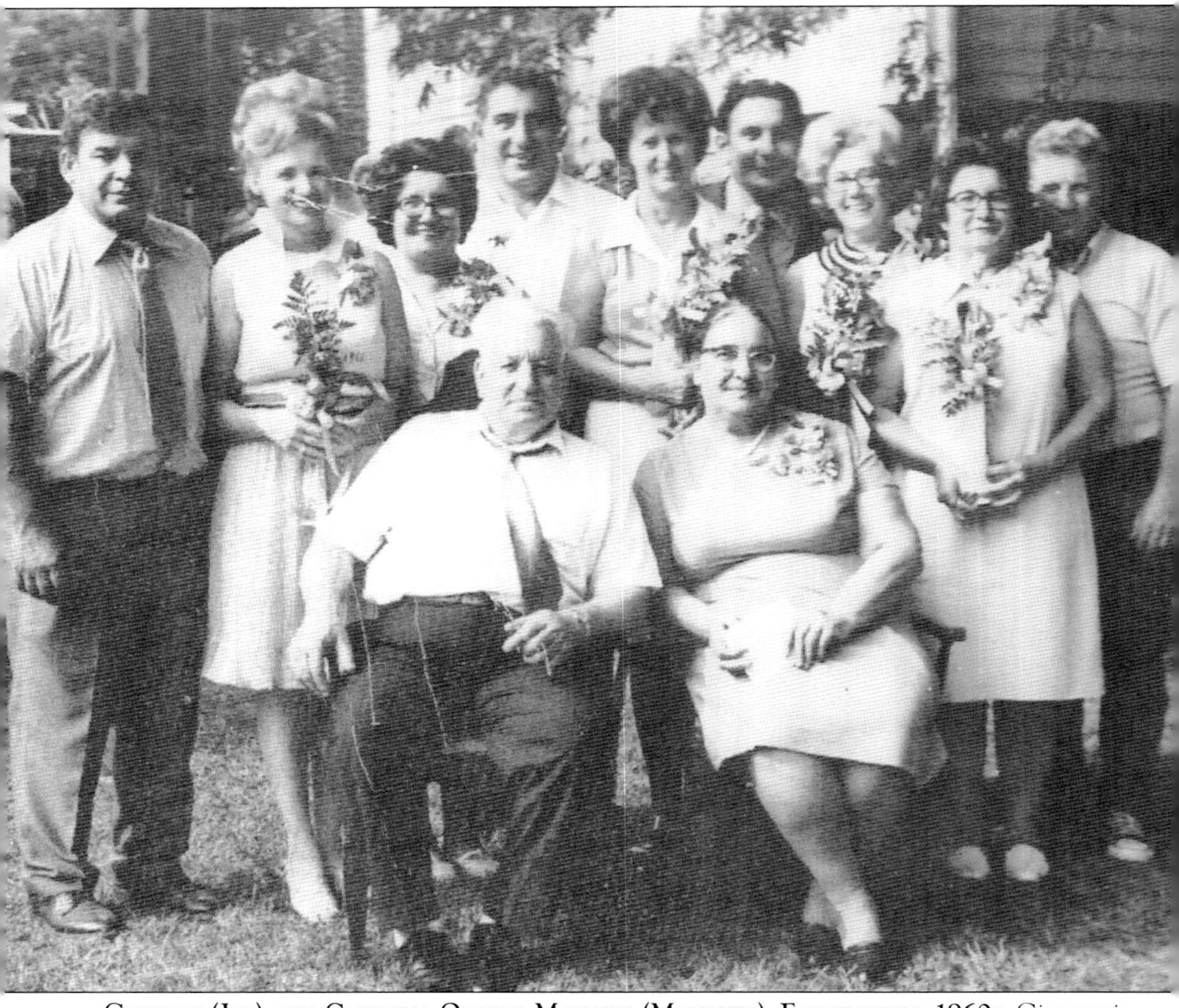

GIUSEPPE (JOE) AND CATERINA OROSCO MANCINI (MANCHIN), FARMINGTON, 1960s. Giovanni and Philomenia Mancini emigrated from San Giovanni in Fiore in 1904. They had two children, a daughter named Constancia and an adopted son named Giuseppe (Joseph), who was born in 1900. As a child, Joseph Manchin completed six years of public schooling and then began working in the mines with his father when he was only 11 years old. Joseph would gather up the bits of coal as his dad chipped them away from the earth. Caterina Orosco and Giuseppe Mancini were married in 1921. The couple had five children—John (1922), twins Frances and Rose (1924), Joe Jr. (1925), and Anthony James (1927). After marriage, Joe entered the business world. He had a automotive repair garage and in 1938 opened up the Manchin Grocery Store. Joe was instrumental in starting up the fire department in Farmington, and he served as the first fire chief. He also served as a constable, a justice of the peace, and the mayor of Farmington. (Courtesy of WVIHF.)

A. James Manchin and Victor A. Basile, Clarksburg, 2001. A. James Manchin, the youngest son of Joe Manchin, served as West Virginia's secretary of state for two terms and then as the state treasurer. He is pictured congratulating Victor A. Basile, the 2001 Italian American Man of the Year, at the WVIHF. (Authors' collection.)

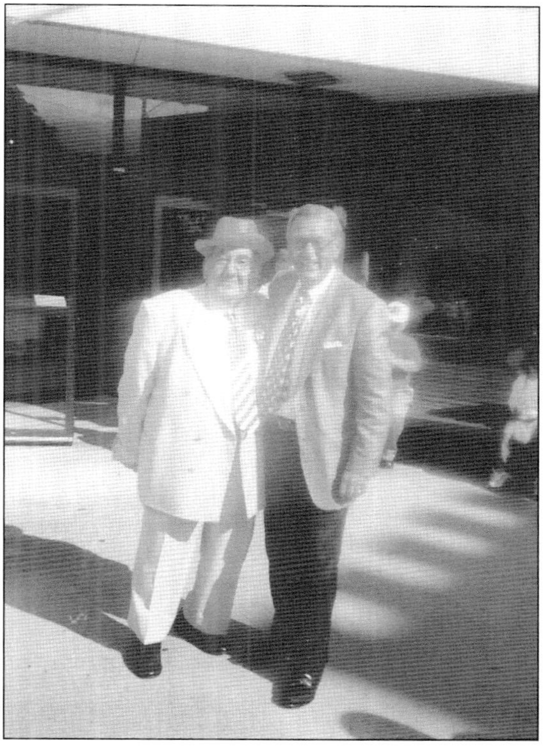

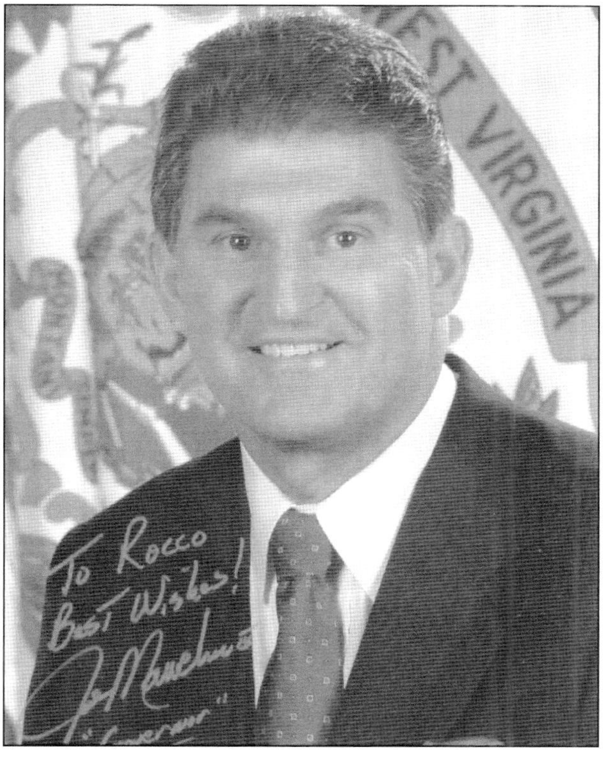

Joe Manchin III, West Virginia's 34th Governor, Charleston, 2005–2010, and US Senator Representing West Virginia, 2011–2013. The grandson of Joe Manchin became the 34th governor of West Virginia. He won a special election in 2010 to fill the seat of Sen. Robert Byrd. Joe Manchin III grew up in the coal-mining town of Farmington and worked in the family's grocery and furniture stores. Family and community have always been important guiding factors in Manchin's personal and political life. (Courtesy of the Rocco Muriale collection.)

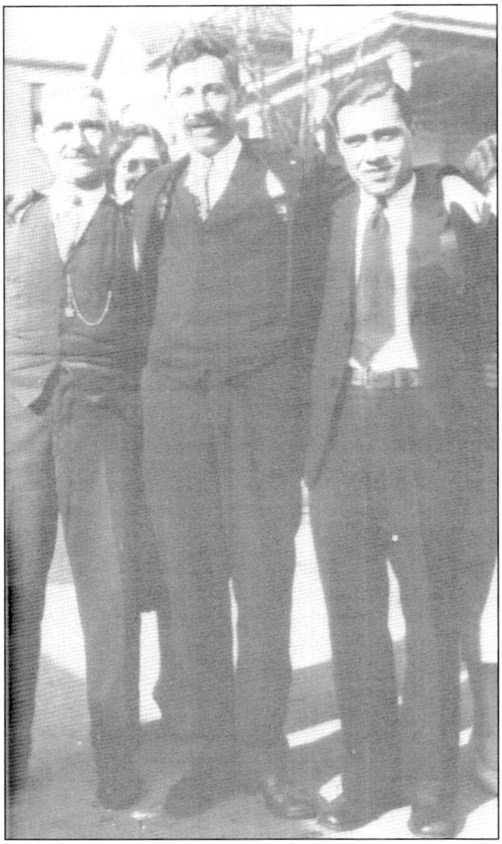

Giuseppe (Poppy), Sam, and Uncle Minardi (Minard) and the Lover Family Photograph, Clarksburg, 1940s. Giuseppe Minardi (left) was born in San Giovanni in Fiore, Italy, around 1900. He met and married Constancia Angotti in 1925 and had nine children. Giuseppe worked in the mines surrounding Clarksburg and was a devoted gardener. The family harvested Giovanni's plentiful produce and shared it with their neighbors. Eventually, the family opened Minard's Italian Restaurant. Giovanni's brother Sam is in the middle; the man on the right is the uncle of West Virginia state senator Joe Menard. The Lovers (pictured below) were a large extended Italian family; they lived in the Glen Elk section at the corner of Bird's Lane and Clark Street. Here, they are pictured downstairs in Frank Lover's home celebrating the Feast of Seven Fishes at Christmastime. (Left, courtesy of WVIHF; below, courtesy of John B. and Mary Ann Angotti.)

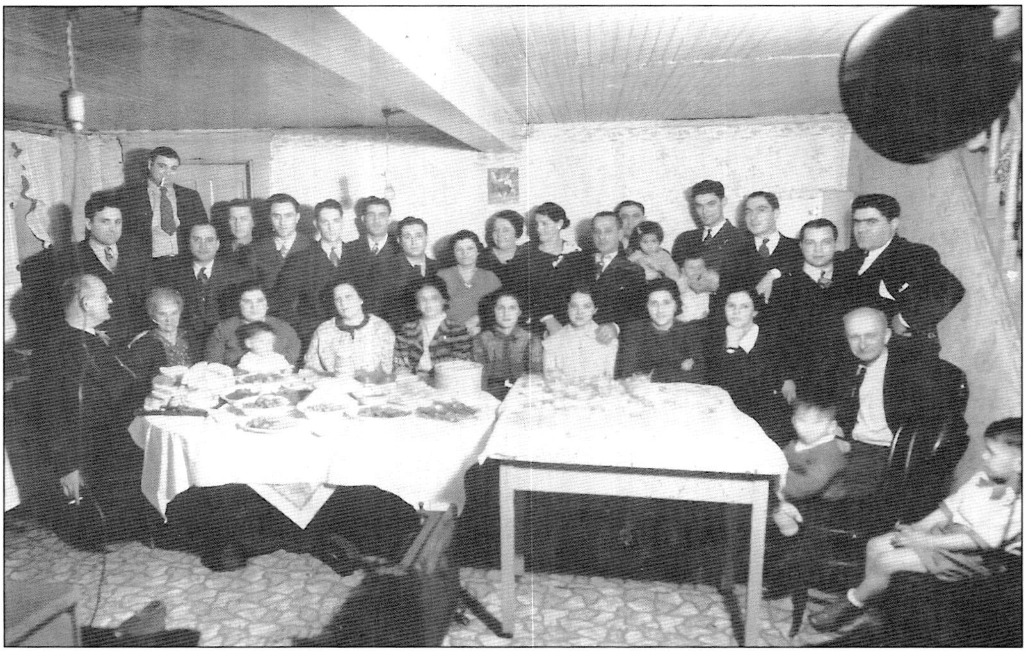

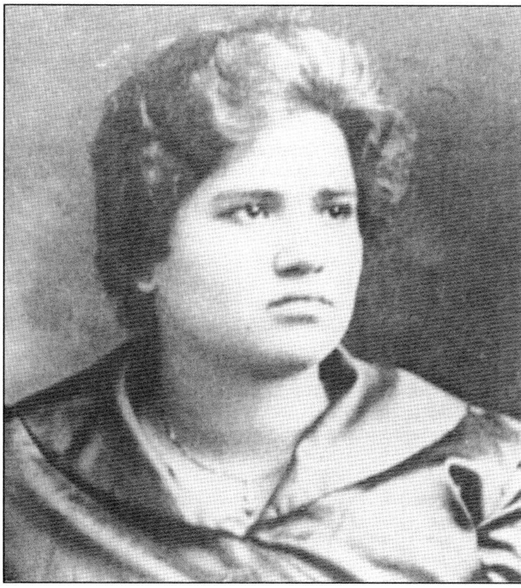

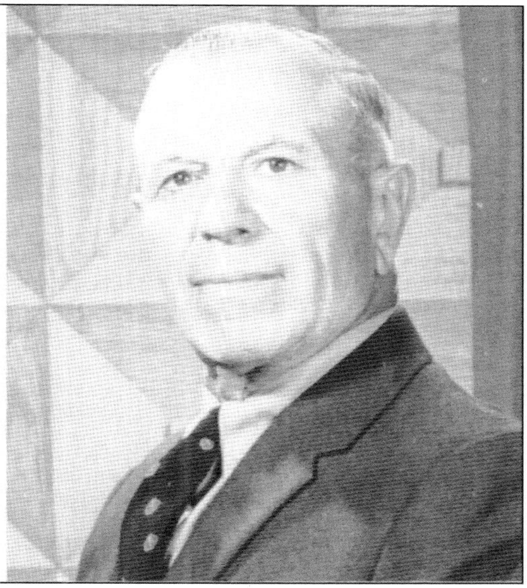

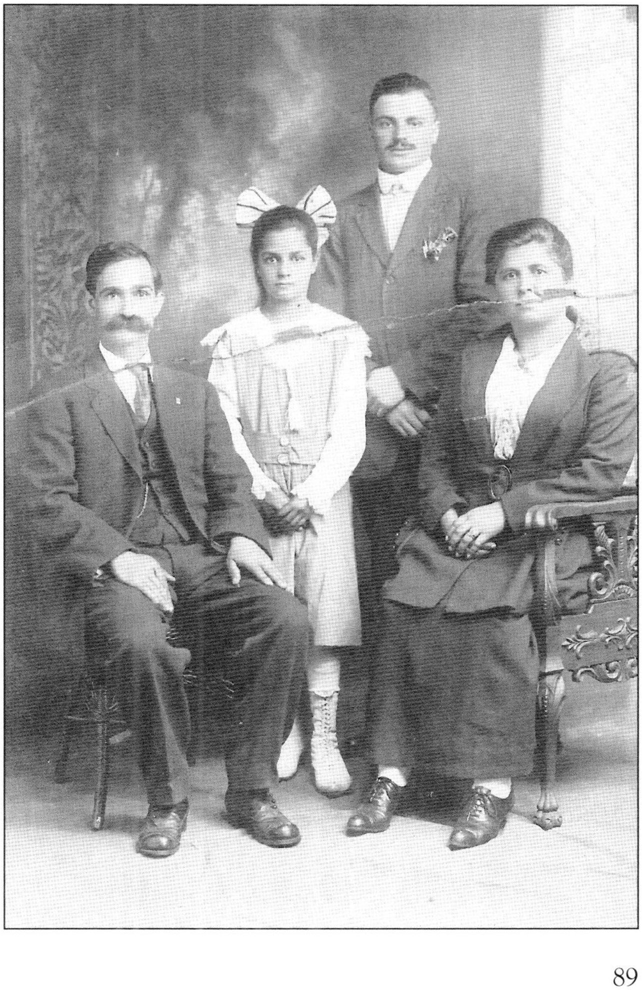

JAMES AND EMILY CAVA LAROSA, CLARKSBURG, AND SALVATORE AND ROSARIA PERRI, ANMOORE, 1900S. James was born in Caulonia, Calabria, in 1891. Emily was born in San Giovanni in Fiore, Calabria, in 1902. In 1916, James rented a storefront from the Cavas where he met Emily. In 1917, they married and had three children—Mary, James, and Virgil. In 1951, James founded LaRosa Fuel, a major West Virginia coal production company. Pictured in the Salvatore Perri family photograph are, from left to right, Salvatore, Vincenza (Reda), Carmen Perri, and Rosaria Perri. Salvatore Perri immigrated in the early 1900s to Anmoore to work for the Grasselli Chemical Company. Rosaria and Vincenza came to join Salvatore in 1912. Carmen Perri immigrated and worked at the Grasselli Chemical Company. He then moved to New York City. (Above, courtesy of the WVIHF; right, Authors' collection.)

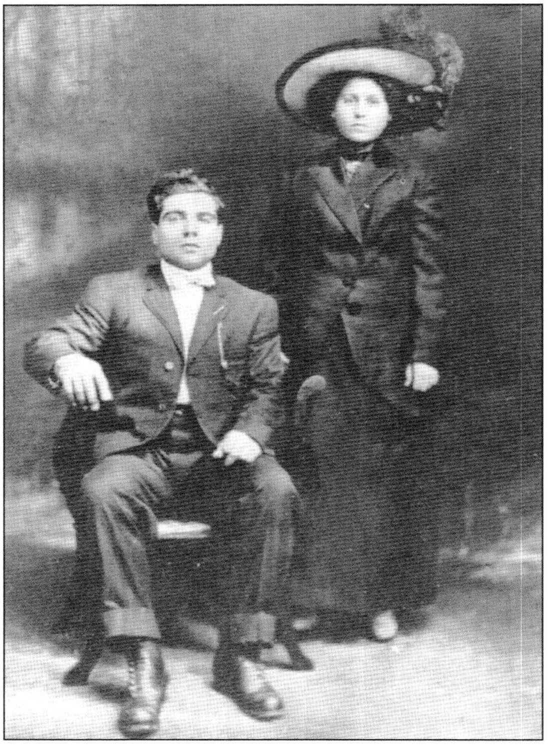

Nicolo and Theresa Puccio DiMasi (Demus), Grant Town, and Felice and Maddelena Gallozzi Maselli, Fairmont, 1920s. Nicolo (left) was born in Caulonia, Italy, in 1885 and immigrated to America in 1898 with his brother Larry. At Ellis Island, the name DiMasi was changed to Demus. In 1912, in Chieftain, West Virginia, he married Theresa Puccio, a young girl he had known in Italy. They had nine children—Nellie, Rose, Joan, Madaline, Larry, Nick, Michael, Theresa, and James. Felice and Maddelena Maselli (below) were married on June 3, 1928, at St. Joseph Catholic Church in Fairmont. St. Joseph was an Italian Catholic church founded in 1909. Over 200 people attended the wedding. They had three children, Anthony James, David August, and Carmen Gene. (Both, courtesy of WVIHF.)

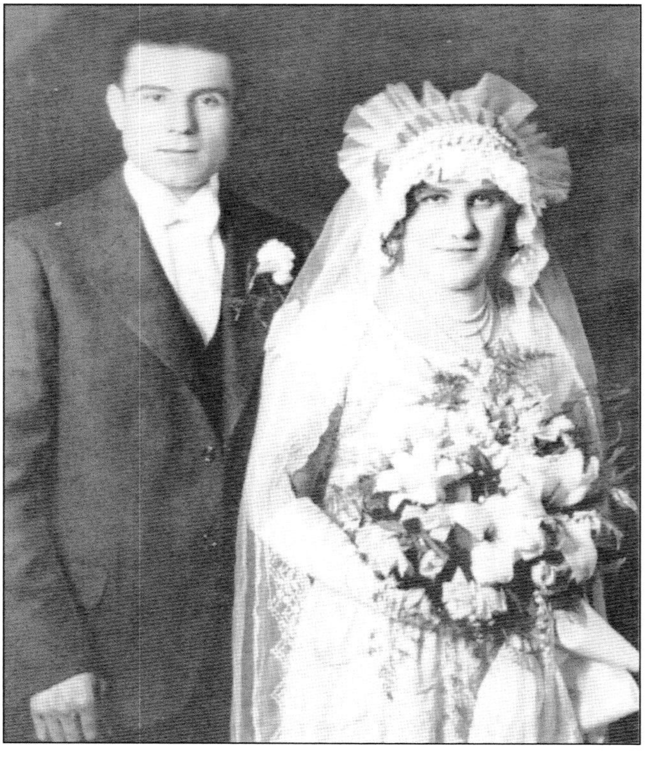

Six

Church and Religion

Italian immigrants brought a strong belief in Catholicism and a rich religious culture to America. They came from towns and villages that had a church or chapel nearby. Italians were accustomed to practicing a religion that was characterized by the belief and veneration of special saints and that had a touch of superstition. The patron saint of the village was particularly special to southern Italians; the religious doctrines that were important to emigrants from Calabria were the teachings of the medieval abbot Joachim of Fiore. In Italian communities, annual religious festivals and processions, known as *feste*, allowed immigrants to venerate the life of a saint or a religious leader. In many instances, these holidays were brought from Italy to America with the immigrant tide.

Italian spirituality stressed pilgrimages, processions, shrines, statuary, and holy cards. Other American Catholics could not understand Italian spirituality; they felt that the Italian spiritual devotions lacked understanding of the great truths of religion. In 1893, the greatest challenge to confront the third bishop of Wheeling, the Reverend Patrick J. Donahue, was how to minister to the growing number of immigrants. The primarily non-English-speaking immigrants were arriving in the dioceses and being sent to regions of the state that were undeveloped and where a Catholic presence had yet to be established. Over 40 missions and 23 parishes were established during his administration. In areas of large Italian populations, Italian Catholic churches were founded, including at Fairmont, Clarksburg, and Wheeling. The immigrant national churches served as transitional institutions that help retain the continuity of cultural traditions in the face of rapid change and forced adaptation. As the Italian American family progressed into the cultural landscape of West Virginia, a new ethnic identity evolved. In smaller, multiethnic coal mining communities, Italian immigrants attended religious institutions patronized by native-born Americas and representatives of a variety of other immigrant groups. By providing a place where Italians interacted with immigrants from countries other than their own, these Catholic churches functioned as vehicles of assimilation. The church also provided a place for religious rites of passage.

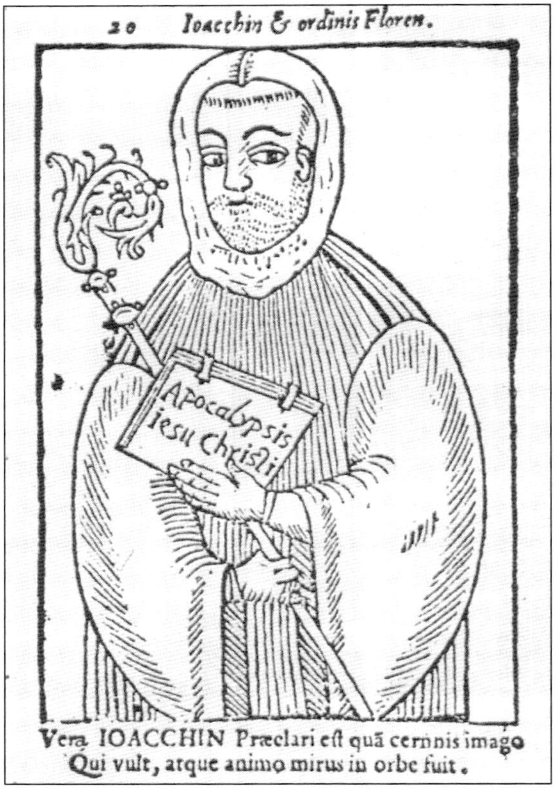

JOACHIM OF FIORE AND THE FLORENS ABBEY OF THE ABBOT JOACHIM, SAN GIOVANNI IN FIORE, ITALY. Joachim of Fiore was a monk from southern Italy who knew kings and emperors and popes; a Cistercian who broke from his order and established a more stringent rule; a visionary exegete of apocalyptic scripture who challenged the Church Fathers in his interpretations; an abbot whose writings were frequently suspect but were not condemned by the Holy See; and a holy man who was never sainted but who was placed by Dante in the Circle of the Sun next to Saint Bonaventure and Saint Francis in the *Paradiso*. However, Thomas Aquinas confuted his theories in his *Summa Theologica*. The Florens Abbey (below) dates back to Joachim of Fiore's trip to La Sila in Calabria in 1188. (Both, Authors' collection.)

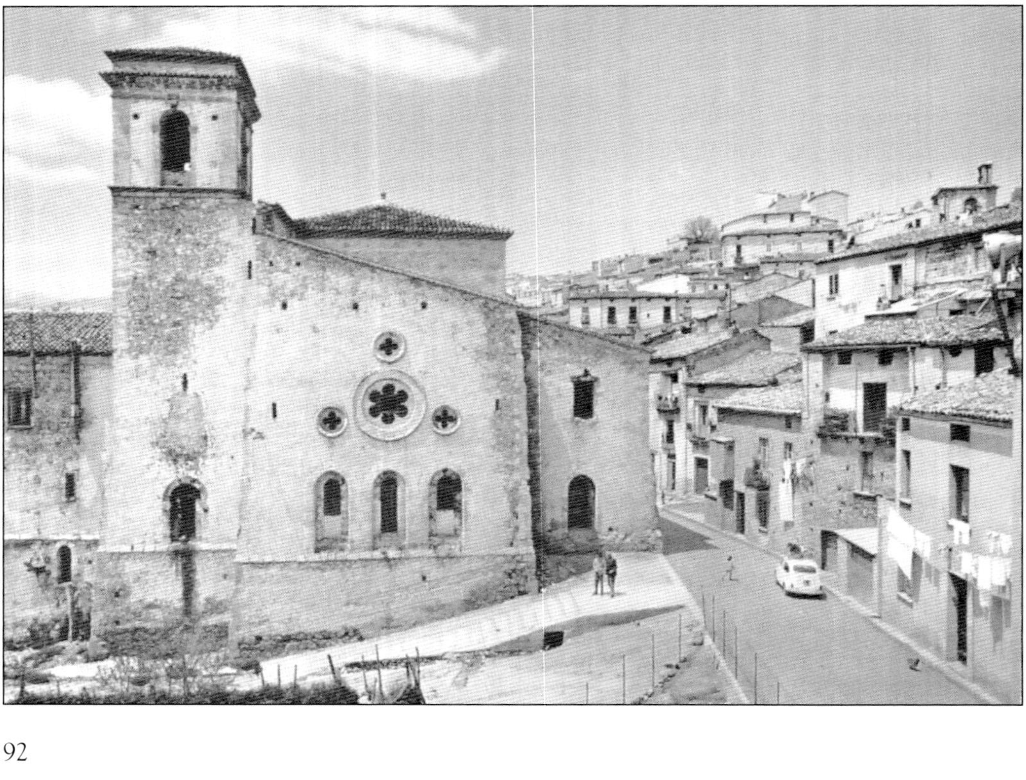

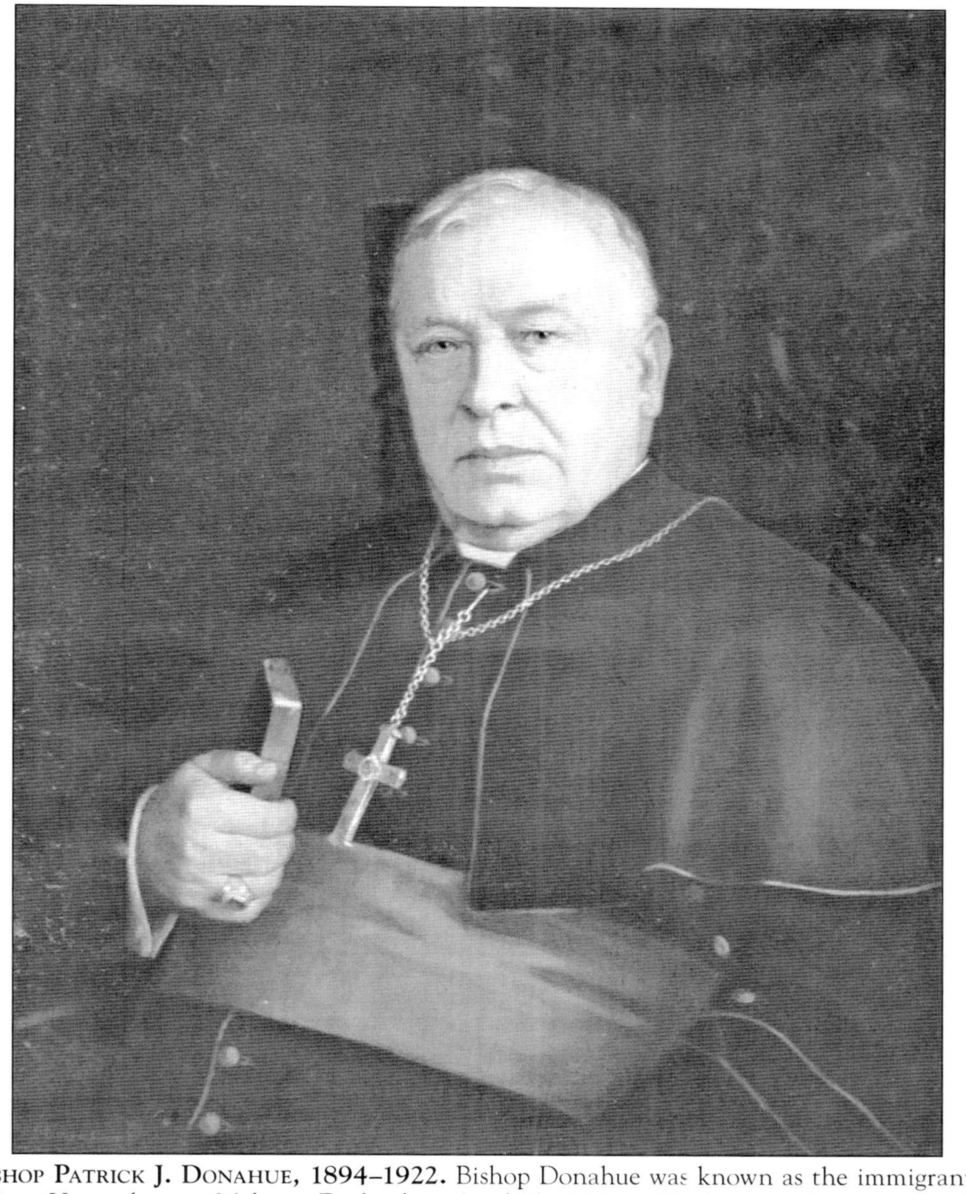

BISHOP PATRICK J. DONAHUE, 1894–1922. Bishop Donahue was known as the immigrants' bishop. He was born in Malvern, England, on April 15, 1845. In 1855, he was ordained a priest by Archbishop James Gibbons. Donahue then spent a year as assistant pastor at St. John's Church, Baltimore, after which he was appointed chancellor of the archdiocese and served as the newly appointed Cardinal Gibbon's secretary. In 1893, Bishop John J. Kain was moved from Wheeling to St. Louis, and on January 22, 1894, Donahue was ordained his successor. During his term as bishop of the Diocese of Wheeling, Bishop Donahue fought for the workingman and the immigrant and endeavored to spread the faith in the most remote parts of West Virginia. He struggled against national conflicts, including friction from immigration and the hardships of industrialization and socialism. By the time of his death in 1922, Bishop Donahue had earned the respect of the communities in which he served and also of politicians and presidents. (Courtesy of the Diocese of Wheeling-Charleston Archives.)

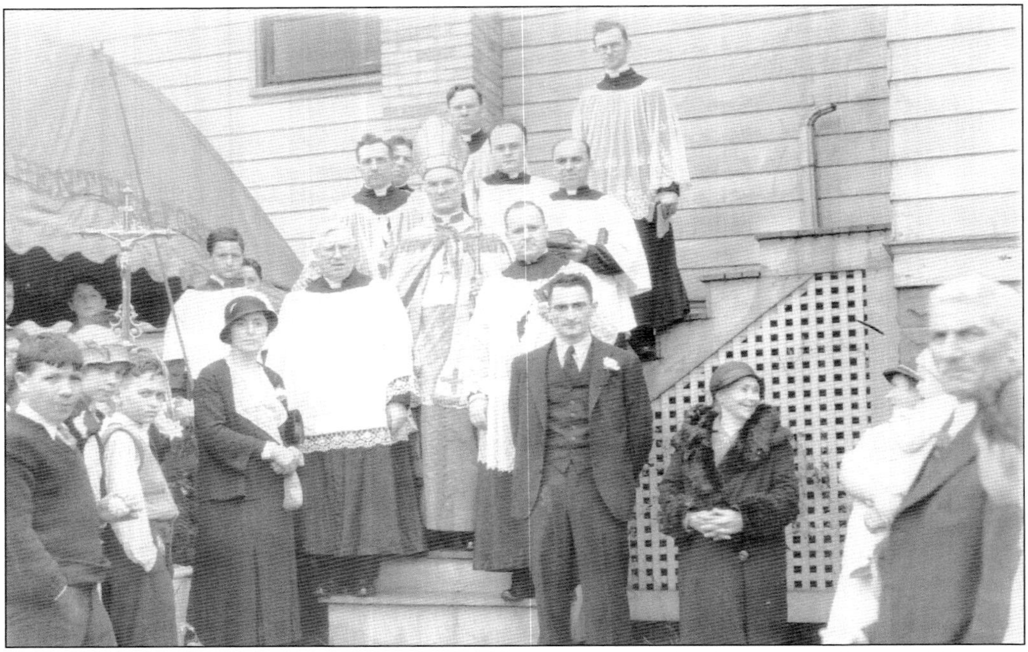

Bishop John J. Swint (1922–1961) and the Dedication of St. Anthony's Parish, Watson, West Virginia. In this image, Bishop Swint is dedicating the Italian mission at Watson in 1933. The mission eventually became St. Anthony's Parish in Fairmont. Bishop Swint was named the fourth bishop of the Diocese of Wheeling, and on the 50th anniversary of his ordination, Pope Pius XII conferred on him the title of archbishop. Nicknamed "God's Bricklayer," Archbishop Swint oversaw the tremendous growth in the diocese. In his 40 years as bishop, the Catholic population doubled, and he oversaw the construction of 100 churches, a new cathedral, a college (Wheeling Jesuit University), 52 elementary and high schools, and five hospitals. (Both, courtesy of the Diocese of Wheeling-Charleston Archives.)

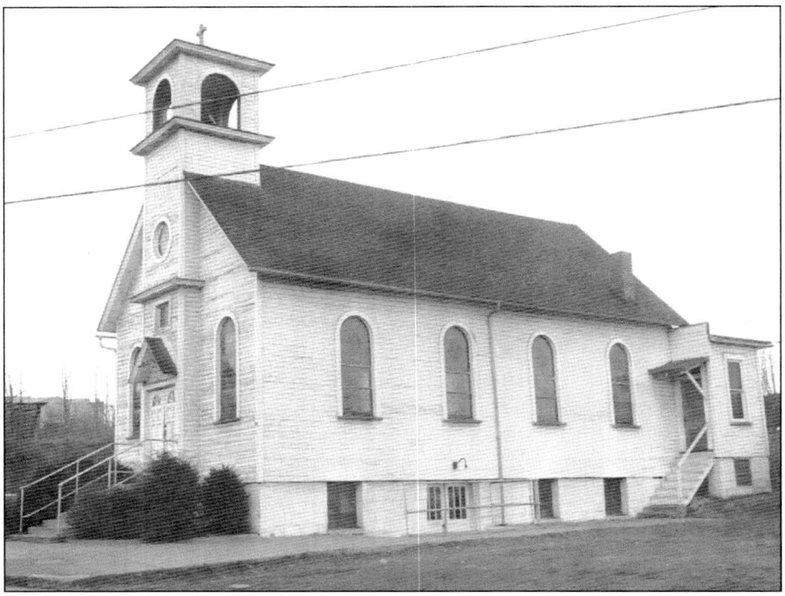

ST. JOSEPH'S CHURCH, FAIRMONT, AND BISHOP THOMAS J. MCDONNELL (1951–1961) WITH DEANERY OF PRIESTS, 1953. St. Joseph Parish in Fairmont was founded in 1909 to serve the growing number of Italian immigrants who came to work in the coal mines of Marion County. The LaSallette Fathers were invited in to the parish in 1924 and served there for the next 40 years. Bishop McDonnell is pictured below with a deanery of priests that served Harrison and Marion Counties, West Virginia. Included in the image are, from left to right, (first row) Rev. George Gocke, Msgr. John B. O'Reilly, Bishop McDonnell, Rev. Peter Flynn, Msgr. John J. O'Brien, and Rev. George Kuhn. Also included are Reverends Francis Ockermann, James Rogers, Joseph Brumfield, Roy Lombard, Leo Werner, Charles R. Carroll, Edmund Weinheimer, Paul Helsley, and Harold Moore. Bishop McDonnell was appointed coadjutor bishop with the right of succession to Bishop Swint. (Right, courtesy of the Diocese of Wheeling-Charleston Archives; below, courtesy of Tom and Louise Cavallaro-Martin.)

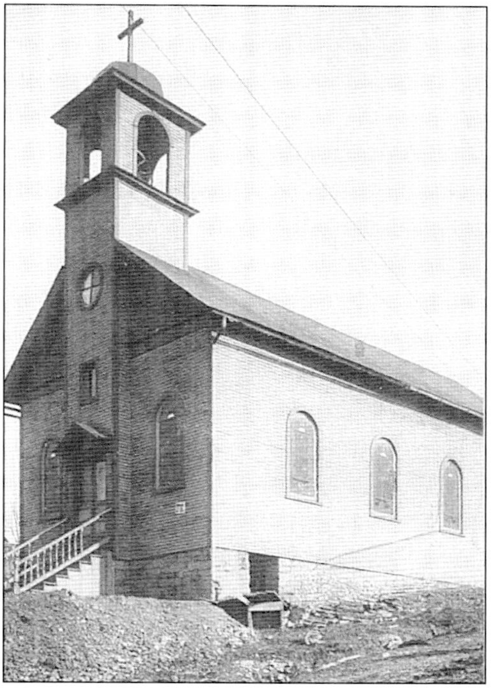

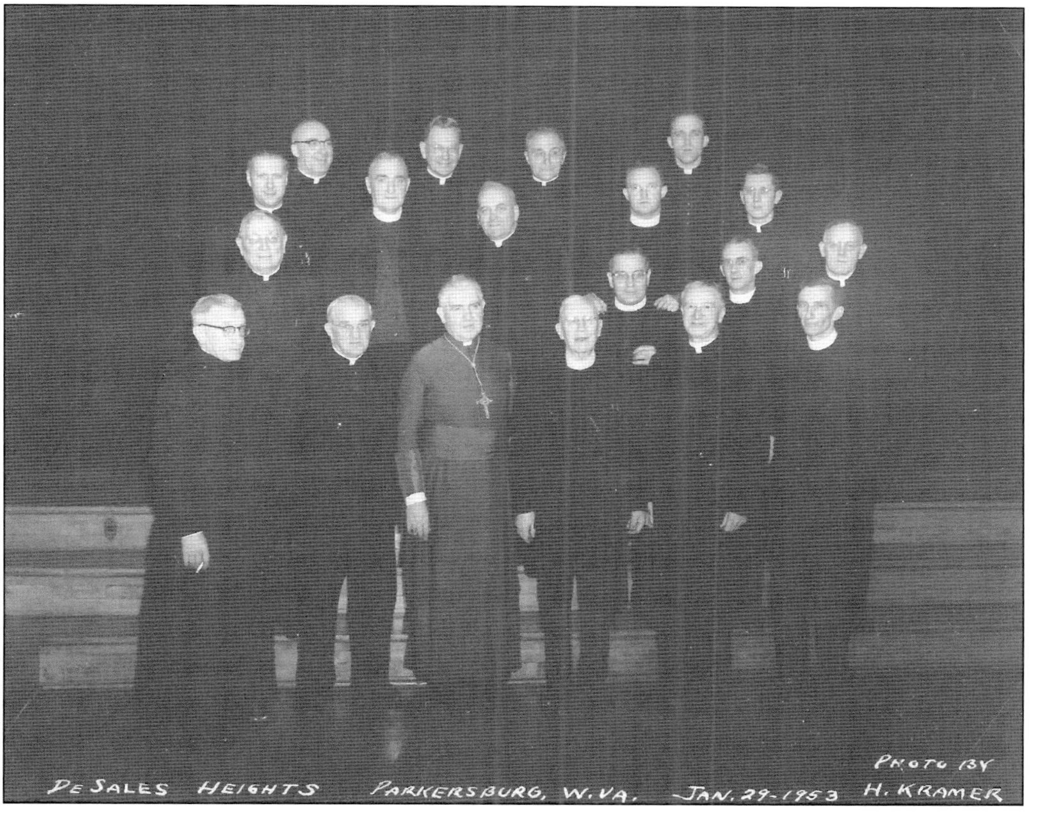

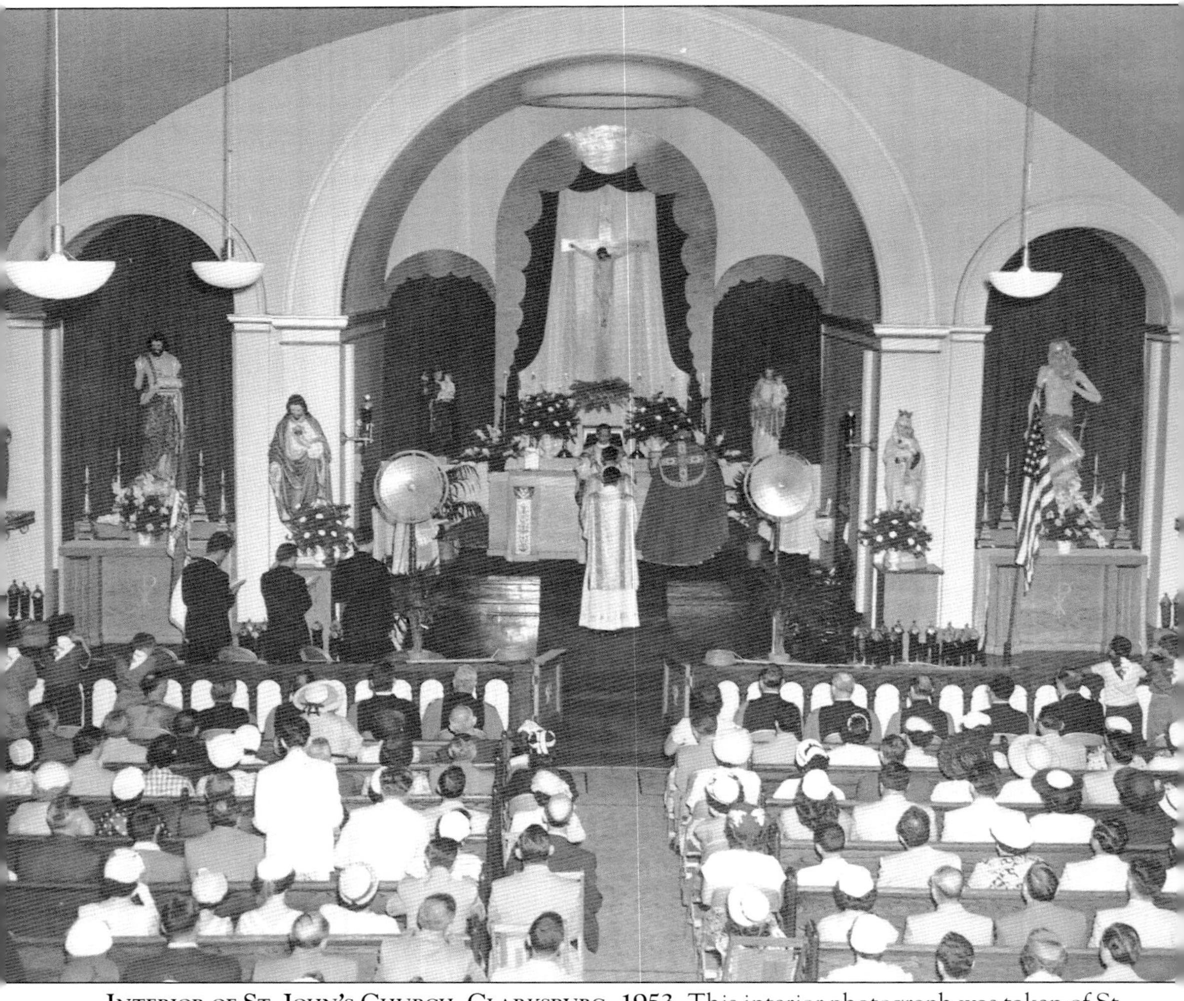

INTERIOR OF ST. JOHN'S CHURCH, CLARKSBURG, 1953. This interior photograph was taken of St. John's, an Italian Catholic church, during the first Solemn High Mass of Rev. Hilarion (Larry) Cann, a native of Clarksburg who was ordained in Rome. The mass was not only a significant celebration in the history of St. John's Church, it was also a remarkable demonstration of Italian American Catholicism. The level of the service has three priests on the altar with elaborate vestments. Italian Catholicism added pageantry and statuary to liturgical services. The 1920 directory of the diocese listed three Italian parishes—Fairmont, Clarksburg, and Wheeling. St. John's Italian Catholic Church was established in the 1920s on Water Street. The Arena, Angotti, and Cann families were influential in establishing a parish in Clarksburg. Early pastors were trained in Rome and spoke Italian. (Courtesy of Rev. Hilarion Cann.)

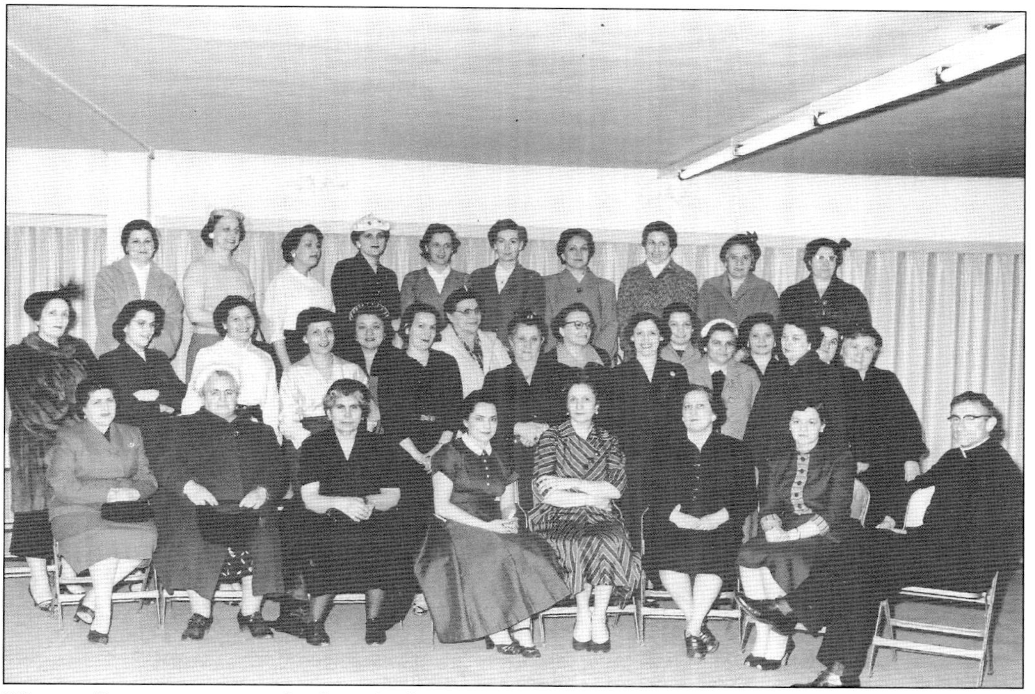

WOMEN PARISHIONERS OF ST. JOHN'S CHURCH, 1953, AND CENTENARY MASS OF ST. ALPHONSUS CHURCH, WHEELING, 1956. Italian women tended to be more dedicated churchgoers; however, both Italian men and women relied on religion to bring guidance and direction to their lives and the lives of their children. These proud, devoted women parishioners were responsible for elevating the solemnity of Rev. Hilarion Cann's hometown mass. Rev. John O'Reilly is seated with the women. He had studied in Rome and was appointed pastor to St. John's by Bishop John J. Swint. Other immigrant churches were highly decorative and reminiscent of Italian solemnity. The proud German community of St. Alphonsus Parish in Wheeling comes to rejoice at its 100th anniversary mass below. (Above, courtesy of Rev. Hilarion Cann and Charles F. Gruber Studios; below, courtesy of Charles F. Gruber Studios.)

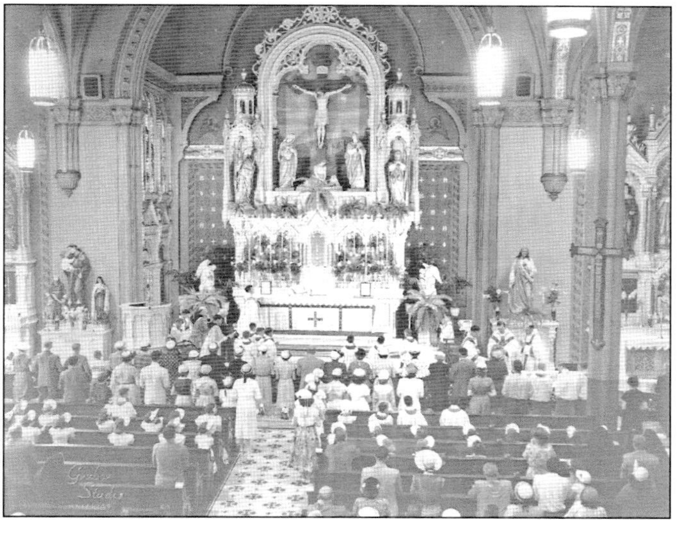

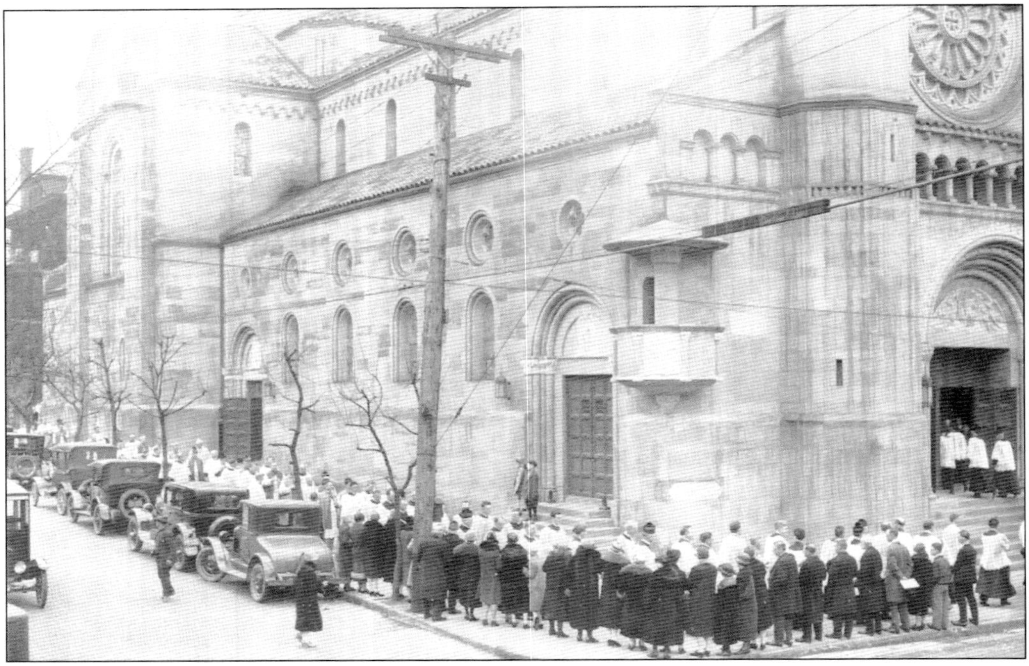

CONSECRATION OF THE NEW CATHEDRAL, WHEELING, 1926, AND HOLY CARD, ST. JOHN'S CHURCH, 1958. Italians loved when the processions and pageantry took place in the streets. It was reminiscent and symbolic of their native Italy. Here, spectators line the streets of Wheeling to view the procession. On April 21, 1926, the new and beautiful limestone cathedral was consecrated by Bishop John J. Swint. On some occasions, the parishioners would join the procession and follow the participants into the church. Holy cards were special to Italians. This 1958 holy card was distributed at St. John's Church on the Feast of St. Joseph the Worker, which is celebrated on May 1 in the liturgical calendar. (Both, courtesy of the Diocese of Wheeling-Charleston Archives.)

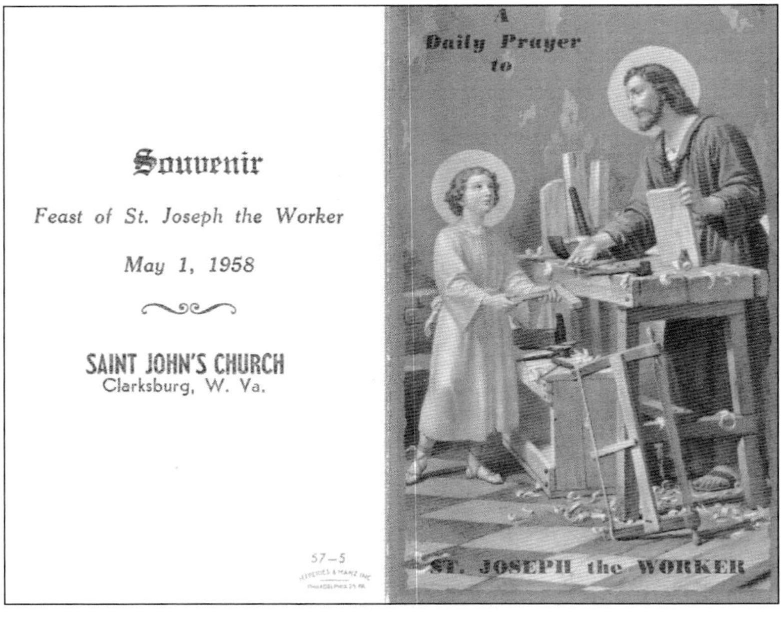

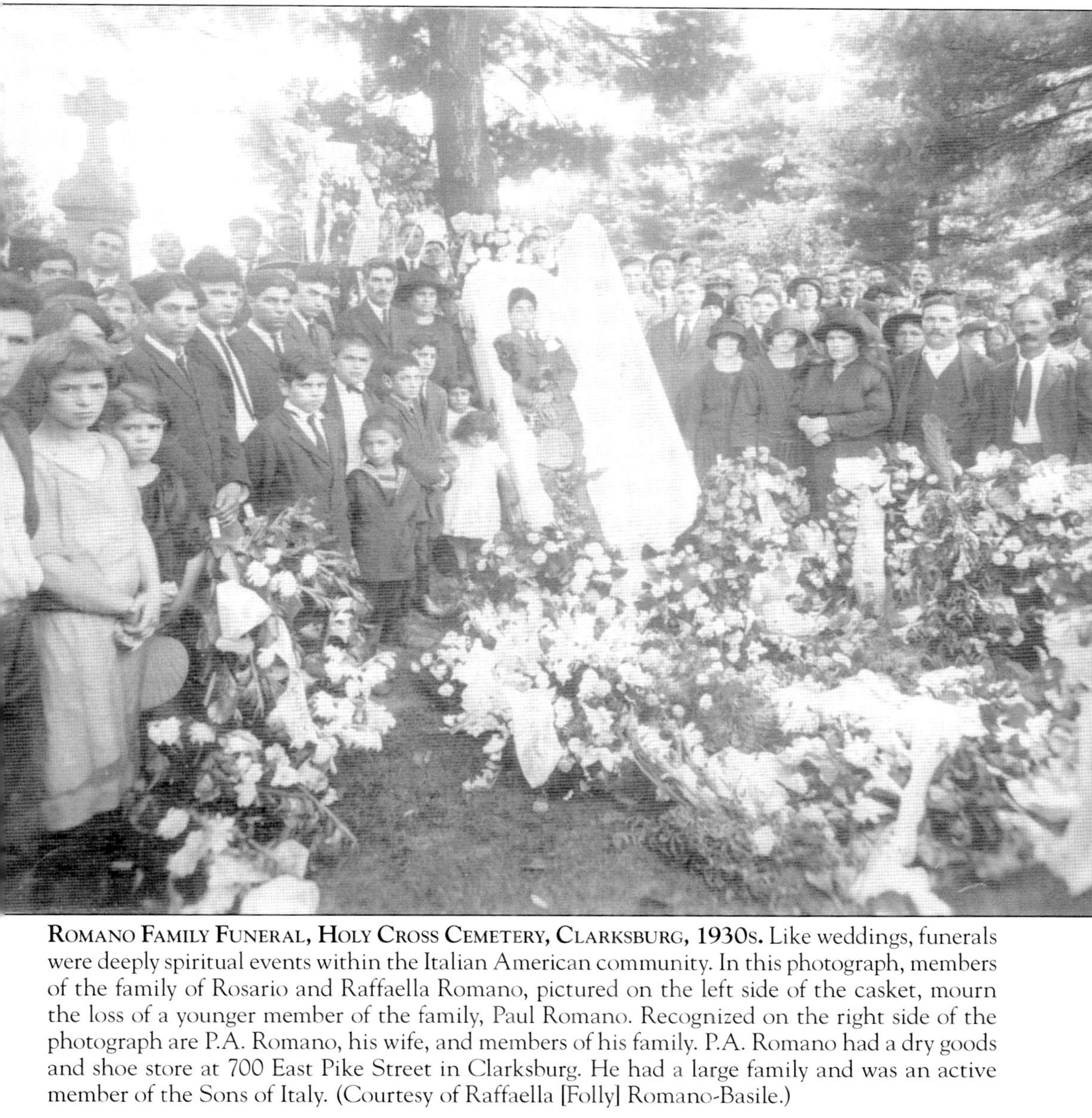

ROMANO FAMILY FUNERAL, HOLY CROSS CEMETERY, CLARKSBURG, 1930S. Like weddings, funerals were deeply spiritual events within the Italian American community. In this photograph, members of the family of Rosario and Raffaella Romano, pictured on the left side of the casket, mourn the loss of a younger member of the family, Paul Romano. Recognized on the right side of the photograph are P.A. Romano, his wife, and members of his family. P.A. Romano had a dry goods and shoe store at 700 East Pike Street in Clarksburg. He had a large family and was an active member of the Sons of Italy. (Courtesy of Raffaella [Folly] Romano-Basile.)

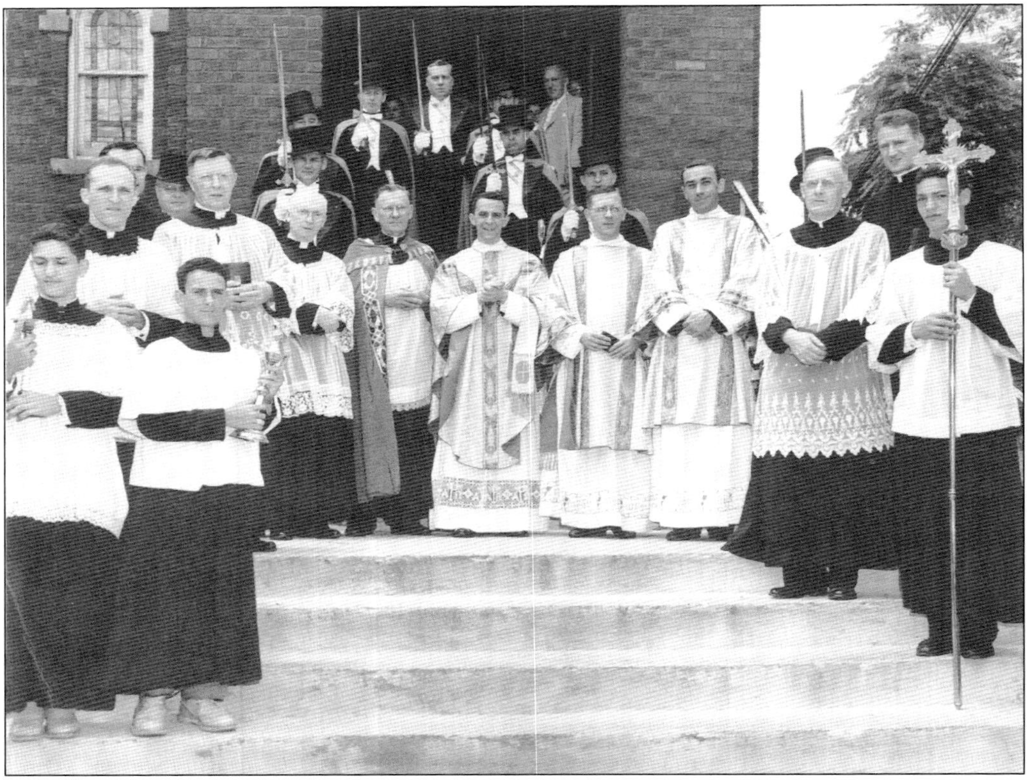

Rev. Hilarion Cann's Solemn High Mass, St. John's Church, and His Class of Seminarians in Rome, 1953. Hilarion Cann was ordained a priest in Rome in 1953. He returned to Clarksburg to celebrate his first solemn high mass. Pictured on the steps of St. John's Church are, from left to right, Joseph Dinaldo and Carmen Romano (alter boys); (first row of participating clergy) Rev. Harold Moore, Rev. P.A. Sikora, Very Rev. John B. O'Reilly, Rev. Paul V. Helsley, Rev. Hilarion Cann, Rev. Robert H. Hickey, Rev. Eugene Schmitt, and Rev. Charles R. Carroll; the priest behind Reverend Carroll is Rev. Warren Hollean, Larry's classmate. The altar boy at right is unidentified. Seminaries studying in Rome are pictured on the steps of the North American College; Larry is in the second row on the left. (Both, courtesy of Hilarion Cann.)

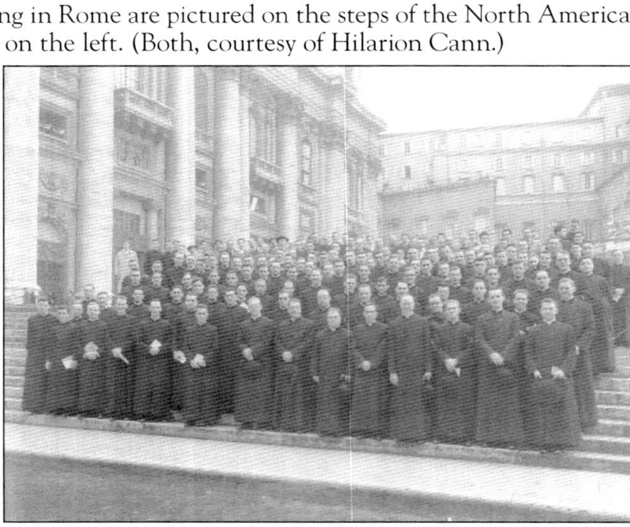

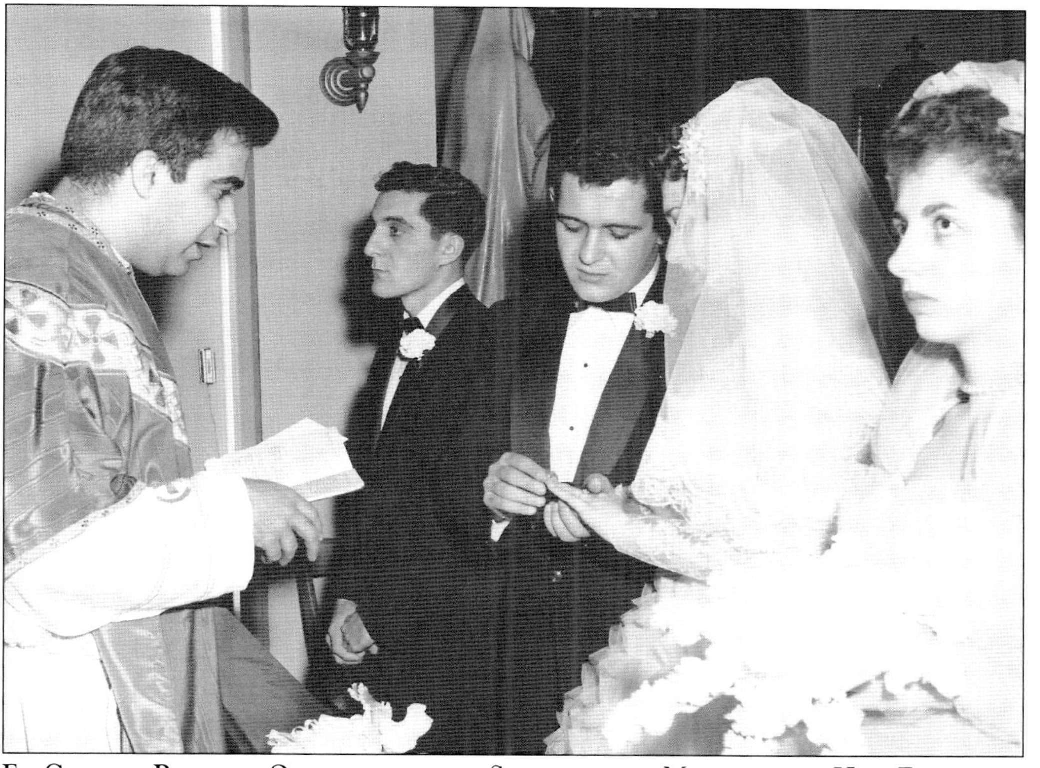

Fr. Colombo Bandiera Officiating at the Sacraments of Marriage and Holy Eucharist, 1950s. Raffaella (Folly) Romano was married to Thomas Paul Basile in 1956 at St. John's Church. Marriages were very significant events in the Italian American community. Rev. Colombo Bandiera, another early Italian American priest in the Diocese of Wheeling-Charleston, is officiating the marriage and standing among the communicants of Holy Eucharist below. Reverend Bandiera was installed as a pastor at St. John's Church in 1953 and served until its closing in 1969, when it was incorporated into the Immaculate Conception Church. In a 2010 conversation with the author, Reverend Bandiera referred to his ministry years at St. John's as "days in Camelot." He is now retired and lives in Morgantown, West Virginia. (Above, courtesy of Thomas and Raffaella [Folly] Basile; below, courtesy of Rev. Colombo Bandiera.)

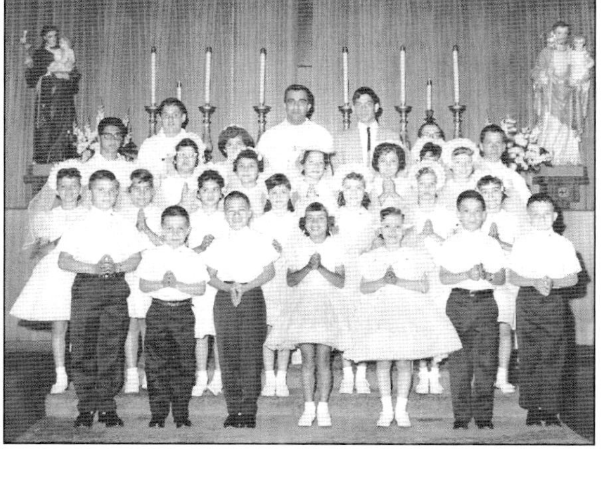

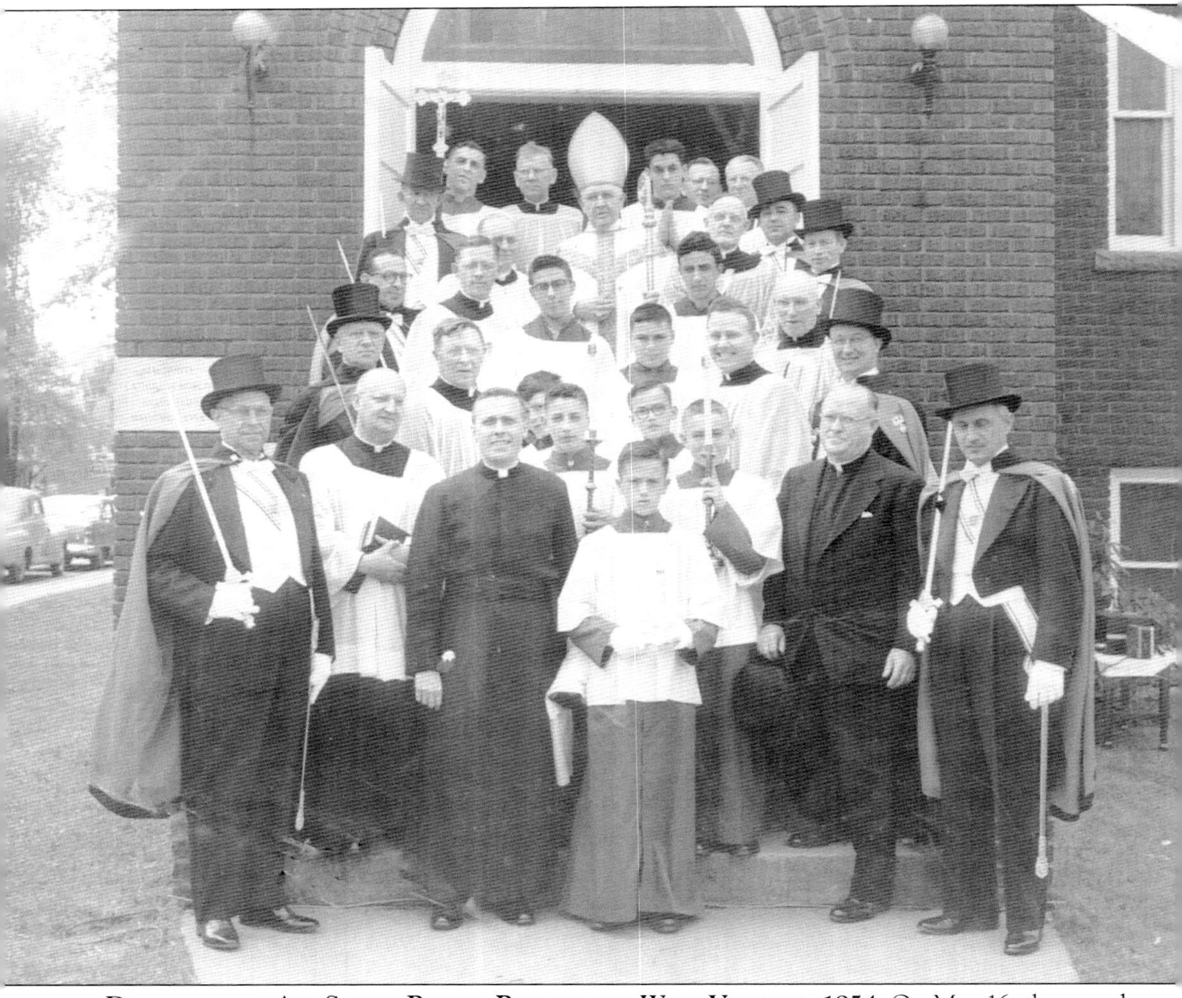

Dedication of All Saints Parish, Bridgeport, West Virginia, 1954. On May 16, the proud parishioners of All Saints Parish in Bridgeport welcomed coadjutor Bishop Thomas J. McDonnell, who officiated over the dedication of a new church. Its members and the diocese purchased an existing Methodist church, and it was consecrated in 1954. Standing in the bottom row at left is Fr. Robert C. Nash, assistant pastor. The pastor, Rev. Charles R. Carroll, is standing to the right of Bishop McDonnell. (Courtesy of Diocese of Wheeling-Charleston Archives.)

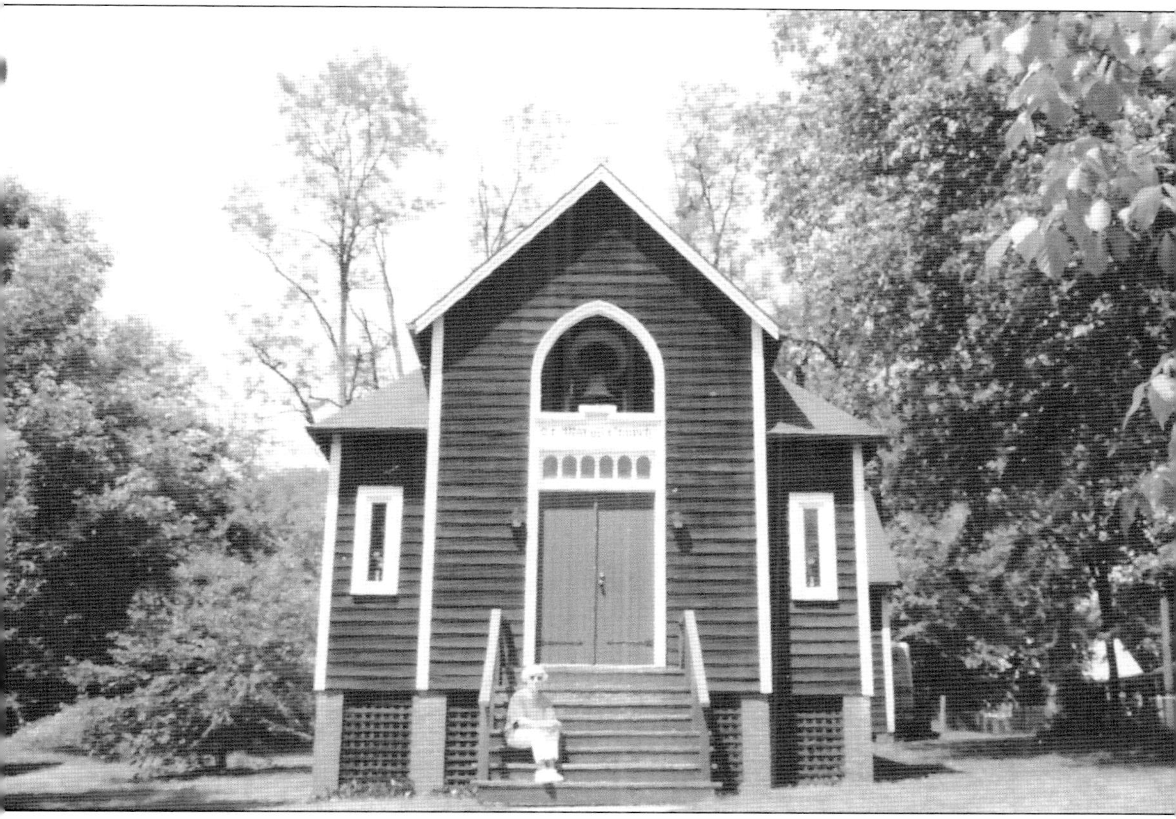

St. Mary's Mission, Rosemont, West Virginia, 1954. All Saints had a number of West Virginia mission churches with diverse immigrant memberships that were incorporated into the parish, including St. Francis Borgia Church (Anmoore), Little Flower Mission (Galloway), St. Joseph Mission (Wendel), Sacred Heart Mission (Brownton), and St. Mary's Mission (Rosemont). Author Lena Pellegrino DeRosa tells that Father Carroll started the St. Mary's Mission Church in a beer garden. The membership consisted of a diverse group of immigrants and natives who worked in the coal mines. On Saturday nights, there were fights, and on Sunday mornings, there were prayers and services. (Courtesy of Mary Ann Basile-Angotti.)

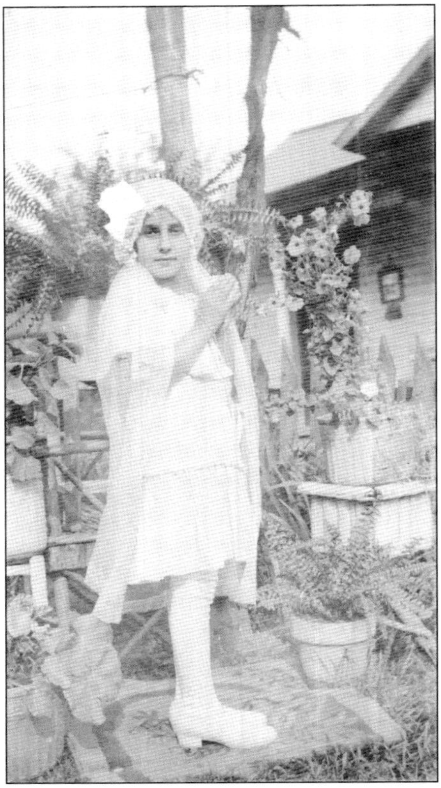

MARY ANN BASILE'S FIRST HOLY COMMUNION PARTY AND A MAY PROCESSION, ST. FRANCIS BORGIA SCHOOL, ANMOORE, 1930S. The Sisters of St. Joseph offered immigrants and their children a softer approach to Catholicism. They prepared them for the religious sacraments and were dedicated, committed educators. Mary Ann Basile's First Holy Communion was certified and recorded in the church records on May 19, 1935. Following the Sunday morning First Communion Mass, the communicants participated in an afternoon May procession honoring Mary, the mother of Christ. A May procession queen was chosen. In the photograph below, Teresa Marino was the May Queen. (Both, courtesy of Mary Ann Basile-Angotti.)

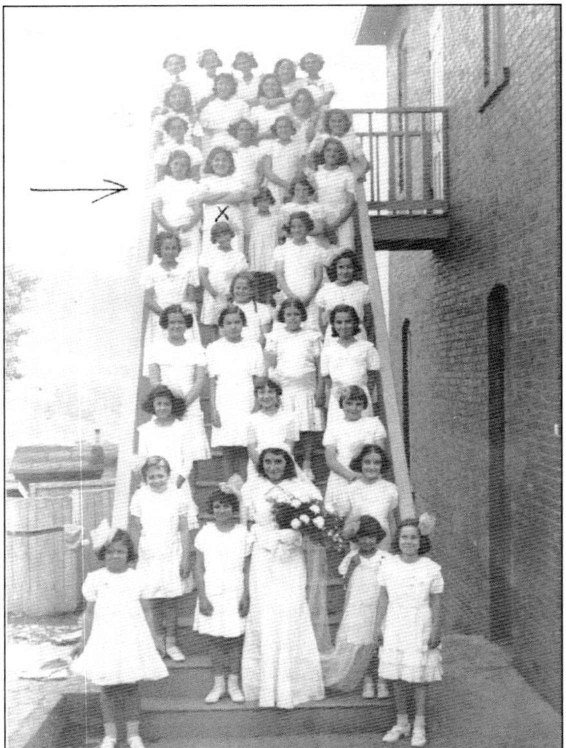

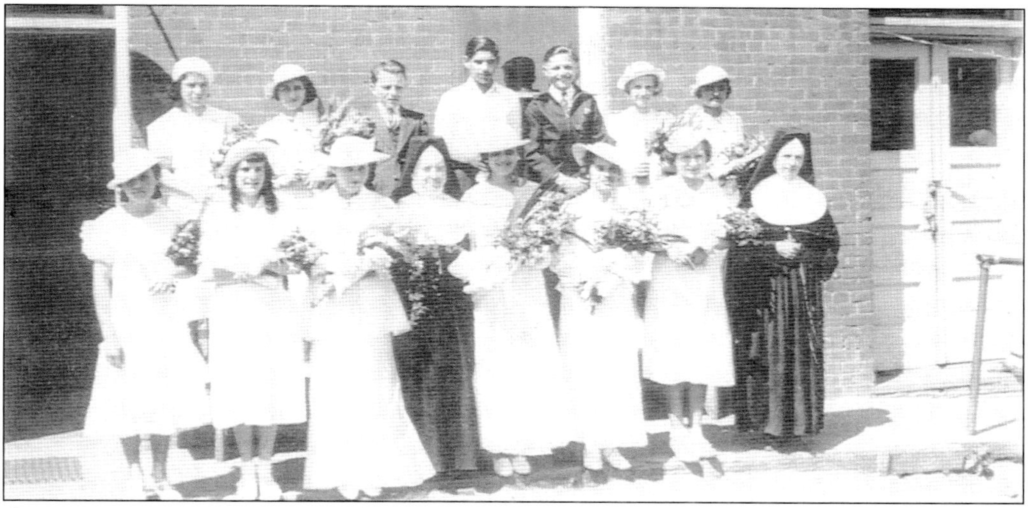

GRADUATION CLASS, ST. FRANCIS BORGIA GRADE SCHOOL, ANMOORE, AND SISTER ANGELINA, SISTERS OF ST. JOSEPH, 1938. The Sisters of St. Joseph's school in Anmoore educated the children of Catholic immigrants from Spain, Italy, and eastern Europe. The school was located on the second floor of a building that had been a Spanish casino. The third floor was adapted to hold services and celebrate mass. The parish was established by Rev. Charles R. Carroll in 1924 and was named after a leading Spanish saint, St. Francis Borgia. The graduating class of 1938 and their teachers are, from left to right, (first row) unidentified, Delta Rodriquez, Helen Powell, Sister Irene, Martha Perri, Mary Nicastro, Mary "Minnie" Grossa, and Sister Juliana; (second row) Alvaro Prieto, Lena Pandora, "Birdie" Grossa, Mr. Vallonga, Fred Fernandez, Consuelo Gonzalez, and Lucia Renzelli. Sister Angelina Cavallaro, pictured below, was among the first students to enroll at St. Francis Borgia School; she entered the Congregation of St. Joseph in 1941. She is pictured with her brothers and sisters at the family homestead. (Above, courtesy of Mary Ann Basile-Angotti; below, courtesy of the Congregation of St. Joseph, Wheeling Center Archives.)

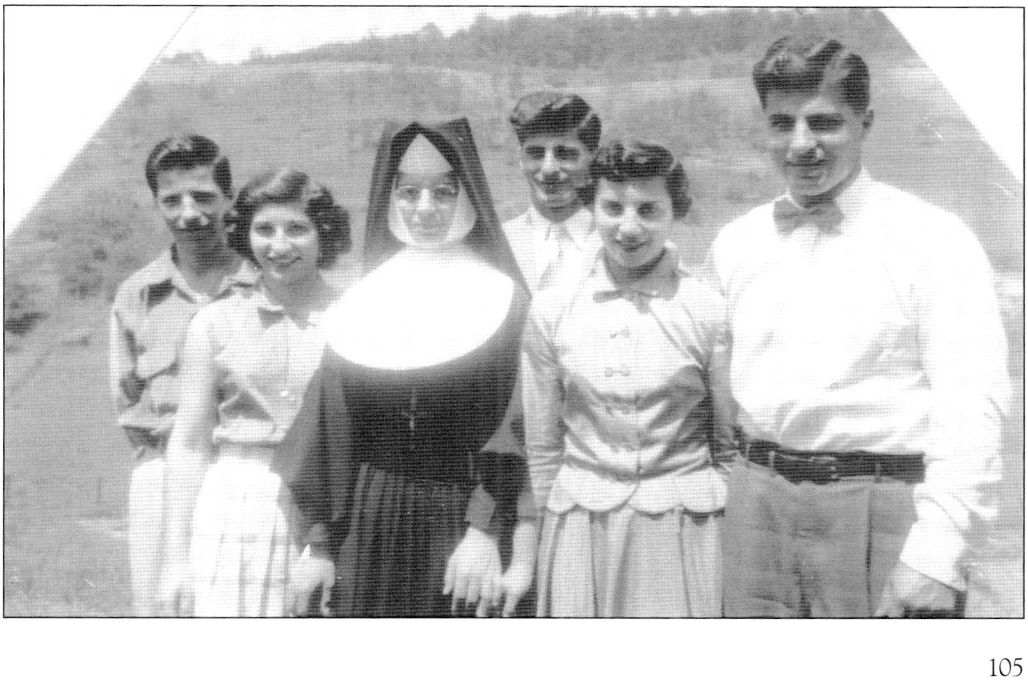

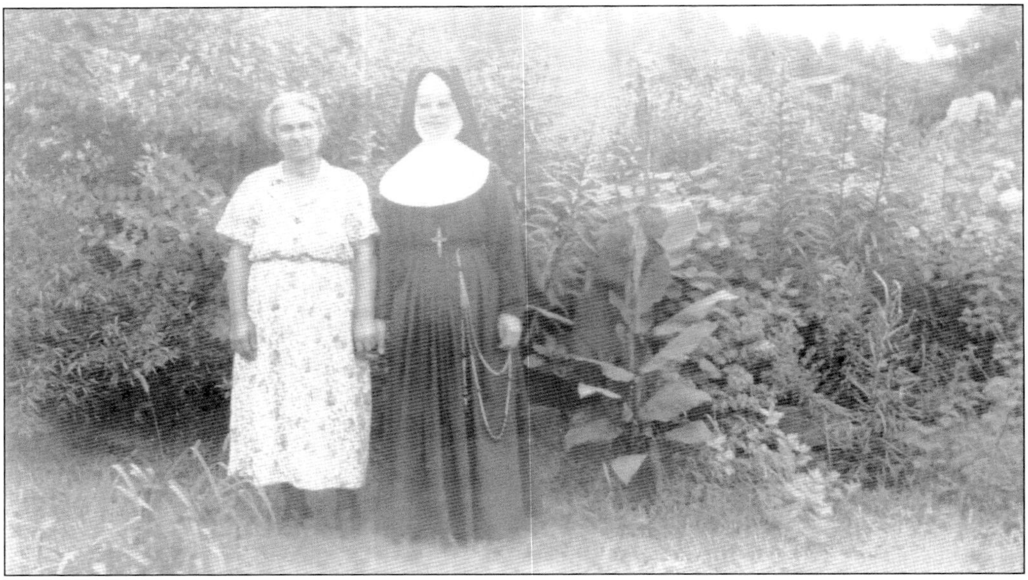

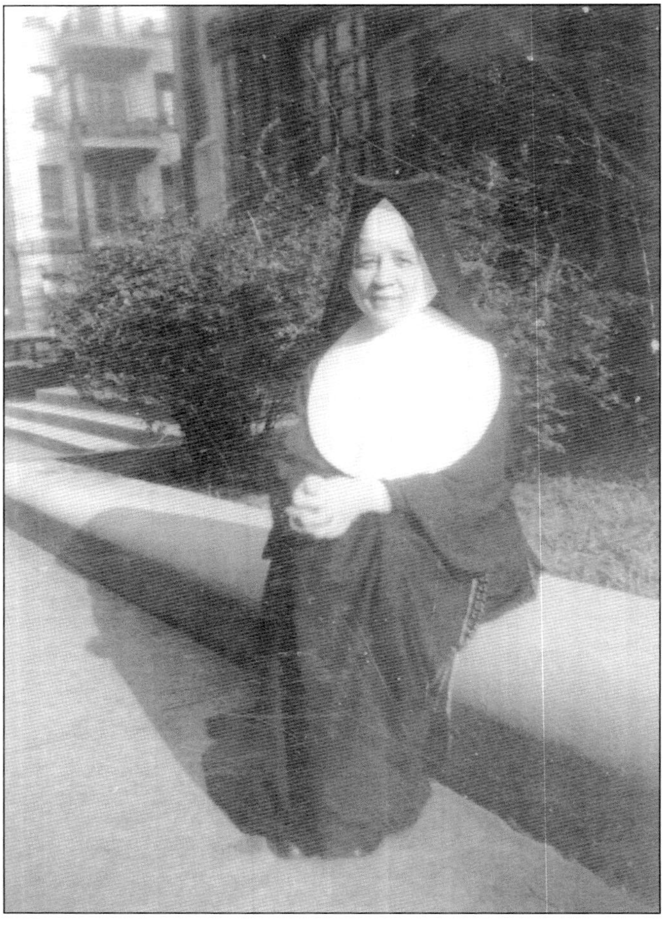

Sisters Vivian Marrama and Francesca DiBacco, Congregation of St. Joseph. Both Sisters Vivian and Francesca were early novices of Italian ancestry to enter the Congregation of St. Joseph. Sister Vivian Marrama is pictured in the garden with her mother, Grace Capranica Marrama. Sister Vivian was born in Monongah, graduated from West Monongah High School, and entered the Sisters of St. Joseph in 1932. She was a member of the congregation for 68 years. Sister Francesca entered the congregation in 1930; she was born in Thomas, West Virginia, the daughter of Paolina DeCesare and Venanzia DiBacco. She attended grade school and high school in Thomas. She studied at Fairmont State and Potomac State and taught school in Tucker County before entering the congregation. (Both, courtesy of the Congregation of St. Joseph, Wheeling Center Archives.)

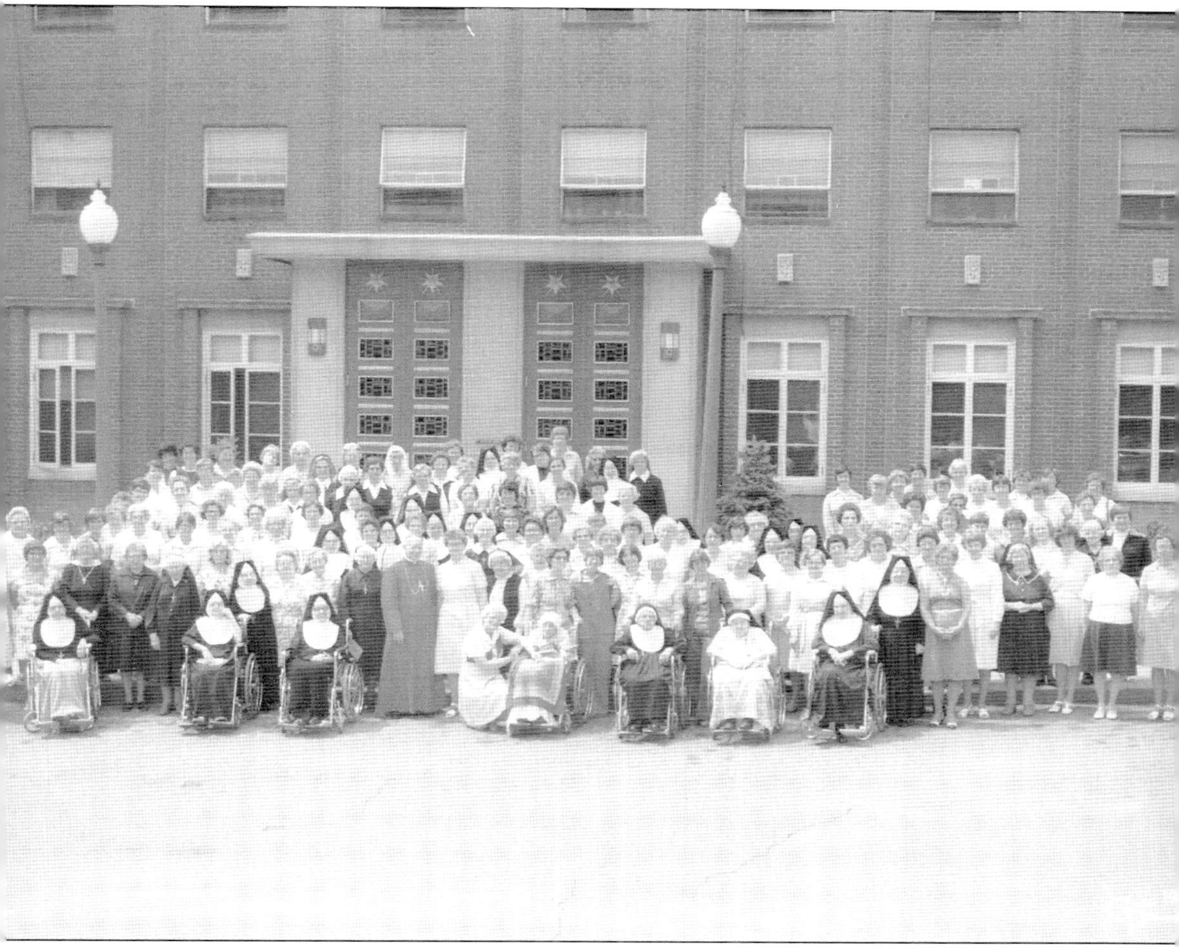

Congregation of St. Joseph, Mount St. Joseph, 1978. Pictured in front of the motherhouse are members of the congregation of the Sisters of St. Joseph in Wheeling. In 1853, Bishop Richard Vincent Whelan requested the Sisters to aid in the work of his new diocese, which had been erected in western Virginia as a suffragan see of the Archbishop of Baltimore in 1850. Four Sisters from Carondelet, Missouri, responded. They arrived in Wheeling on April 13, 1853. They were immediately put in charge of the new Wheeling Hospital. On May 4, 1860, the Sisters became the first and only religious order to be incorporated in the diocese. Today, the Sisters of St. Joseph of Wheeling continue to reach out to West Virginians through a variety of ministries. (Courtesy of the Diocese of Wheeling-Charleston Archives.)

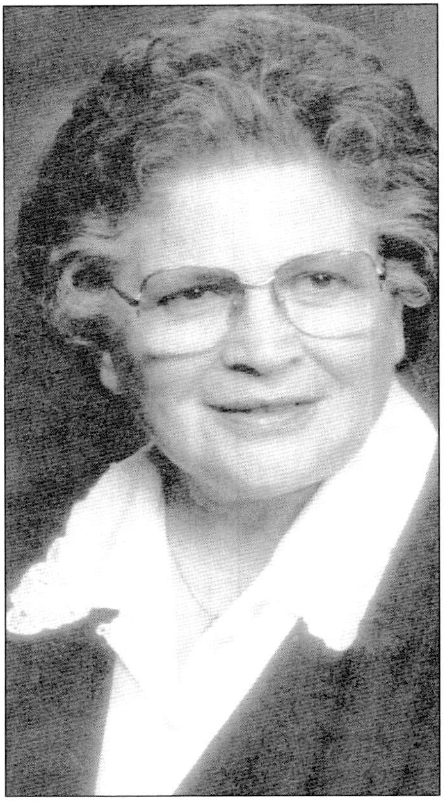

Sister Sandra Peraldo, CSJ, and Italian American Woman of the Year, WVIHF, 2001. Sister Sandra was the Italian American Woman of the Year at the 23rd WVIHF, held in Clarksburg. She is pictured below at the table accepting the award for her outstanding ministry in education. She is the daughter of the late Plinio and Lina Peraldo of Beckley. She entered the Sisters of St. Joseph after receiving her degree in education from Concord College. She taught in the Diocese of Wheeling-Charleston Schools for several years and then began parish work in Hinton, Bridgeport, and later Elizabeth, West Virginia. She completed her master's at Catholic University and is a certified chaplain and member of the National Association of Catholic Chaplains. (Both, courtesy of the Congregation of St. Joseph, Wheeling Center Archives.)

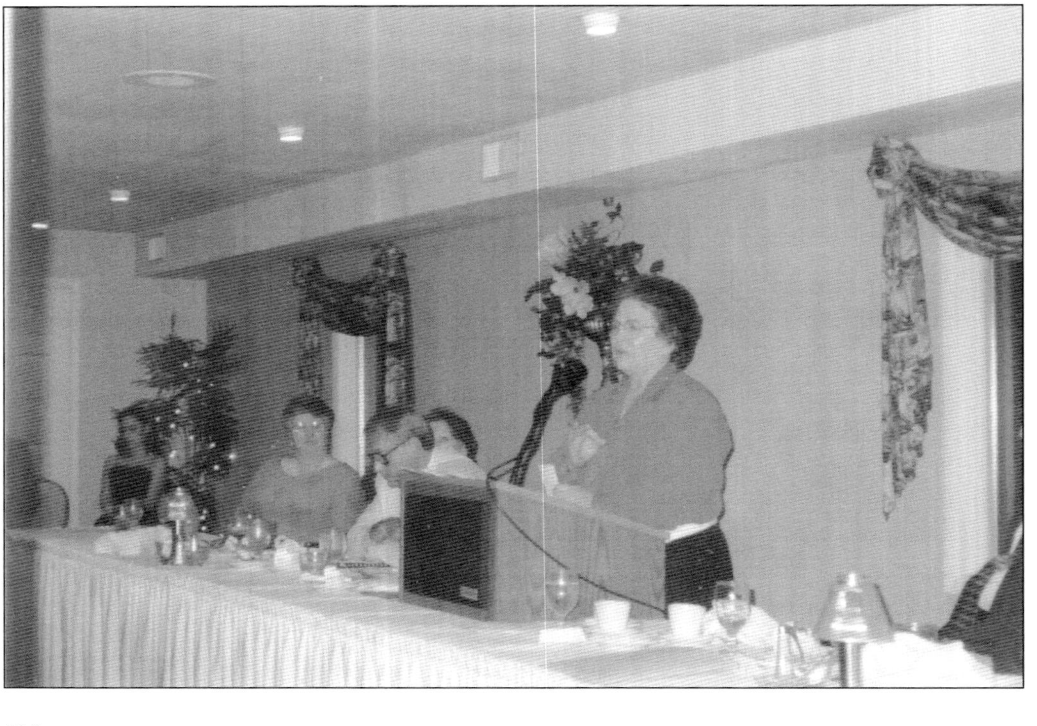

Seven

The Italian American Festive Spirit Today

Since the late 1970s, Italian heritage festivals have celebrated Italian culture and pride in areas of West Virginia containing Italian Americans. The Clarksburg Italian Heritage Festival came first, in 1979, followed by festivals in Wheeling and Bluefield. More recently, the Calabria–West Virginia Italian Heritage Association and the Audia Caring Foundation have focused on preserving Italian cultural identity while developing broader civic, philanthropic, and educational agendas. Currently, educational institutions are reacting to the interest in heritage culture by providing Italian language and cultural instruction in West Virginia, as well as by creating student exchanges sending American students to Italy and bringing Italian students to America. West Virginia University has student exchanges with the University of Trento, while Fairmont State University exchanges students with the University of Calabria.

Italian American writers from West Virginia interpret the ancestral pilgrimage in various ways, some writing from the heritage perspective. One of the most important themes is la dolce vita, or the customs evoking foods and consummation. Rosalyn Queen Alonso explores family memories through recipes in *Arrivederci: Customs and Recipes Every Italian Girl Takes from Home*. Not only did Robert Tinnell study his memories of the Christmas Eve feast in the Italian household in his *Feast of the Seven Fishes*, he also developed a winter festival in Fairmont on the theme. Other writers focus on the struggles and triumphs inherent in the typical American success story. Poet Russell Marano unfolds the realities of growing up poor but proud in Glen Elk, the Italian section of Clarksburg, while Dr. Joan Saverino of Fairmont has studied such features of the Italian American experience as the Monongah mine disaster. Denise Giardina and Jean Battlo both came of age in the southern coal camps of McDowell County. Giardina's novels, *Storming Heaven* and its sequel, *The Unquiet Earth*, reveal the indomitable Italian spirit prevailing over economic adversity and ethnic prejudice during the turbulent years of the mine wars. Battlo, a playwright, poet, novelist, and historian, sees her writings as vehicles to dispel the negative stereotyping of the people of her native state. To her, the Italian spirit and the Appalachian spirit are one.

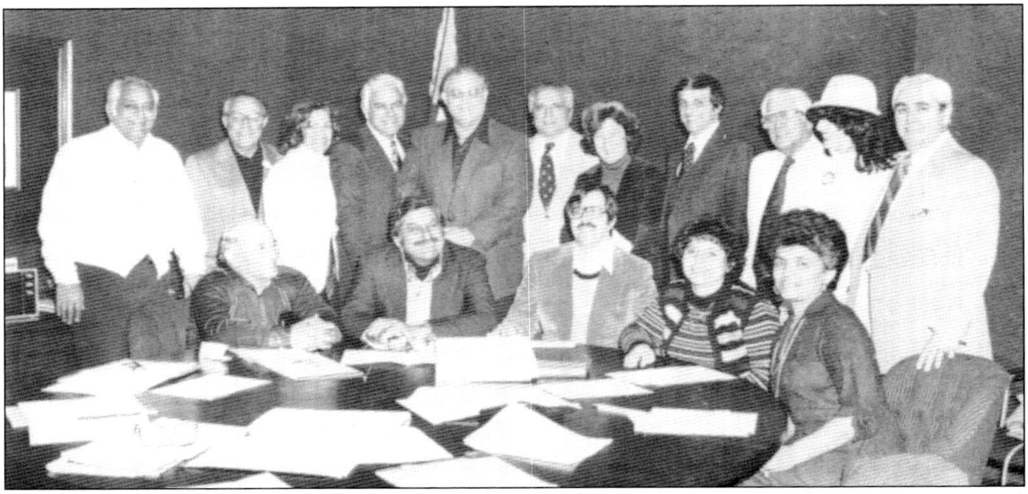

BOARD OF DIRECTORS, WVIHF, 1979. This oldest of Italian festivals in West Virginia was conceived in Clarksburg, in the heart of the state's largest ethnic populace. It was initially sponsored by the Clarksburg Public Library under the guidance of Merle Moore and six "founding fathers," Sam Chico, Sam D'Annunzio, Frank Iaquinta, James D. LaRosa, John Manchin, and Louis Spatafore. Together with other community leaders, the early board of directors decreed Labor Day weekend as the time for what became an annual event of homecoming, remembrance, and celebration. Pictured are, from left to right, (first row) Louis Petitto, Russell Bonasso, Thomas Kupec, Betty Audia, and Rosalyn Queen; (second row) Joe Minard, Russell Lopez, Loretta Mazzie, Frank Iaquinta, Bernard Folio, James D. LaRosa, Merle Moore, Louis Spatafore, Victor Gabriel, Lenora Riley, and Sam Paletta. Not pictured are Sam D'Annunzio, Mike Audia, Sam Bonasso, Homer Carmichael, Sam Chico, C.E. Compton, John Manchin, and Joe Casabona. (Both, courtesy of the WVIHF archives.)

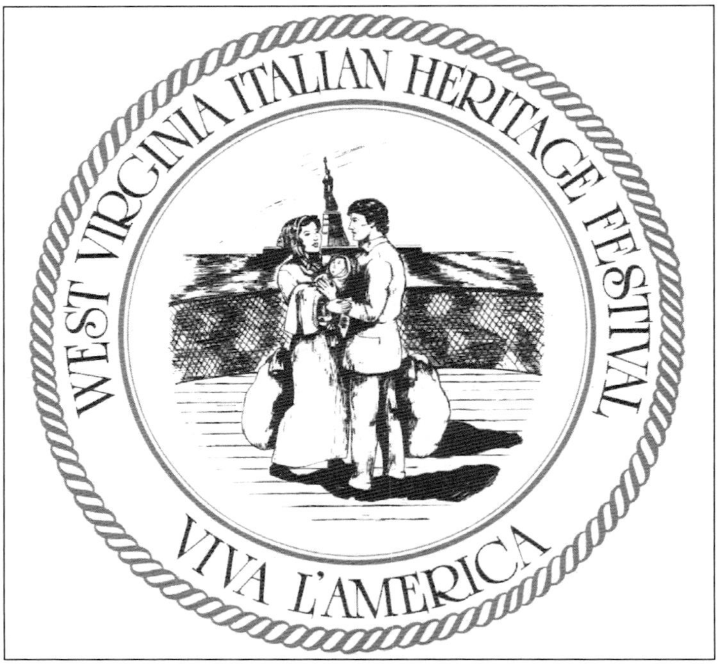

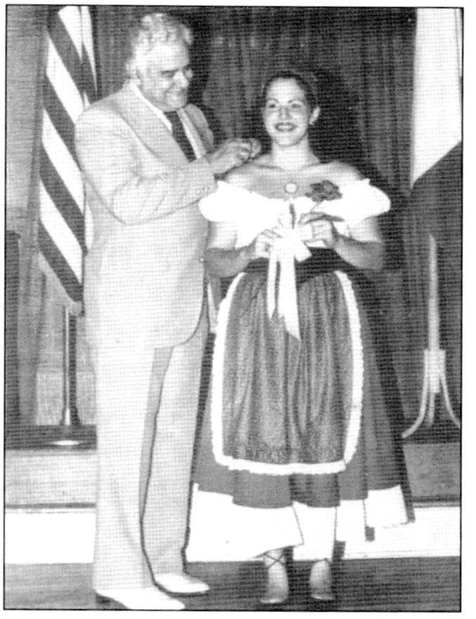

Regina Maria I, Mary Frances Beto, 1979. Selected because of her Italian ancestry and her desire to perpetuate her heritage, the queen, along with her court, is one of the central symbols of the festival that has been named among the top 100 events in North America by the American Bus Association and among the top 20 events by the Southeast Tourism Society. The WVIHF opens on Friday with the crowning of the queen, who is also given the festival medallion by the festival president (Frank Iaquinta in 1979). Regina Maria I was dressed in an interpretation of a traditional southern Italian costume. Each year, Mary Frances has returned to the festival as a featured vocalist. (Courtesy of the WVIHF archives.)

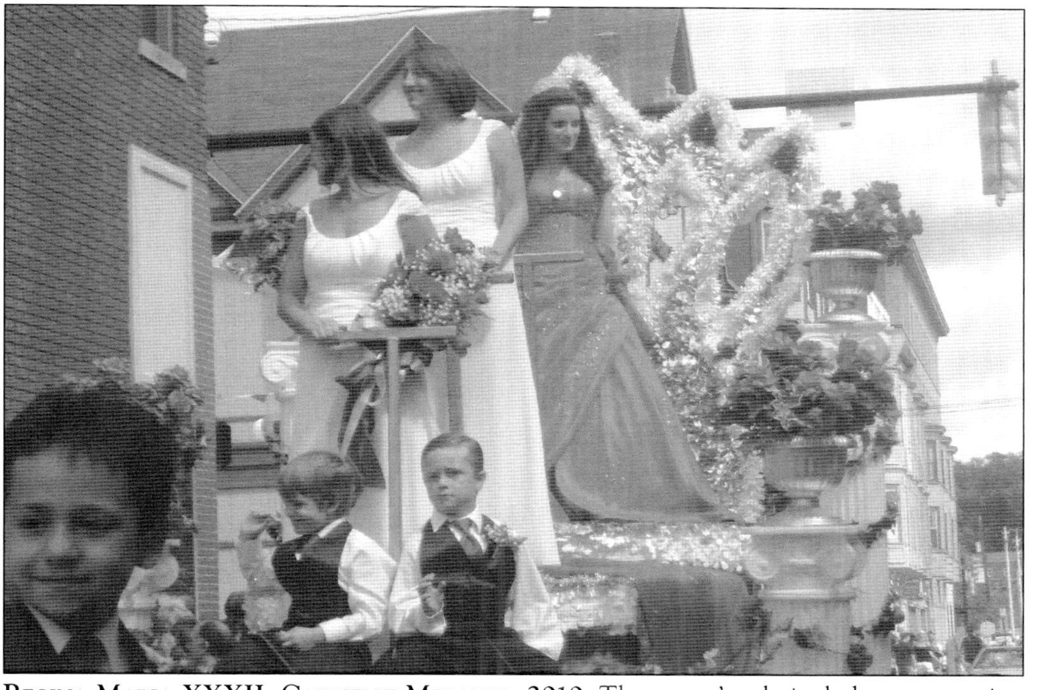

Regina Maria XXXII, Gabrielle Merandi, 2010. The queen's role includes representing contemporary Italian heritage in West Virginia throughout the coming year. She encourages the learning of the Italian language, travel to Italy, and the preserving of Italian customs. She helps with festival fundraisers and the promotion of scholarships for Italian American youth. As queen, Gabrielle is continuing a family tradition; her grandfather, Sam Chico, was one of the festival founders, and her mother, Constance Chico Merandi, was Regina Maria II in 1980. Today, even though Regina Maria wears a personally designed red gown and crown, she still dons the traditional festival medallion and leads the Saturday morning parade through the streets of Clarksburg. (Authors' collection.)

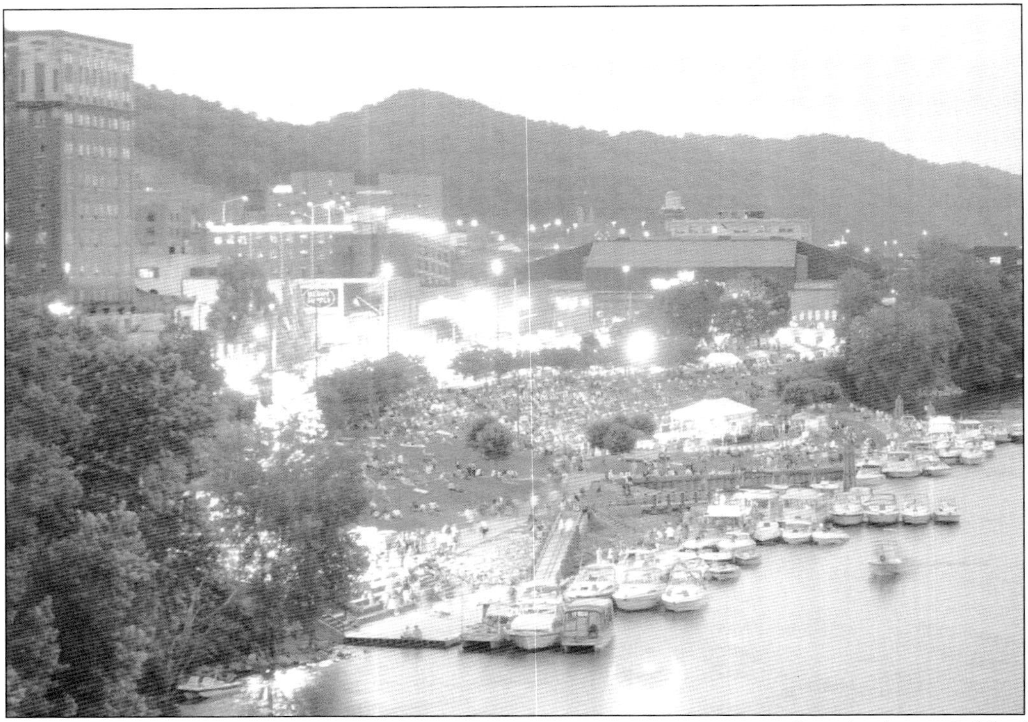

The Upper Ohio Valley Italian Heritage Festival, 1983. It started as the brainchild of Anthony Zambito, Vincent Colaianni, Anthony Iannarelli, and Benny Battistelli, who, after visiting the WVIHF in Clarksburg in 1982, yearned to begin such a great tradition in northern West Virginia. They gathered a team of volunteers from the Italian American Clubs throughout the Ohio Valley and placed the event in Wheeling on Market Street during the third week of July. With a special emphasis on awarding scholarships for Italian American youth, the popularity of this festival soon outgrew its location. In 2001, it relocated to the Heritage Port waterfront and has become the second largest Italian festival in the United States. (Both, courtesy of Kim Smith, Ohio Valley Italian Heritage Festival coordinator.)

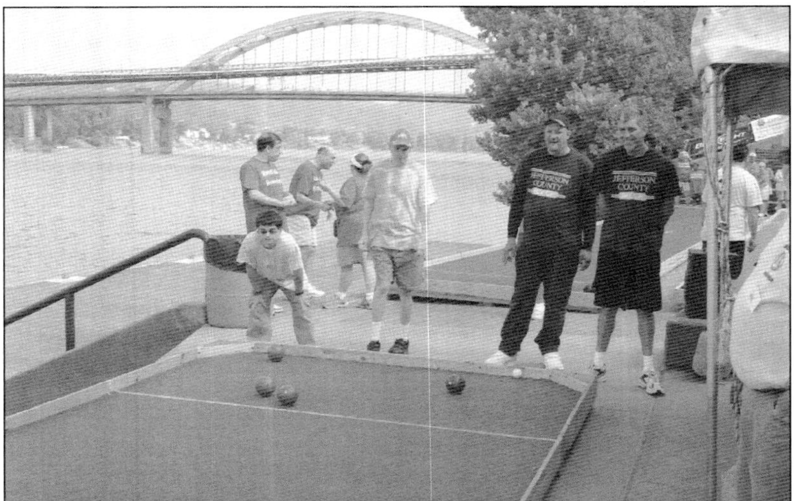

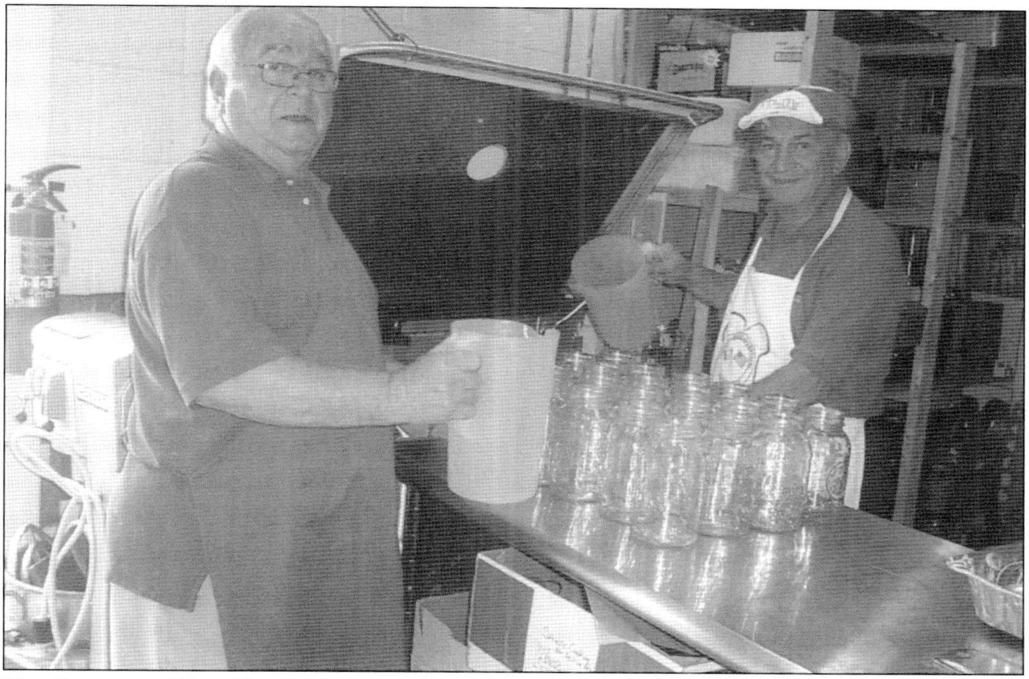

The Southern West Virginia Italian Day Festival, 1994. Inspired by its northern counterparts, the Order of Sons of Italy in America Lodge No. 2631 developed its own southern celebration in Princeton with a special emphasis on rewarding educational scholarships to Italian American youth. Under the leadership of Nick Ameli as lodge president, the festival established Bluefield as its annual site. It is held on the first weekend in October. Over the years, it has become a popular reunion event for the entire community, offering food, dancing, and entertainment. During the festival and at least four times a year, the lodge members make their spaghetti sauce and meatballs that have become famous throughout Mercer and McDowell Counties. (Both, courtesy of Nick Ameli and Christina Willis.)

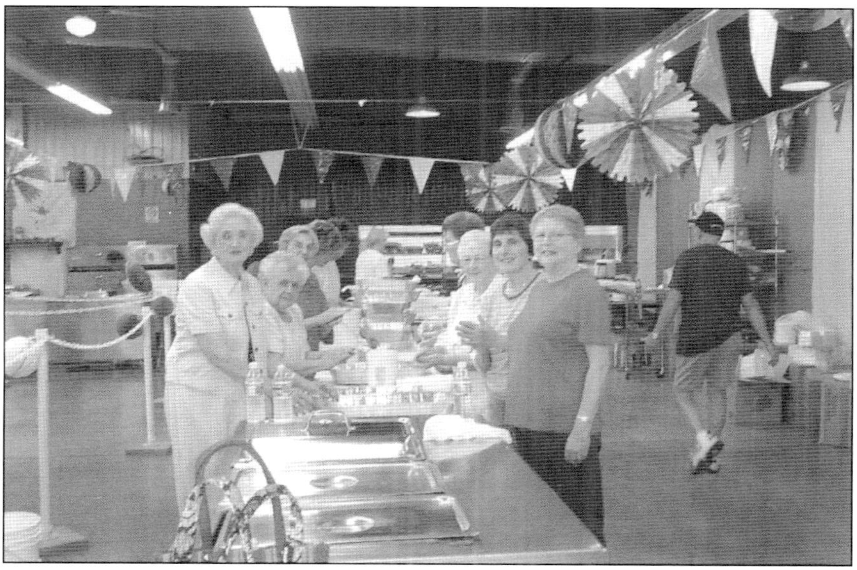

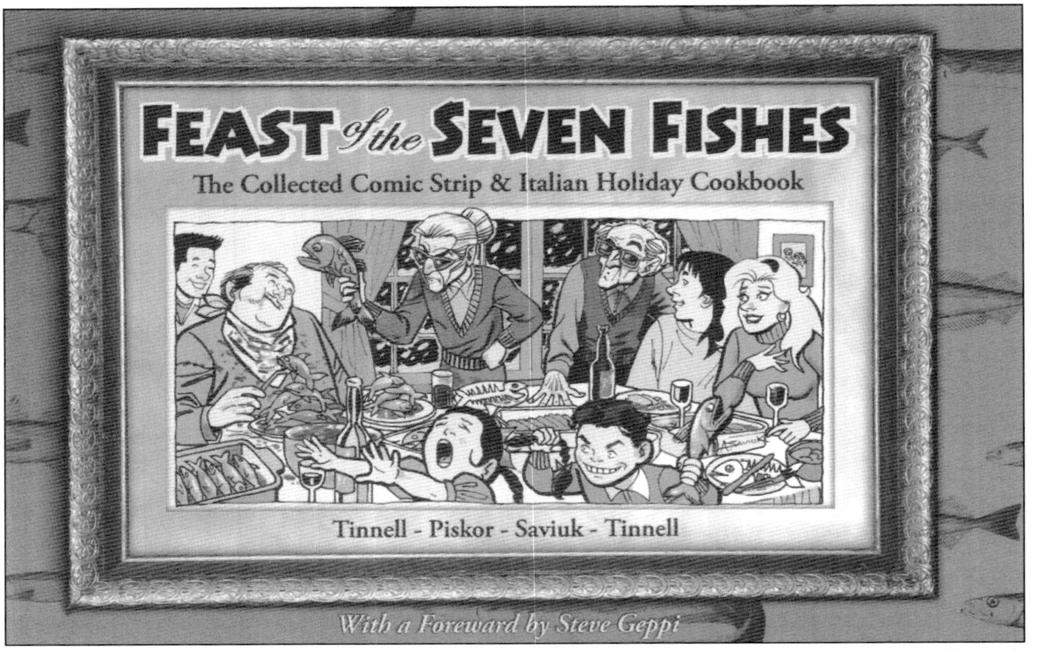

FEAST OF THE SEVEN FISHES, 2006. In Fairmont, West Virginia, a one-day winter street festival, usually on the first Saturday in December, commemorates a Christmas Eve custom of southern Italians by substituting fish for meat as a vigil preparation for Christ's birth. The festival was the brain child of Robert Tinnell, a graphic artist and film producer, and his wife, Shannon, who had coauthored with Ed Piskor and Alex Saviuk a graphic novel/cookbook in comic-book form that recounted what they had learned from their own southern Italian families. (Courtesy of Robert Tinnell.)

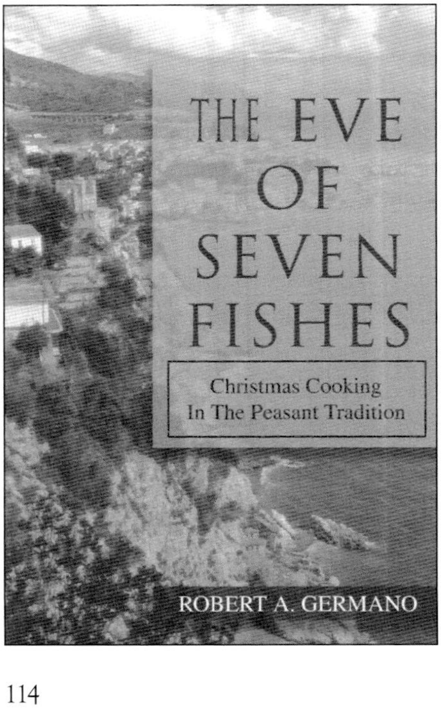

THE EVE OF SEVEN FISHES—CHRISTMAS COOKING IN THE PEASANT TRADITION, 2005. Robert Germano, a loyal participant of Fairmont's Feast of the Seven Fishes, teamed up with Bob and Shannon Tinnell in the cooking-school portion of the festival, using recipes from his cookbook that is also reminiscent of the festival's theme. The recipes are simple and reflect the menu of dishes the Germano family had on Christmas Eve. (Courtesy of Robert Germano.)

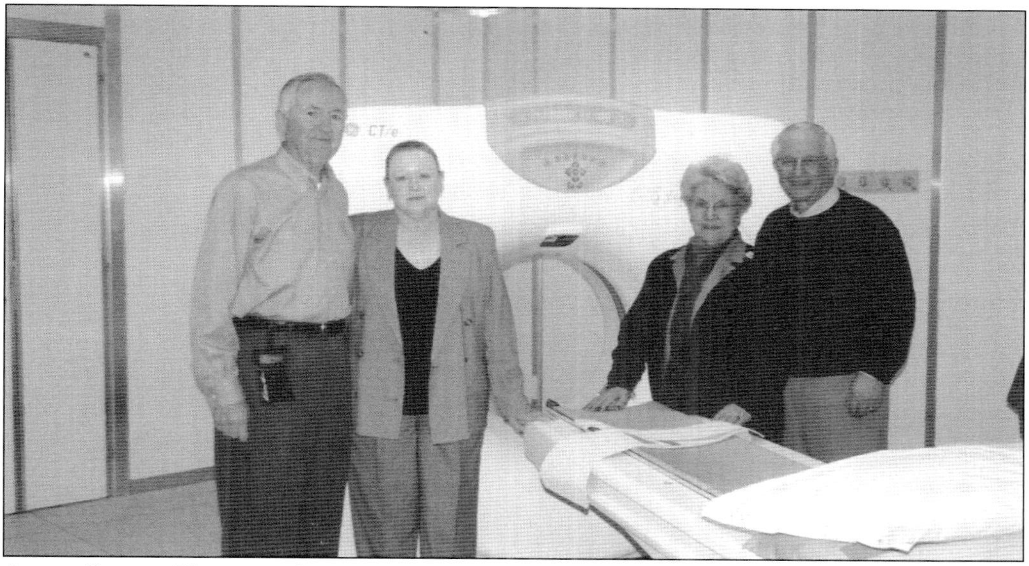

Audia Caring Heritage Association, 2000. The mission of this philanthropic organization is to assist communities in need and to improve their quality of life. It started in 2000 under the leadership of Albert Andy from Washington County in southern Pennsylvania. He wanted to thank the people of San Giovanni in Fiore for their hospitality when he visited the hill village of his ancestors and other parts of Calabria. A West Virginia chapter, headquartered in Morgantown and headed by John Angotti, helped Audia Caring Heritage Association to raise almost $500,000 to purchase medical diagnostic equipment for the hospital in San Giovanni in Fiore in 2002. Members of the delegation who traveled to the hospital to deliver the CAT scanner include, from left to right, Albert and Terry Andy and Sera and Frank Merandi. (Both, courtesy of Rosalyn Queen Alonso.)

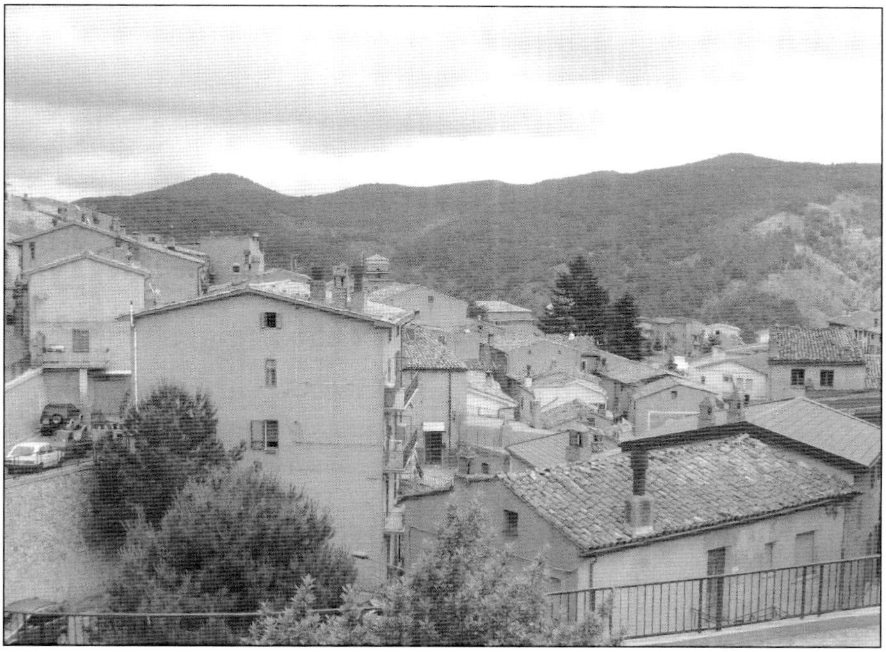

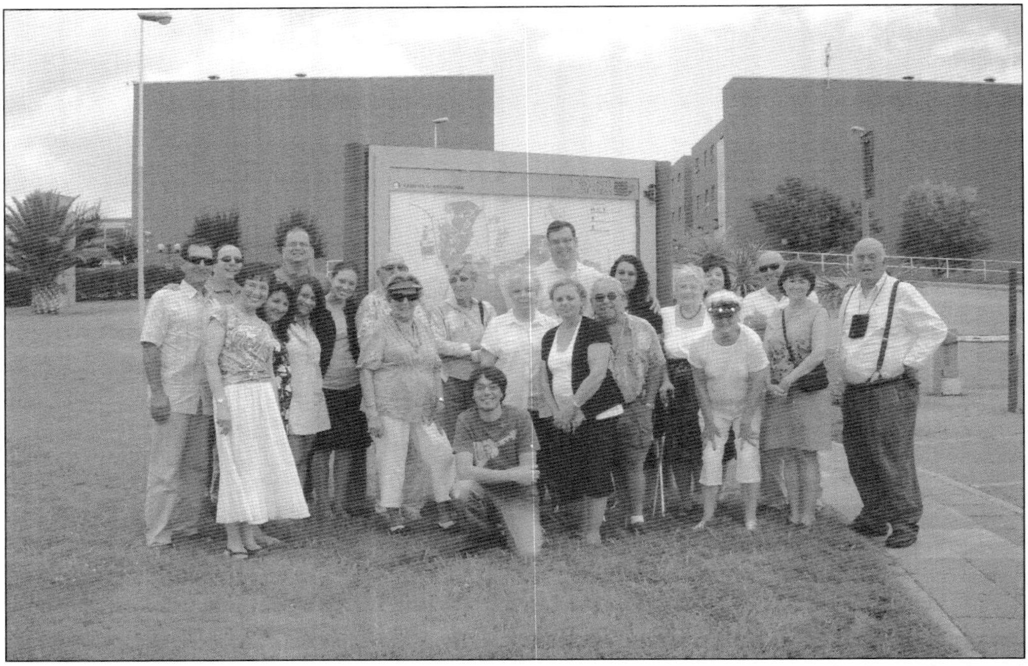

CALABRIA–WEST VIRGINIA ITALIAN HERITAGE ASSOCIATION, 2005. This newly formed cultural organization, with Louis R. Spatafore from Clarksburg as president, is a chapter of Heritage Calabria International, which was founded by Dr. Francois Xavier Nicoletti. The association is affiliated with the Frank and Jane Gabor West Virginia Folklife Center at Fairmont State University. Its mission is to preserve and perpetuate Italian heritage in West Virginia through Italian arts, language, literature, history, and folklore, along with encouraging study throughout Italy, such as the student exchange with the University of Calabria, Cosenza. In June 2009, the association sponsored a tour through Calabria and Sicily. One of the highlights of the two weeks of travel was to visit the University of Calabria. Engineering student Carlo Salatino, kneeling in front, was the campus guide for the 28 travelers. (Both, Authors' collection.)

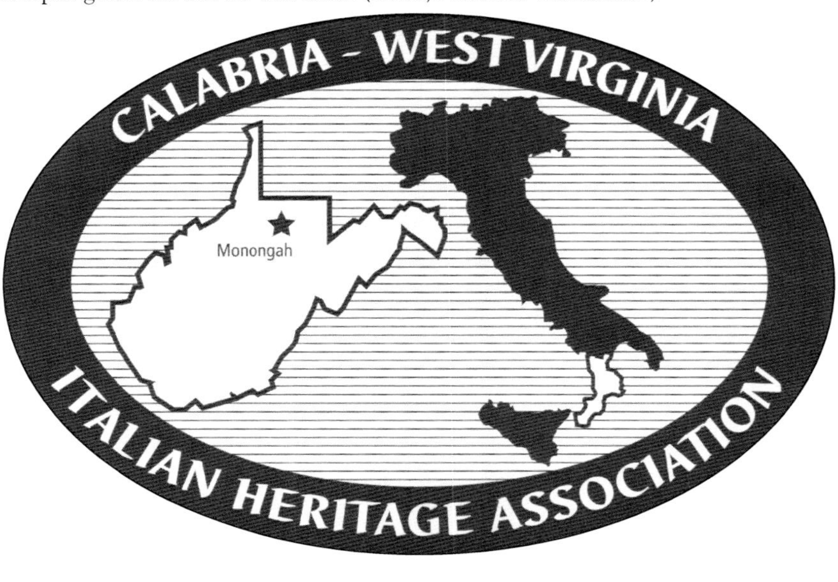

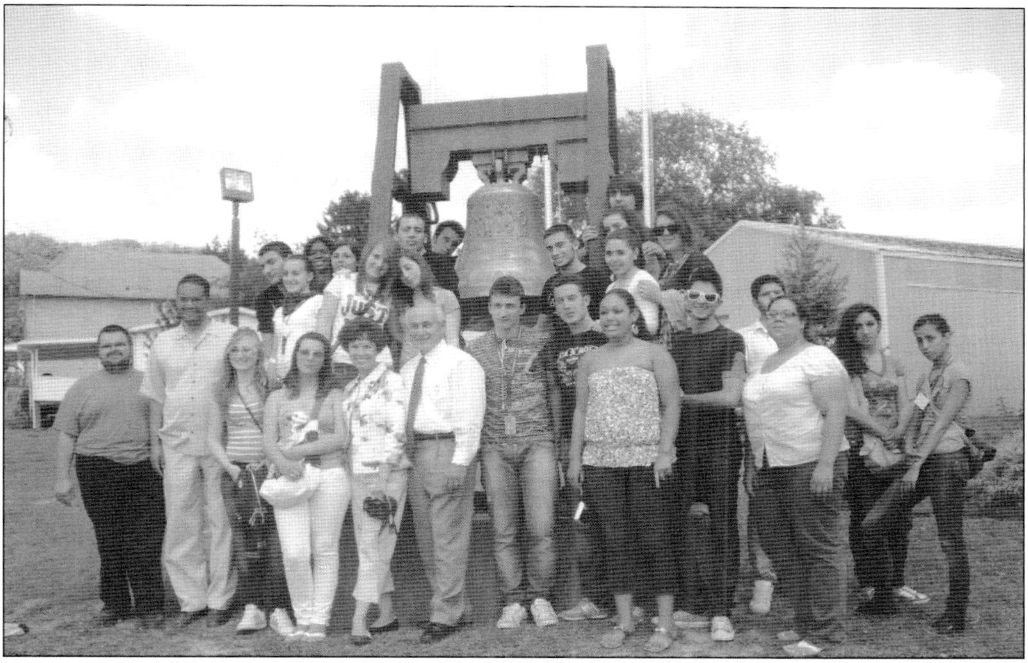

Mountains to Mountains from La Sila to Appalachia: Italian to American Cultural Camp, June 2010. A full 23 Italian high school students participated in the first English language immersion summer program in West Virginia, which was sponsored by Fairmont State University under the direction of Michael Belmear, vice president of student affairs. The students, from Liceo Scientifico Statale in San Giovanni in Fiore, learned about the cultural connections between Italy and north central West Virginia. Throughout the three-week camp, the students, accompanied by their English teacher from San Giovanni in Fiore, Teresa Bitonti, studied American literature, West Virginia history, theater, and English as a second language. Many Italian American community leaders opened their hearts to the students. Rocco Muriale, owner of Muriale's Italian Restaurant in Fairmont, was delighted to have the students sample the many dishes he features from his ancestral region of Calabria. Another highlight of the camp was meeting West Virginia state senator Roman Prezioso for a walking tour and discussion in Monongah of the mining disaster that occurred there. (Both, Authors' collection.)

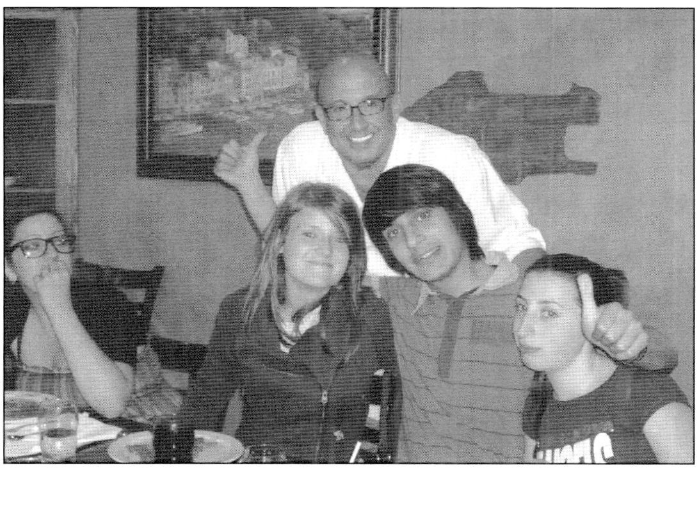

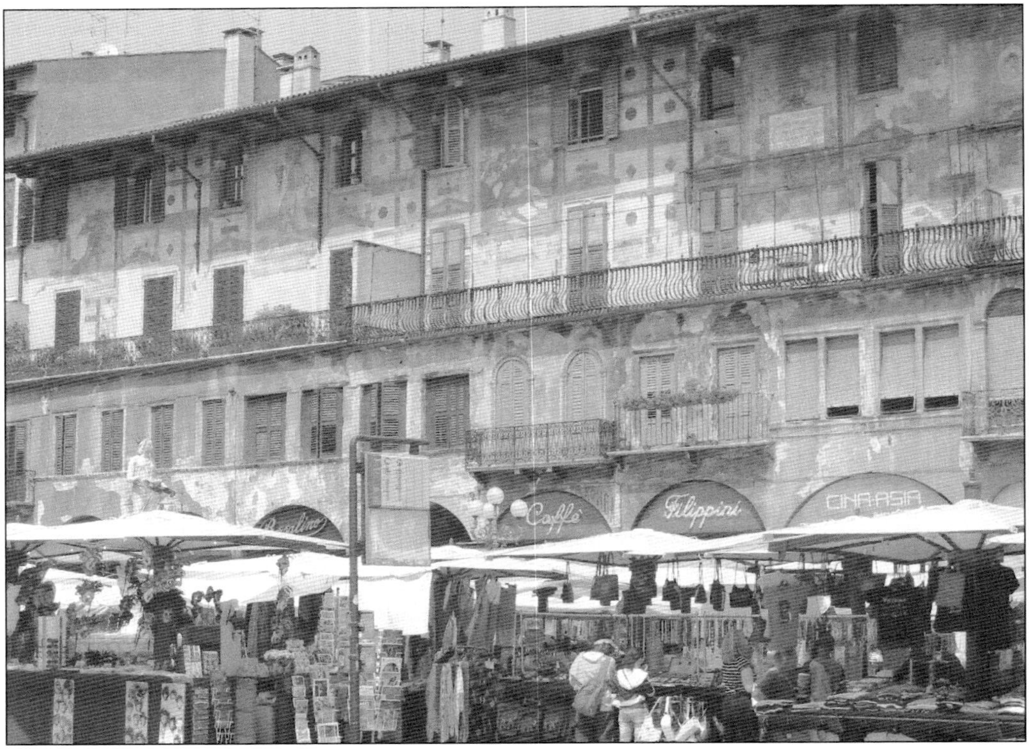

ITALIAN STUDIES PROGRAM AT WEST VIRGINIA UNIVERSITY. In the Eberly College of Arts and Sciences, West Virginia University students can participate in the Italian studies program that contains a newly developed major along with its traditional minor. They can also participate in the Italian studies club, called Circolo Italiano, which offers events, including a pasta-making evening, learning to play the Italian card game scope, a pepperoni-roll-making afternoon, a bocce tournament, and Italian movie nights. Students also have several immersion opportunities in northern Italy, such as an exchange program with the University of Trento that permits West Virginia University students to spend a semester or a year abroad. This special program was initiated with the support of the West Virginia Italian American communities. (Courtesy of Leisa Muto.)

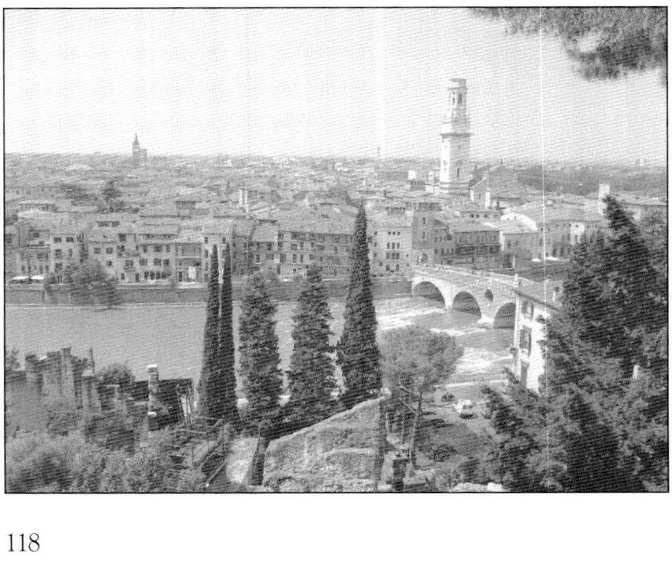

SUMMER SHORT COURSE IN ITALY. Students who have completed one semester of college-level Italian (or the equivalent) are eligible to participate in a four-week faculty-led summer program located in Nettuno, a seaside town one hour from Rome. During this time, students take excursions to Rome, Ostia Antica, Cerveteri, Subiaco, Castelli Romani, and Florence. (Courtesy of Leisa Muto.)

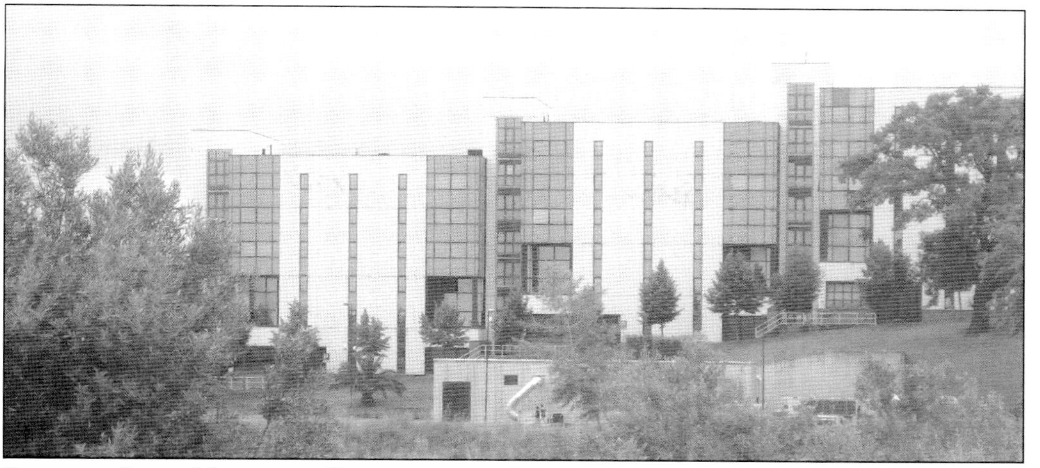

Fairmont State University Established an Italian Studies Program, 2007. Through the help of Heritage Calabria International, under the leadership of Dr. Francois Xavier Nicoletti and the Regional Council of Calabria, Fairmont State University established a partnership with the University of Calabria after a travel-abroad program to Italy in the summer of 2007 titled Roads to Appalachia, sponsored by the Frank and Jane Gabor West Virginia Folklife Center at Fairmont State University. Through the Department of Language and Literature in the College of Liberal Arts, students can participate in an Italian studies program that has a 12-hour liberal studies emphasis along with the opportunity to spend a semester or a year studying in southern Italy. (Authors' collection.)

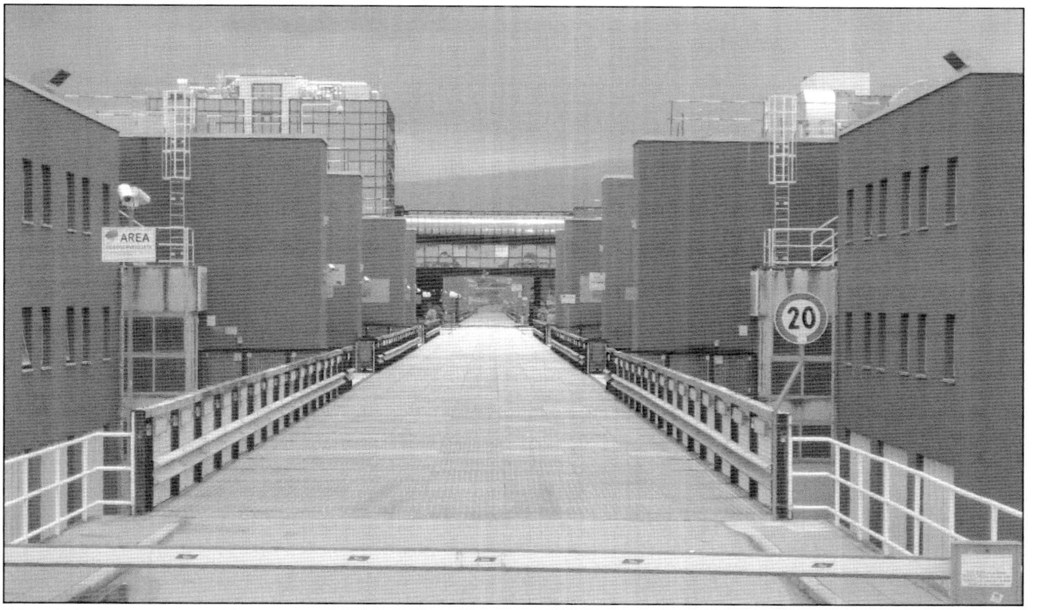

The University of Calabria. This school is a middle-sized, state-run university in Arcavacata di Rende, a suburb of Cosenza, Italy. It is the only residential university campus in Italy. It was founded in 1972, and its rector is Dr. Giovanni Latorre. The student poplation of 30,000 is supported by 450 teaching and research staff and about 700 administrative staff. The buildings line a suspension bridge, and students live in residential blocks surrounded by the green hills of Arcavacata. (Authors' collection.)

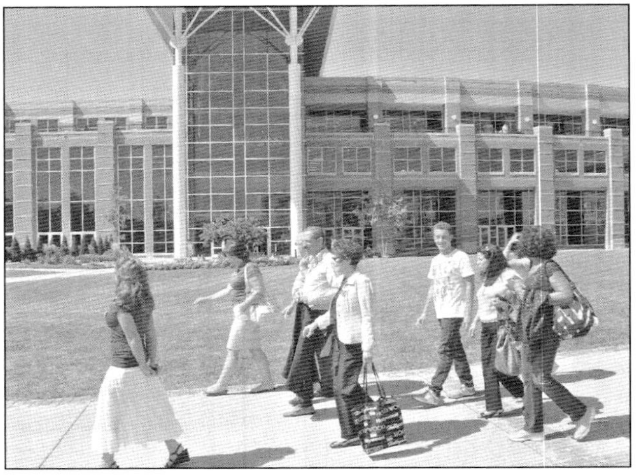

GOVERNMENT DELEGATIONS FROM CALABRIA EXTEND EDUCATIONAL PARTNERSHIP BETWEEN FAIRMONT STATE UNIVERSITY AND SOUTHERN ITALY, 2009. Officials from local and provincial governments have visited the campus of Fairmont State University to see the potential of educational exchanges with their regional university (University of Calabria) and also with high school summer programs in English-language proficiency. The student center on campus offers many recreational facilities. (Authors' collection.)

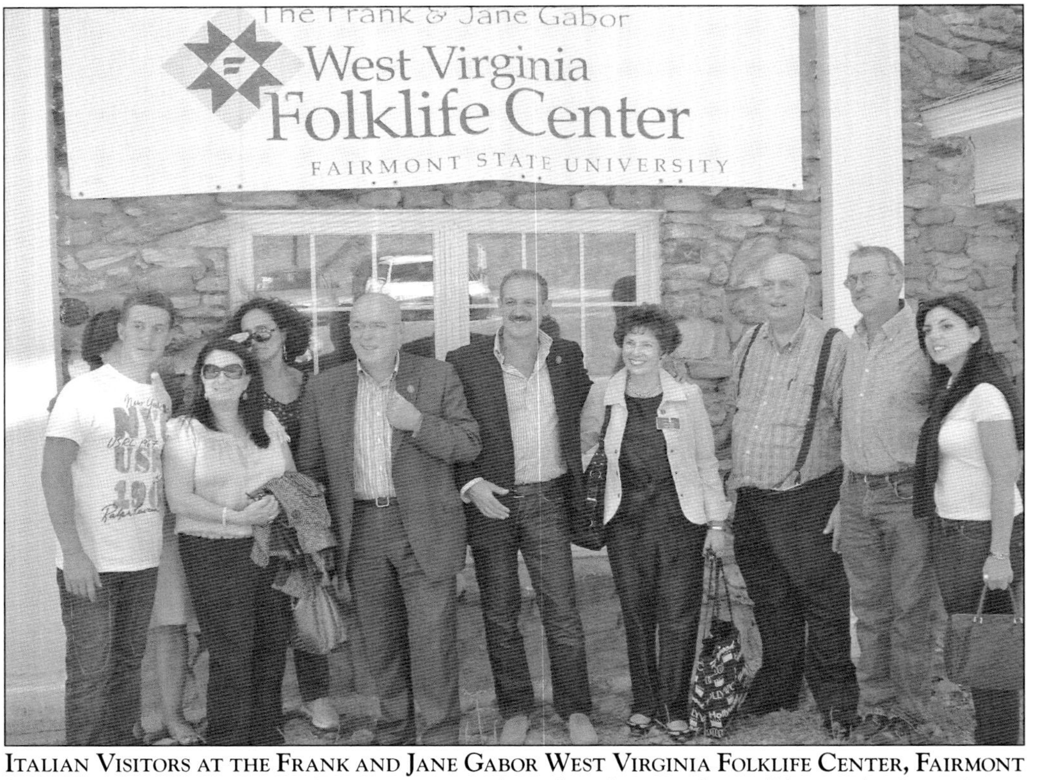

ITALIAN VISITORS AT THE FRANK AND JANE GABOR WEST VIRGINIA FOLKLIFE CENTER, FAIRMONT STATE UNIVERSITY, 2009. Italian visitors tour the cultural center that will house the Great Room of Cultures, which will honor all the different groupings of people who settled in West Virginia. There will be an exhibit section devoted to the immigrants from southern Italy. Standing are, from left to right, Giuseppi Nicoletti, high school student from San Giovanni in Fiore who became a member of the first Mountains to Mountains Summer Language and Culture Camp; Rose Mazza, Italian instructor, Fairmont State University; Mario Oliverio, president of the province of Cosenza; Dr. Antonio Nicoletti, mayor of San Giovanni in Fiore; Dr. Judy Prozzillo Byers, director of the center; Michael Oliverio and John Oliverio, hosts for the visitors; and Laura Oliverio, University of Rome student. (Authors' collection.)

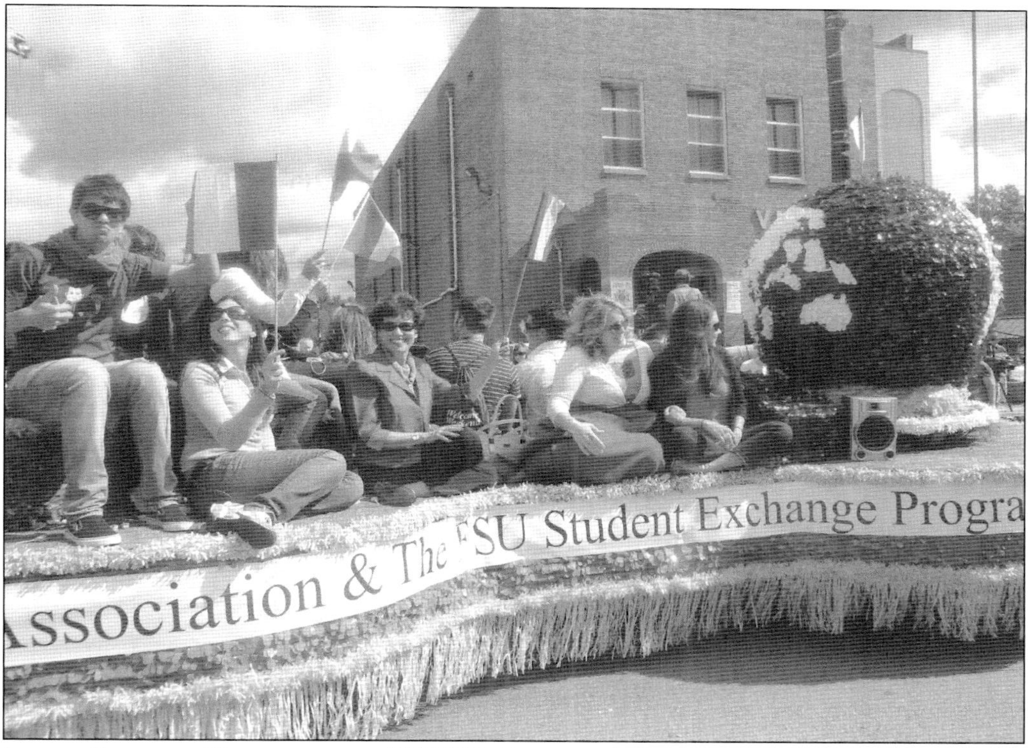

ITALIAN STUDENTS HONORED AT THE WVIHF, CLARKSBURG, LABOR DAY WEEKEND, 2010. Within days of arriving at Fairmont State University from the University of Calabria, the Italian students were honored guests of the festival and featured in the annual parade on a special float called "It's a Small World." Throughout the fall semester, they were immersed in the American culture, which they soon realized was much like theirs in Calabria, since north central West Virginia is heavily populated with people of Italian lineage. Through the leadership of the Calabria–West Virginia Italian Association and Fairmont State University, many Italian American families throughout the tri-city area of Clarksburg, Fairmont, and Morgantown invited them on Sunday afternoons for traditional family dinners. The students marveled at how similar the climate and topography of West Virginia was to that of Calabria. (Authors' collection.)

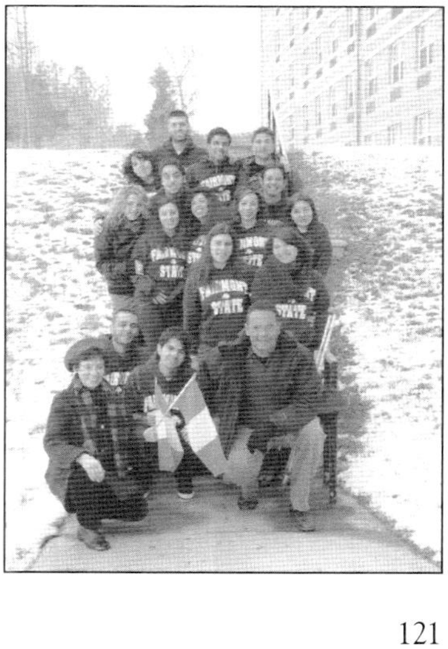

ITALIAN EXCHANGE STUDENTS AS ADVOCATES FOR GLOBALIZING EDUCATION, 2010. Bittersweet were the farewells as the first class of Italian exchange students ended the 2010 fall semester at Fairmont State University. They had successfully completed their study program, perfected the English language, befriended many college students, and actively participated in campus life. They had traveled throughout America to Washington, DC, New York City, and Los Angeles. In West Virginia, however, which they considered their American home, they had become ambassadors for internationalizing education. They had visited elementary and secondary schools, encouraging local youth to learn other languages and cultures and to travel and study abroad. (Authors' collection.)

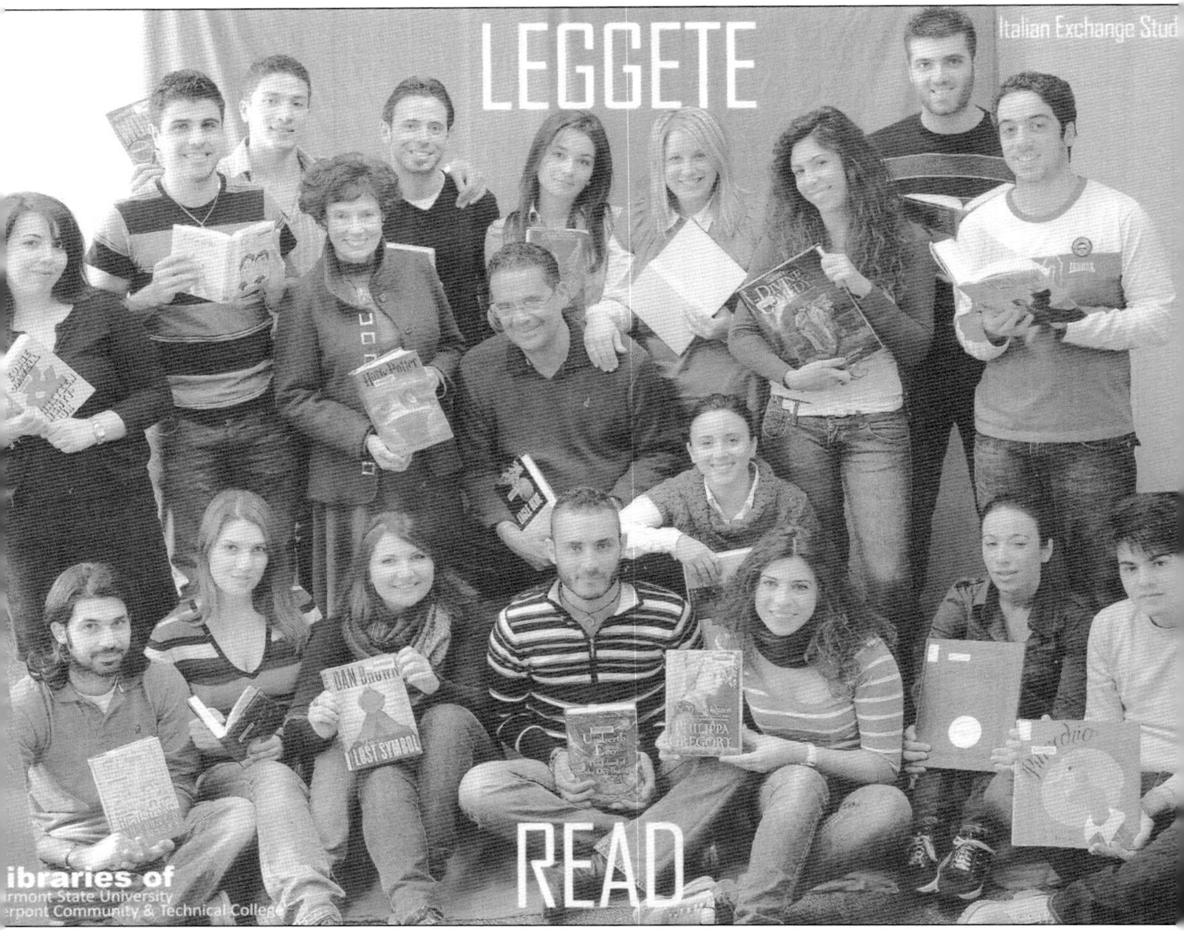

First Class of Italian Exchange Students from University of Calabria, Fall Semester, 2010. As a regional university, these students represented many of the provinces within the region of Calabria. Pictured are, from left to right, (first row) Antonio Mola (Cosenza), Antonella Sestito (Cosenza), Serena Rinninella (Catanzaro), Giuseppe Sgró (Reggio Calabria), Rosella Morgante (Lamezia Terme), Stefania Giovinazzo (Reggio Calabria), Mariapina Bloise (Cosenza), and Giuseppe Peluso (Cosenza); (second row) Giuseppina Scarpino (Catanzaro), Alfredo La Serra (Crotone), Dr. Judy Prozzillo Byers (Fairmont State University advisor), Michael Belmear (Fairmont State University vice president of student affairs), Mariateresa Aloisio (Cosenza), and Emanuele Carnevale (Cosenza); (third row) Francesco Ruberto (Catanzaro), Antonio Morgante (Lamezia Terme), Teresa Cattolico (Cosenza), Leisa Muto (Fairmont State University advisor), and Mario Francesco Mirabelli (Cosenza). (Courtesy of Lingbing Hang, Fairmont State University.)

ROSALYN QUEEN ALONSO PRESERVED ITALIAN TRADITIONS THROUGH A LITERARY COOKBOOK. *Arrivederci: Recipes and Customs Every Italian Girl Takes from Home* collects the customary lore surrounding foods traditionally practiced in southern Italy, especially in Calabria, and transmitted to America by immigrant families. Through her own family practices and extensive oral history interviews, these recipes are basic to daily cuisine and influenced by the growing seasons. She learned most of these recipes at the knees of her mother, Florence Roberti Burnett, and her grandmothers, Giovannie Iaquinta Brunetti and Anna Audia Veneziano. The cover of the book is an original painting by Raffaella (Folly) Basile. Alonso, a native of Harrison County, was the executive director of the WVIHF and was honored as the Italian Woman of the Year. She has also served on the Christopher Columbus Fellowship Foundation. She maintains a popular weekly column on heritage and news called "The Grapevine" that appears in various North Central West Virginia newspapers. (Courtesy of Phyllis Moore's Literary Collection, Fairmont State University.)

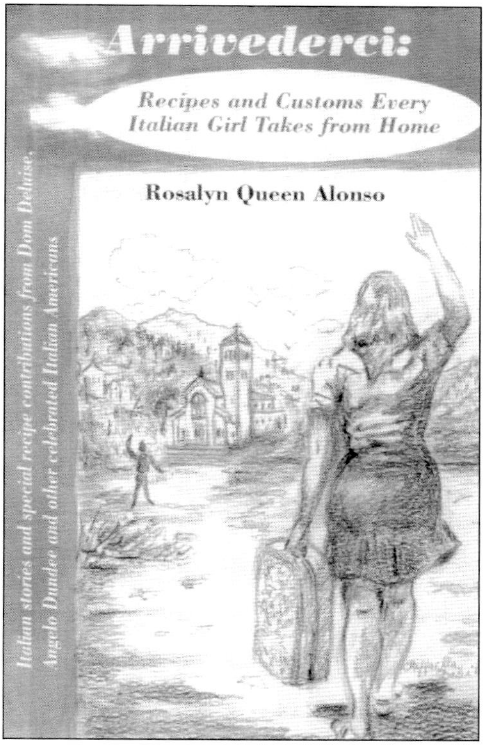

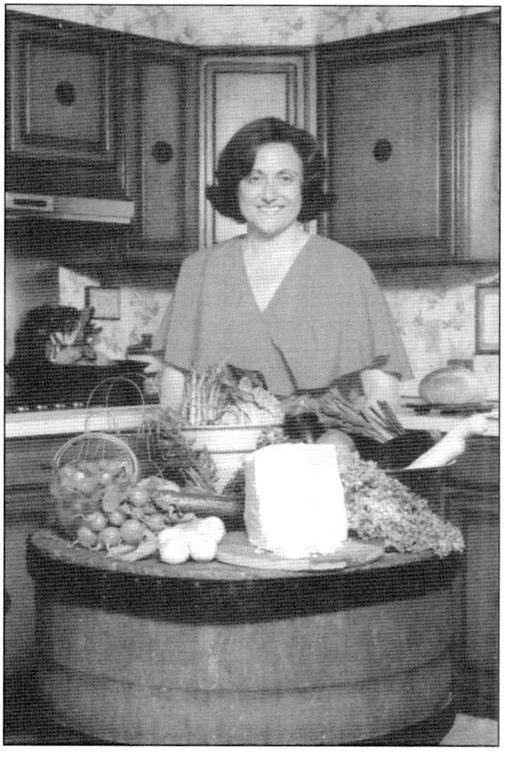

ROSALIE FUSCALDO GAZIANO: FOOD AND FAMILY AS INGREDIENTS FOR LIFE. Combining the food traditions from two distinctly different parts of southern Italy, Rosalie Fuscaldo Gaziano, a native of Charleston, West Virginia, created a family cookbook, *Seasons and Celebrations: Cooking Secrets of Italian Villages Deliciously Translated for the American Table* (1982) to honor her Calabrian heritage and also that of her husband, who is from Aragona in Sicily. When she herself was just a little girl, she delighted in the sights and smells of the Italian kitchen and the artistic ways of food presentation. This cookbook salutes food as the heart of the Italian family. A dozen years later, Gaziano wrote a travelogue of her family's year of world adventures in honor of her Italian parents, who had first introduced her to the joy of family travel, called *It's Your Turn, Chickadees* (1996). In 2002, Gaziano was named National Mother of the Year and authored *Mothers Speak . . . For the Love of Family* (2005), a lasting tribute to the power of family. (Courtesy of Phyllis Moore's Literary Collection, Fairmont State University.)

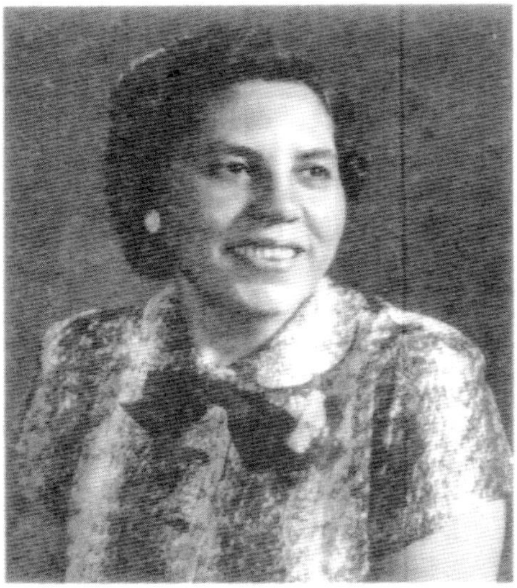

Regina M. D'Ariano

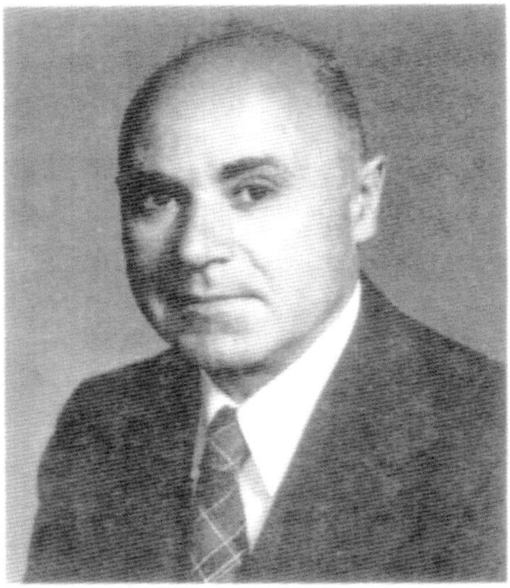

Roy D'Ariano

Roy and Regina D'Ariano: Romantic Expressions of Italian Culture. Rizieri (born 1896) and Regina (born 1902), brother and sister, were born in the province of Benevento in the town of San Bartolomeo. After learning the shoemaking trade, Roy immigrated to Monongah, where he was able to own his own shoemaker's shop. A few years later, he sent for his sister, who eventually became a teacher. They both advanced their educations, earning degrees from Fairmont State University and West Virginia University. Using a romanticized view of traditional life in the old country, Regina transcribed the folk poems from her childhood memories and Roy put the ballads and lyrics to music to produce *Italo-American Ballads, Poems, Lyrics, and Melodies* (1976). They also produced prose books titled *The Country Lass, I'll Strike It Rich, The First Landing of Columbus*, and *Enchanting Stories*. The D'Arianos retired in Fairmont, and until their deaths, they enjoyed attending the WVIHF as members of the Immigrant Honor Council. (Courtesy of Phyllis Moore's Literary Collection, Fairmont State University.)

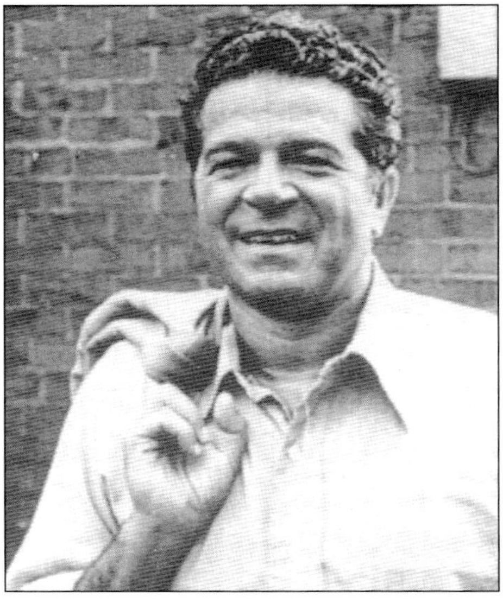

Russell Marano: Poetic Realities of Italian Immigrant Segregation. In his collection *Poems from a Mountain Ghetto* (1979), Russell Marano recalled the realities of growing up poor and Italian in Glen Elk, a segregated section of Clarksburg inhabited by those not yet fully assimilated into the community. In his poetry, Marano introduces the reader to all the members of the ghetto, including families, winos, gamblers, priests, and prostitutes, as well as the proper people across the bridge in Clarksburg. After leaving the ghetto, Marano migrated to Chicago, earned a degree in philosophy from Northwestern University, and taught. Years later, while dying of a brain tumor, with the help of his loving wife, he produced another collection of poems, *Pockets of Love*, which explored the deep need for love both human and divine. (Courtesy of Phyllis Moore's Literary Collection, Fairmont State University.)

JEAN BATTLO AND DENISE GIARDINA: LITERARY ADVOCATES OF SOCIAL JUSTICE. Giardina and Battlo have much in common. They are both natives of McDowell County, born into the Italian culture, and raised in the southern coalfields. Giardina's novel *Storming Heaven* (1987) and its sequel *The Unquiet Earth* (1992) present the historical struggles of West Virginia coal miners, in which the Italian immigrants and their descendants have played main roles. Giardina is a professor in the English department of West Virginia State University Institute. Starting with what she knew best, the community, Battlo has told and retold the struggles of the mining industry, especially in historical drama for Theater West Virginia. In 1999, she produced *Life: A Celebration*, a play with music that chronicled the joys and struggles of an Italian immigrant couple and their family from 1920 to 1988. When not writing, Battlo teaches workshops on playwriting for Theater West Virginia. Both writers have a history of community involvement and support for labor issues and environmental protection. They also support the fair taxation of coal and absentee-owned land. (Both, courtesy of Phyllis Moore's Literary Collection, Fairmont State University.)

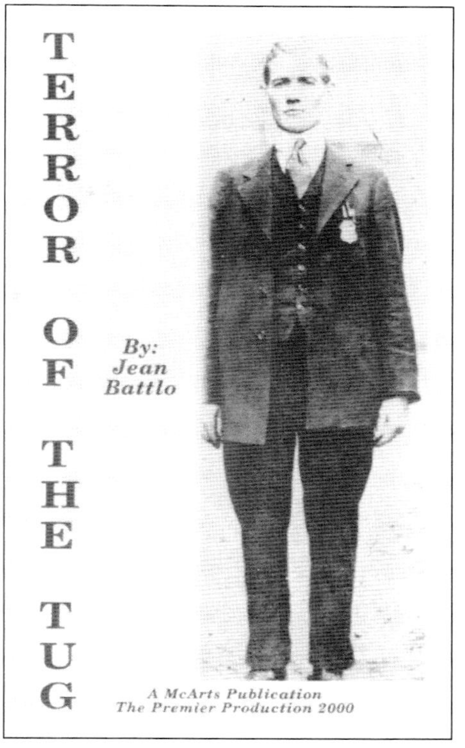

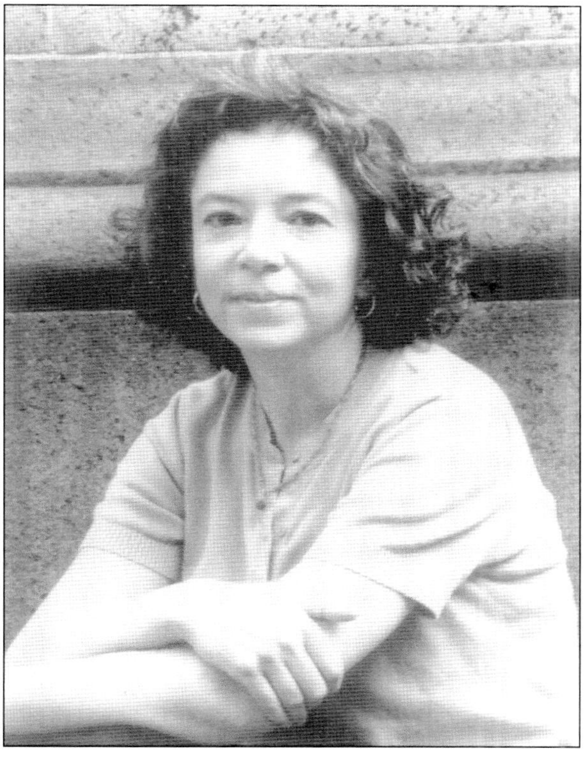

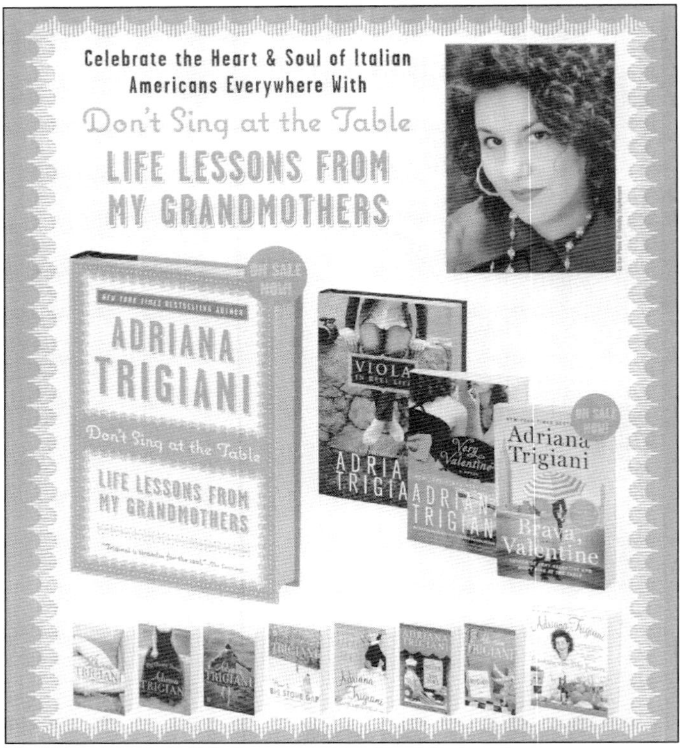

LIFE LESSONS FROM MY GRANDMOTHERS, ADRIANA TRIGIANI, 2010. West Virginia Italian Americans would like to salute internationally recognized bestselling author Adriana Trigiani. Although she is not exactly a West Virginian, she hails from southwestern Virginia. In her early novels, *Big Stone Gap*, *Big Cherry Holler*, and *Milk Glass Moon*, Trigiani explores the struggle and challenges of her protagonist, Ave Maria Mulligan MacChesney, and her family. She has a deep understanding of her character and is able to express all her emotional nuances. (Courtesy of Adriana Trigiani.)

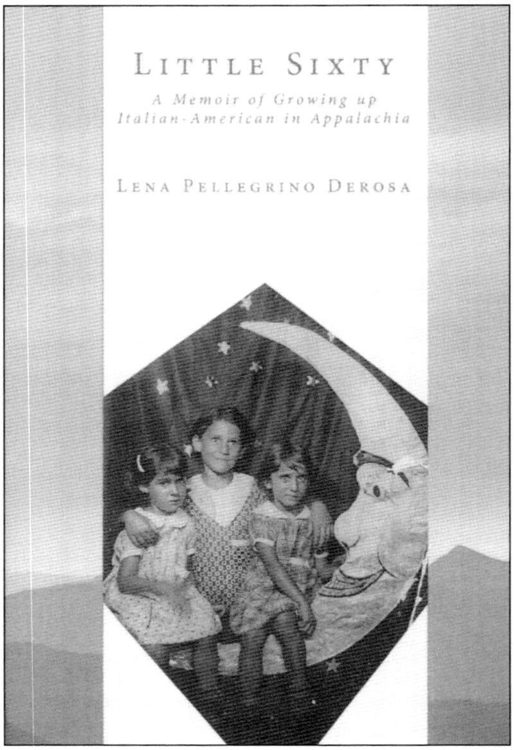

LITTLE SIXTY: A MEMOIR OF GROWING UP ITALIAN-AMERICAN IN APPALACHIA, 2010. Lena Pellegrino Derosa's recent work is one person's written story of what Images of America: *Italians in West Virginia* conveys pictorially. Derosa's family were immigrants from Lattarico, Cosenza, Calabria. In 1920, her father came to Rosemont, West Virginia, and went to work in coal mining, After eight years, he had saved enough money for the passage of his wife and three children. When they arrived at Ellis Island in 1928, he was waiting for them. Four more children were born, including the author. In Rosemont, the family carved out a life among strangers with strange ways and strange foods, but they survived the Great Depression, ethnic prejudice, and World War II. Derosa's story can be the tale of any Italian coming of age in the heart of Appalachia before the 1960s. It is filled with courage, faith, and above all, great spirit. (Courtesy of Lena Derosa.)

Bibliography

Bonasso, Russell F. *Fire in the Hole*. Fairmont, WV: Russell F. Bonasso, 2003.

Cannistraro, Philip and Gerald Meyers, eds. *The Lost World of Italian American Radicalism*. Westport, CT: Praeger, 2003.

Choate, Mark I. *Emigrant Nation: the Making of Italy Abroad*. Cambridge, MA: Harvard University Press, 2008.

Fones-Wolf, Ken and Ronald L. Lewis, eds. *Transnational West Virginia: Ethnic Communities and Economic Change, 1840–1940*. Morgantown: West Virginia University Press, 2002.

Gentile, Vincenzo. *La Calabria Strappata*. Milano: Libre ARE, 2009.

McAteer, Davitt. *Monongah: the Tragic Story of the 1907 Monongah Mine Disaster*. Morgantown: West Virginia University Press, 2007.

Olivito, Salvatore. *San Giovanni in Fiore*. San Giovanni in Fiore, Italy: Edizioni Pubblisfera, 2005.

Order of Sons of Italy in America (OSIA), Souvenir Booklet of the State Convention, Clarksburg, WV, 1925.

Rittenhouse, Ron. *Monongah Coal Mine Disaster 1907–2007; Pictorial History of a Monumental Tragedy*. Morgantown: Morgantown Printing and Binding Company, 2007.

Saverino, Joan. *"Il Fuoco di Minonga:" The 1907 Mine Disaster and the Making of Transnational Identity of West Virginia*. Presentation given at the Darkest Month Coal Mining Symposium, Heinz History Center, Pittsburgh, December 1, 2007.

Schoener, Allon. *The Italian Americans*. New York: Macmillan, 1987.

Swick, Gerald D. *Historic Photos of West Virginia*. Nashville: Turner Publishing Company, 2010.

Zurzolo, Anna P. *Bread, Wine and Angels*. Winnipeg, Manitoba: Turnstone Press, 1997.

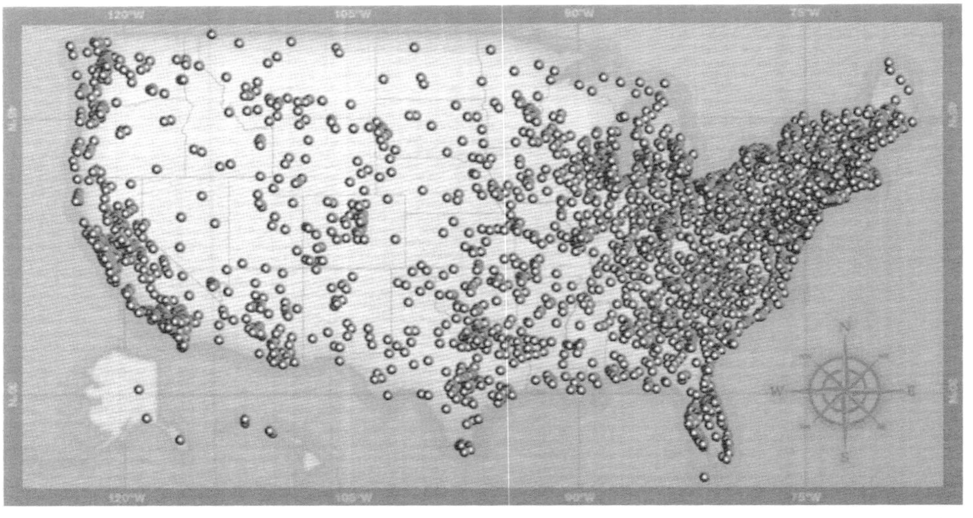

Consistent with our mission to preserve history on a local level, this book was printed in South Carolina on American-made paper and manufactured entirely in the United States. Products carrying the accredited Forest Stewardship Council (FSC) label are printed on 100 percent FSC-certified paper.

MADE IN THE USA